D0932714

THE ARCHITECTURAL THEORY OF
VIOLLET-LE-DUC

THE ARCHITECTURAL THEORY OF VIOLLET-LE-DUC:
Readings and Commentary

edited by M. F. Hearn

Second printing, 1992
© 1990 Massachusetts Institute of Technology

All rights reserved. No part of this book may be
reproduced in any form by any electronic or mechanical
means (including photocopying, recording, or information
storage and retrieval) without permission in writing from
the publisher.

This book was set in Sabon by Achorn Graphic Services,
Inc. and printed and bound in the United States of
America.

Library of Congress Cataloging-in-Publication Data

Viollet-le-Duc, Eugène-Emmanuel, 1814–1879.
    [Selections. English. 1990]
    The architectural theory of Viollet-le-Duc: readings
and commentary / edited by M.F. Hearn.
        p.   cm.
    Selections translated from French.
    Bibliography: p.
    ISBN 0-262-22037-7.—ISBN 0-262-72013-2 (pbk.)
    1. Viollet-le-Duc, Eugène-Emmanuel, 1814–1879—
Philosophy. 2. Viollet-le-Duc, Eugène-Emmanuel,
1814–1879—Criticism and interpretation. I. Hearn,
M.F. (Millard Fillmore), 1938–   . II. Title.
NA 1053.V7V47   1990
720—dc20   89-34629
                                                CIP

For John and Susannah

Contents

Illustrations

Acknowledgments

First and foremost, I am indebted to Gail Phillips for transcribing the texts, interpolating the commentary, and entering numerous corrections in the course of rendering the entire manuscript in neat and legible form. Without her untiring cooperation this project would never have come to fruition.

For assistance with my translation of the letter that concludes this volume, I would like to thank Professor Catherine Hebert of The Pennsylvania State University at New Kensington.

For arranging a grant to cover the cost of the illustrations, I am obliged to Dr. Leonard Kuntz, Office of Research, University of Pittsburgh; for actual production of the illustrations, to Geoffrey Cepull and Blaine Walker, University Center for Instructional Resources.

Finally, I would like to thank Dr. Bertrand Davezac, now of the de Menil Collection and Foundation in Houston, for introducing me to the writings of Viollet-le-Duc in the early days of my graduate study.

Preface

Viollet-le-Duc is generally acknowledged to be the premier theorist of modern architecture, yet few among those familiar with his reputation have actually read his work. There are good reasons for this discrepancy: all his books have been out of print during much of the twentieth century and several of them are not readily available even in research libraries. Moreover, the number of pages—running into the thousands—is daunting: even the tireless reader will be faced with numerous repetitions and lengthy digressions. Still, the experience can be rewarding, for the best passages contain brilliant insights and are written with a delightful lucidity. The obstacles are that these passages are not easy to locate and that the people who have the greatest reason for reading them—architects and students in professional architecture curricula—have no time to search for them. Even the newly reissued *Discourses on Architecture* is nearly a thousand pages long and too diffuse to sustain interest all the way through. The result is that the most imaginative and inspiring theorist of architecture in the modern era is little known in our own day.

Long fascinated by Viollet-le-Duc's work as both scholar of Gothic architecture and theorist, I have combed his books on architecture and drawing in order to extract the passages in which his major ideas about the theory of architecture are most cogently expressed. Arranging and interpolating them in a sequence of topics that follows his line of reasoning, I have assembled these readings with a connecting thread of interpretive commentary. Today's reader can thereby become acquainted with Viollet-le-Duc's theory in his own words.

The passages selected are those that seem best to represent the historical insights and practical principles that made his thought so useful to the first two generations of modern architects. While there may be additional gems of expression or nuances of definition contained in works not widely circulated—letters, journal articles, untranslated books—I have restricted the coverage (with one exception) to that portion of his writing that was generally available and broadly influential. By coincidence, these are the works that were translated into English before 1900 and can now be quoted here without limitation. The other criterion for inclusion has been that the passages should also be capable of addressing the present, for this volume is intended to communicate Viollet-le-Duc's ideas to architects of the present and future as well as to readers whose interest is largely historical.

With the exception of the topic of restoration concluding this volume, the arrangement of the quoted passages follows a sequence that reflects Viollet-le-Duc's own experience in evolving a theory of architecture. He began with a period of serious travel, when he studied the monuments of earlier centuries; accordingly, the readings open with a long section on the lessons to be learned from architecture of the past. Next he was concerned about the best way to proceed with his own education and training for a professional career, so the second section begins with passages on the preparation of the architect. Because he approached the theory of architecture in terms of principles rather than rules, the application of those principles required the formulation of a method, an explanation of which completes the second section. The individual principles—devoted to composing structure, handling materials, devising ornament, and conceiving designs—are set out in the third section. Their order is not dictated by an internal logic; they could be arranged in a different sequence without altering their meaning. A section on restoration has been included at the end because this topic is of current concern, not because it was regarded earlier to be a crucial part of Viollet-le-Duc's theory of architecture.

Regarding transcription of the passages, several alterations have been made that ought to be acknowledged. The spelling of words and names has been changed to conform with current American usage, as have some points of punctuation and syntax. In a number of instances, passages separated by several paragraphs in the text have been combined into one paragraph, with elisions indicated (. . . .). All figure numbers have been altered to conform to the order of their appearance in this text. The sources of the translations are given at the end of the introductory essay.

Finally, I would like to point out the programmatic limitations I have imposed upon this project. First of all, because this collection is meant to address only Viollet-le-Duc's theory of architecture there has been no attempt to represent the full range of his multifaceted life work or even of his thought about architecture. The passages are intended to convey the substance of his theoretical discourse, not to frame literary treasures. For that reason, any portion of a passage that digressed into other issues or into matters (now obscure) of only local concern has been omitted. My aim has been to provide the late-twentieth-century reader with a collection of ideas that were crucial to the development of the theory of modern architecture and remain relevant to modern practice; hence the *history* of Viollet-le-Duc's ideas—embracing their origins, their reception, and their transformation after his lifetime—is not the subject of this volume. Because the translations offered here were (with one exception) made either in Viollet-le-Duc's lifetime or shortly after, they exude a somewhat Victorian quality, but they convey his ideas faithfully and with something of the spirit of his era. For these reasons I have not judged it necessary to undertake a project of making new translations.

THE ARCHITECTURAL THEORY OF VIOLLET-LE-DUC

Viollet-le-Duc: A Visionary among the Gargoyles

Monday, March 11, 1844, was the day of destiny in the life of Eugène-Emmanuel Viollet-le-Duc. On that date, a few weeks after his thirtieth birthday, he was awarded—along with his collaborator, Jean-Baptiste-Antoine Lassus—the commission to restore the Gothic cathedral of Notre-Dame de Paris. Nearly two years earlier, these two young architects had submitted to the Commission des Monuments Historiques their proposal for the restoration project, where it was considered in competition with several others. Perhaps the award was never seriously in question, for the head of the Monuments Historiques, Prosper Mérimée (otherwise known to us as the author of the novella *Carmen*, on which Bizet's opera was based), had long been an intimate of Viollet-le-Duc's family. But as Mérimée well knew, it was an award of merit also, for during the previous year he had visited Viollet-le-Duc's restoration in progress at the historic Romanesque abbey of Vézelay and found both the organization of the project and the work itself to be exemplary. He had, in fact, been so deeply impressed that he invited the young architect to accompany him on his official visitations to historic sites throughout France, the result of which was that they became fast friends, despite the eleven years' difference in their ages.[1]

The Notre-Dame commission profoundly affected every aspect of

1. Francis Salet, "Viollet le Duc et Mérimée," *Les Monuments Historiques de la France* 11 (1965), 19–32.

Viollet-le-Duc's career. Although he had already accepted another dozen restoration jobs, this was by far the most prestigious, the one that would be most closely scrutinized by the public, and therefore the one most demanding of his knowledge and talents. It marked the moment when he became Mérimée's protege and was put on the track to a central position in the Parisian cultural establishment. Henceforth, his thought and work in the field of architecture were to be grounded in the Gothic tradition, as opposed to the classical orientation of prevailing taste and practice. For the next few years at least he would also be drawn into participation in the Gothic revival, heralded in France by Victor Hugo, whose novel *Notre-Dame de Paris* had contributed substance to that movement since its publication in 1831. Indeed involvement in the movement was part of the job, by virtue of the fact that Hugo was a member of the board that had selected the architects for the restoration. Viollet-le-Duc's architectural practice would now be focused primarily on restoration of historic monuments rather than on the design of new buildings. The Notre-Dame project would prompt him to write about architecture, beginning with a partisan interpretation of Gothic. In due course it would also lead him to view the field of architecture and to prophesy its future in terms of what he had learned from Gothic architecture.

But when he sat down to dinner that March 11 he could not know all that. (Indeed, he did not learn of the commission until May 14, while working at Vézelay!) Although he was a very energetic and ambitious man he also did not realize that he would become one of the most important contributors to the historiography of architecture in the nineteenth century as well as the most important theorist of architecture in the modern era—some say, ever. What were the conditioning factors that made this possible? And how did these factors happen to get organized in such a way as to prepare him for these accomplishments?

Let us acknowledge at the outset that Viollet-le-Duc's were bourgeois pursuits—that is, requiring high culture and high professional ability but not conferring the highest level of prestige. In order to pursue them, he was lucky enough to be situated in a bourgeois family in the ultimate bourgeois city during the great century of the bourgeoisie. To do what he did he could not have been better placed. Born on the day of the year that had produced a Mozart fifty-eight years earlier—that is, on January 27—he was bright, intense, and utterly focused. He grew up in a household that was comfortable, cultivated, and connected. Located on the Right Bank near the Palais des Tuileries, the five-story house belonged to his maternal grandparents, who lived on the first floor above street level. Eugène's family lived on the next floor, his mother's younger sister and her husband on the third, and his mother's bachelor brother on the top. The grandfather was a successful contractor who had built, among several conspicuous buildings, the Théâtre Français at the Odéon. Our subject's father, Emmanuel, was a civil servant who was soon to be in charge of all the royal palaces. He was a royalist at heart and a rational classicist by disposition, and he and his wife maintained a Friday evening salon of like-minded people. Upstairs, Eugène's uncle, Etienne Delécluze, an artist who had become a well-known critic, was, on the other hand, a republican of romantic disposition who was at home on Sunday afternoons, to an equally distinguished assembly, including Prosper Mérimée. The young Viollet-le-Duc, then, was exposed from early youth to people who either built or preserved important structures, who wrote and conversed about art and architecture, and who were involved in shaping the culture of Paris, which was, after all, the leading center in Europe.

When Eugène was eleven, he and his younger brother Adolphe were sent away to a boarding school near Fontenay-aux-Roses, chosen by his uncle for its staunchly republican and anticlerical philosophy. The uncle even moved to Fontenay to see that all went well. Back home in Paris, Eugène received the *baccalauréat* at age sixteen from the Collège de Bourbon, and shortly afterward his childhood facility for drawing came to the fore. As the son of the superintendent of the royal palaces, his drawings had been admired by King Louis Philippe, who gave the teenage boy permission to observe and sketch royal events, albeit from a discreet vantage point. Following a brief internship in the office of a neighbor, Jean-Jacques-Marie Huvé, he declared his intention of becoming an architect. Against the advice of his family he decided not to be trained at the Ecole des Beaux-Arts but through work in the office of a friend of the family, Achille Leclère. The following year he took the first of several extended trips, this time to the Auvergne and Provence, with his uncle. His skill in drawing was certainly cultivated in the architect's office and practiced while traveling. Thus it is that an interest in architecture as a profession and in drawing as an avocation got him started on his way.

In 1834, at age twenty, Viollet-le-Duc married and took on an additional job teaching drawing in a minor private institution, the Ecole de Dessin de Paris. A son was born to the young couple during the next year, but in 1836, in the manner so typical of European gentlemen of that time, he decided to embark on an extended trip to Italy with a male friend to see the great architecture of the past. After a few weeks, though, his wife sent word that she was on her way to join him, leaving the baby in the household of the now-widowered father-in-law, Emmanuel Viollet-le-Duc, then residing as palace governor in the Palais des Tuileries. During a sojourn of eighteen months Viollet-le-Duc had an opportunity to study at first hand and draw representative buildings of much of the history of Western architecture, including the Greek Doric temples of Paestum and Sicily, the Roman ruins of Pompeii and Rome, and the great Renaissance churches and palaces of Rome, Florence, Venice.

Returning to Paris, he received employment with the Conseil des Bâtiments Civils, most notably working on the Hôtel des Archives. Meanwhile, each summer he visited more sites of great medieval architecture in France, filling out his experience with the Romanesque and Gothic periods. At this point it is difficult to say whether or not he had a distinct interpretation of the historical styles in mind. Indeed, when he got the commission to restore the abbey of Vézelay in 1840, at age twenty-six, he was most probably approaching the project more as an architect than as a dedicated medievalist. Yet he was keenly aware that restoration was a new activity in human civilization and that it represented a complex and delicate interaction with history. But within the next four years, as he embarked on a series of additional restoration jobs, the Romanesque or Gothic content of the buildings became more and more the subject of his career.

In 1842, Mérimée appointed Viollet-le-Duc as second inspector of the restoration of the Sainte-Chapelle in Paris, where he became well acquainted with the first inspector, Jean-Baptiste-Antoine Lassus. In the course of that year the two of them worked up a prospectus for the restoration of Notre-Dame, during which time Lassus proselytized Viollet-le-Duc to the rationalist interpretation of architecture in general and of Gothic architecture in particular. By the time they received the commission to restore Notre-Dame in 1844, Violet-le-Duc had developed his position and begun publication of polemical articles on Gothic architecture, interpreting it as a logical structural system. His momentous adventure among the gargoyles was under way.

The Notre-Dame project involved a church much altered since its creation in the late twelfth and early thirteenth centuries and much neglected since the Revolution, when its sculpture was severely damaged. Viollet-le-Duc and Lassus had to decide which aspects of the fabric design to retain and which to alter. While it may well have been an equal partnership in decision making, whatever blame was involved has fallen on Viollet-le-Duc, in large part because Lassus died in 1857 before the project was finished. For reasons that have not become clear, Viollet-le-Duc changed the form of the flying buttresses along the nave, the earliest universally acknowledged buttresses in Gothic architecture, the original form of which was therefore historically important. We can still see at the end of the west side of the south transept arm a trace of the original design, so the fact of the change is indisputable.[2] Observing in the same area a series of virtually identical scars in the masonry of the clerestory, he deduced that the traceried windows of the thirteenth century had replaced a shorter, plain window and a roundel under the window that represented the third story in a four-story elevation. Accordingly, he decided to "restore" the original wall configuration in the bays adjacent to the crossing. He was, of course, removing genuine thirteenth-century work in order to make manifest the elevation he thought had been there at the outset. While no one seriously challenged the supposition that this had been the actual original design, it was shocking to many that he would presume to reverse history. His decision was all the more questionable because the later windows had involved lowering the roofline, with the result that the roof would no longer cover the roundels, which originally opened into the dark area over the gallery vaults. Undaunted, he filled the roundels with stained glass, thereby treating them in a manner in which they had never been seen in the Middle Ages. More was to come: where all the statues of biblical kings had stood on the west front—in the embrasures of the portals and on the gallery of kings—he ordered replacements for those vandalized in the antiroyal riots of the Revolution in the 1790s. Ironically, other features he created have become among the most-cherished

2. William Clark and Robert Mark, "The First Flying Buttresses: A New Reconstruction of the Nave of Notre-Dame de Paris," *Art Bulletin* 66 (1984), 47–65.

aspects of the cathedral: the grotesques on the tower balustrades had weathered to an unrecognizable nubbin and he replaced them with original figures that are perhaps the most memorable on the entire cathedral. Also, aware that until 1792 the crossing had been accented by a spire, or flèche, he replaced it, approximating the design and adding the figures of the apostles and archangels at the angles of the roof.

On the other hand, the reputed intrusion of modern anachronisms has been proven false. Contradicting popular legend, his granddaughter has established that the figure that turns to look at the spire does not after all represent the architect himself, but one of the Apostles. Also, because the spire was painted with red lead just after construction, the Parisian populace assumed that Viollet-le-Duc had constructed it of modern cast iron. Actually, though, it is made of wood and had merely been treated to protect against predatory insects.[3] Thus two features of the project that have been imputed to egotism were misjudged because of the audacity of his other decisions.

These various modifications of the cathedral have been pointed out in order to indicate that Viollet-le-Duc's theory of restoration was neither to bring a building back to the end of its living evolution—in this case, its state at the end of the Middle Ages—nor to restore it to a pristine version of its original twelfth-century design. Rather it was, in his words, "to reestablish it in a complete condition that may never have existed at any given moment." Such a policy may seem shocking to us, and indeed it made him very controversial in his own lifetime, but, as he cautioned: "It is only from the second quarter of our century that attempts have been made to restore the edifices of another age, and we do not know if architectonic restoration has been clearly defined" *(Dictionnaire raisonné,* VIII, 14).

For him, returning ruined structures to full order was not simply a case of a bright detective completing a jigsaw puzzle. Rather, he had a remarkably detailed knowledge of history and a wonderfully intuitive imagination with which he peopled these monuments and envisioned them in use. He was not, then, either facile or ignorant in his reconstitutions. The flaw, if one must be attributed, was in second-guessing the

3. Geneviève Viollet-le-Duc, "La flèche de Notre-Dame de Paris," *Les Monuments Historiques de la France* 11 (1965), 43–50.

medieval builders and imputing to them his own systematic interpretation of the intentions behind medieval architecture.

Among the French and in volumes of the *Guide Michelin*, Viollet-le-Duc is chiefly remembered as a restorer. While he was always controversial in that capacity, his reputation has also fluctuated with the changing of ideas about restoration, tempered by an awareness that the buildings he restored would not otherwise have survived until today. But he is equally prominent as an architectural historian, in which field he looms as a giant among nineteenth-century savants; indeed, his interpretation of Gothic structure, which is almost as controversial as his restorations, has colored deliberations up to the present day.

By the late 1840s Viollet-le-Duc must have been aware that his activities as restorer, together with his systematic travels with Mérimée, were providing him a highly privileged familiarity with medieval buildings and that there might be good reason for him to set down both his special knowledge and his general understanding of medieval architecture. Each building had been meticulously recorded as he found it and each had required a detailed and painstaking set of drawings for the restoration, so he had accumulated a vast fund of concrete information. In due course he decided to codify this information alphabetically, treating individually each of the elements of structure and decoration as well as generalities such as "cathedral" and "construction." It was organized in a work that he titled *Dictionnaire raisonné de l'architecture française du XIe au XVIe siècle,* published in ten volumes that appeared between 1854 and 1868.

His explanation of Gothic architecture began with the assumption that the urge to construct high vaults had been the generating imperative. His interpretation of the statics of the high vault convinced him that the pointed arch and the diagonal arch rib had been adopted together by Gothic builders in order to facilitate the covering of rectangular and odd-shaped spaces, rather than just squares, and to guide the unavoidable lateral pressures to the corners of the vaults, where they were received by the walls. Such an ordering of vaults implied a supporting structure composed of a series of isolated points rather than a continuous mass of masonry, hence the emergence of a highly articulated bay system. Even so, the lateral pressures of vaults necessitated external resistance, arranged perpendicular to the wall, resulting in the development of the flying buttress. Because the intervals between vertical supports were thereby relieved of a load-bearing function, they could be reduced to a series of arches that connected the supports, thus permitting the evolution of a skeletal structure. The coordinated formulation of moldings on the arches and of shafts on the supports was intended to make the composition intelligible as structure and, indeed, to serve in part as actual structure. Consequently, both the ensemble of functional elements and the decorative features—such as blind arcades on aisle walls and bar tracery in the windows—served a functional purpose. The beauty of Gothic architecture, then, was the result of a systematically rational approach to building rather than of aesthetic or iconographical considerations. It is ironic that a subject that inspired so much romantic sentiment in others evoked such a cerebral response from Viollet-le-Duc. Yet it was this response that awakened the visionary in him, which showed itself in his ideas about modern architecture.

In the course of restoring buildings and writing the *Dictionnaire raisonné,* Viollet-le-Duc believed that he had discerned principles that could be applicable to architecture at any time, principles that would make it possible for modern architecture to transcend the stale academic classicism of the Ecole des Beaux-Arts. Although he conceded that he and others of his generation would not likely be able to create the new forms, he felt compelled to lead the younger generation in that direction. Accordingly, in 1857 he set up an atelier on the rue Bonaparte, next door to the Ecole des Beaux-Arts, where he undertook to train young men in the profession. For this purpose he worked up a curriculum of study including an examination of the history of architecture that would promote the adoption of principles from the past rather than the imitation of classic forms. As it turned out, the teaching venture was not a success, but Viollet-le-Duc published the historical essays and continued to write others, which he collected and issued in 1863 under the title *Entretiens sur l'architecture,* known in English as *Discourses on Architecture.*

In the history of architecture he discerned three models of key importance: the Greek Doric temple, the complex structures of the imperial Romans, and the Gothic cathedrals of medieval France. The Doric temple he interpreted as a sublimely rational approach to the formulation of structure. In his estimate, every member was shaped according to its function in the structural system and was logically related to the adjacent members and to the whole. It was, however, an architecture determined by its mode of assembly rather than by its purpose as a building; the system was inflexible and difficult to adapt to formats other than rectangular and round peripteral temples. Roman architecture, on the other hand, best exemplified by huge complexes such as the great third-century baths of Caracalla, began with a program of functional requirements and proceeded then to devise various structural solutions to the problems raised by the different sizes and shapes of spaces in a complex arrangement. Yet, while the structural schemes were ingenious the builders always ended by decorating them with a luxurious but irrelevant veneer of Greek forms. Although the Romans had what was probably the superior method of design the Greeks were more authentically artistic. The virtues of both traditions, however, were to be found in the late-twelfth- and early-thirteenth-century Gothic cathedrals of France. Beginning with a program of liturgical requirements, the builders had to devise a structure for a complex spatial scheme. But the formulation of the structural elements had the fine-tuned rationality and the inherent beauty of the historically unrelated Doric tradition. As Viollet-le-Duc described it, though, the Gothic cathedral was actually as much a purely structural conception as the Doric temple, primarily because his anticlerical views had atrophied his interest in its liturgical purpose. Ignoring this inconsistency of interpretation, he nevertheless represented Gothic architecture as being a fully rational structure conceived to fulfill a functional program. In addition to the French Gothic cathedral he also admired the French Renaissance chateau, which he deemed to have been formulated on purely functional considerations, beginning with the program of domestic requirements. By the same token, he had only scorn for the palaces and houses built in the classical tradition during the baroque era and later, for he regarded their symmetrical facades as preconceived images that took precedence over interior spatial arrangements, usually to the detriment of comfort and convenience. At the end of this parade of historical examples the vision of the future was not yet limned, but the impulse to do so later was probably prompted by events in the year following the publication of these essays.

For, in 1863 also, in large part due to Viollet-le-Duc's instigation, a reform of the Ecole des Beaux-Arts was announced by the government and Viollet-le-Duc was appointed professor of the history of architecture. Unfortunately for him, he was associated with unpopular aspects of the reform and the result was that he was shouted down by the students. It was during the brief period of five months when he persisted in delivering his lectures that he began to formulate his prophecy for a modern architecture. In the immediately preceding years, Viollet-le-Duc's modernity was ambivalently manifested in the tentative novelty of his own architectural designs. In 1861 he had entered the state competition, generally thought to have been rigged in his favor, for the new Paris Opera, but things went awry and he did not win. By contrast with Charles Garnier's victorious entry, Viollet-le-Duc's was much more straightforward in its general formulation, avoiding historicism in its formal vocabulary, eschewing grandiloquence in its ceremonial areas, and aspiring to better sight lines and acoustics than decor in its auditorium. It was, on the other hand, noncommittal with regard to both functional and formal meaning: not only did it not guide the operagoer from the entry to a seat but it also offered nothing to evoke the drama of opera or the glamour of attending it. In 1862, he built at 68 rue Condorcet a multistoried townhouse for himself and his wife, including his design office. The asymmetry of the entrances and of the third-floor window openings asserts his concern for the primacy of function in design, and the ornamental facings carefully avoid repetition of historical embellishments. Yet, despite the modernity of its formulation, it possesses no distinction. In 1864 he designed the church of Saint-Denis de l'Estrée, employing a basically medieval format and formal vocabulary, albeit in an archaic version that virtually ignores the concept of rational structure in its composition. This sample of three designs does not reveal him as a revolutionary architect. Yet in 1864 he wrote and published the two essays that were to become the core of his theory of modern architecture. While the full articulation of his theory of architecture would be worked out over the course of the remaining fifteen years of his life, he was mostly preoccupied by other matters throughout the 1860s.

While the 1850s had been primarily devoted to restoration projects and the almost incessant traveling they required, the 1860s were years in which he was most active as a practicing architect. During this decade he continued publication, in installments, of his *Dictionnaire raisonné* of French medieval architecture and wrote additional essays on the education of architects and on architectural ornaments (which would later appear in the *Discourses*) as well as numerous reports and reviews. In order to accomplish so much work he maintained a rigorous schedule, described by one of his English contemporaries:

He enters his studio at seven in the morning, where he is engaged till nine in getting in readiness the work that will be called for, and preparing for his visitors, whom he receives from nine till ten, during which he takes his frugal breakfast standing. At this hour will be found lying ready the manuscript for the publisher, a pile of wood blocks for the engraver—who has only to follow and cut between the sharp lines of the finished drawings which cover them—plans for the builder, designs for the sculptor and blacksmith, and cartoons for the decorator or glass painter—every one of which is the product of his own hand. For each of his staff as he arrives, after his *"Voila, monsieur, vôtre affaire"* and verbal instructions, he has a kind word of friendly inquiry, encouragement, or advice. At ten his studio is closed, and he works at his drawings without interruption until his dinner hour at six. At seven he retires to his library, where he is engaged with his literary pursuits till midnight. Thus, his daily life at home, is but little varied when away. He generally travels by night, often taking journeys of several hundred miles; for he visits every building upon which he is engaged once a month.[4]

Meanwhile, on days of rest or as occasions arose, he enjoyed the good life of Paris in most of its social and cultural forms. He stood high in the favor of the Emperor Napoleon III and the Empress Eugénie and, in consequence, was often asked to design the arrangements for special court events. Under Mérimée's prompting he had become virtually a courtier in the regime of the Second Empire.

But in 1870, the ill-fated Franco-Prussian war brought all this to an end. The fifty-six-year-old Viollet-le-Duc was mobilized as an artillery officer and oversaw the defense of portions of Paris during the brief military campaign. Following the fall of Napoleon III he was, due to his close association with the imperial regime, condemned to death by the Commune; accordingly he fled to the provinces until the demise of that government a few weeks later, at the end of May 1871. The aftermath of the war brought on a deep national depression and a sense of crisis in French culture, with which Viollet-le-Duc empathized.

Personally he felt remorse for the extent of his collaboration with the Second Empire, into which he had gradually drifted without reflecting on the degree of his involvement. Perhaps the death of his patron

4. Charles Wethered, "Restoration of Historical Monuments in France," *Viollet-le-Duc's "On Restoration"* (London, 1875), 101–102.

Mérimée, in 1870, made him feel exposed in this regard. In any event, he virtually withdrew from public life, curtailing his restorations to a minimum and not resuming his architectural practice. Except for some civic duties—in 1874 he was elected to the municipal council of Paris to represent the IXe arrondissement (Montmartre) and appointed to the fine arts and historic monuments commissions of Paris—he devoted the years after 1871 to a torrent of writing.

In 1872 he published the second volume of the *Discourses on Architecture,* which included his proposals for a modern architecture and architectural education. During the next seven years he produced the last five volumes of his work on medieval decorative arts (initiated in 1858), seven books on various architectural topics, and a volume on the geology of Mont Blanc. Among these were three titles in which he raised theoretical issues. *How to Build a House,* 1873, set out a method for creating a design, in contradistinction to the traditional type of book that prescribed rules for the design itself. *The Habitations of Man in All Ages,* 1875, analyzed all the vernacular traditions of world architecture that were then known. Some were judged to be conservative, others progressive, and it was of course for the latter that he reserved his most positive assessments. Finally, in his last year, 1879, he published *Learning to Draw,* in which the skill of visual representation is presented not as artistic expression but as the basis for analytical observation that leads to problem solving. For him, the art of designing was ultimately a rational activity in which beauty is largely a by-product.

It is only when we take all these works together that we discover the totality of Viollet-le-Duc's visionary theory of architecture. Viewed in this manner it can be resolved as a logical system of principles, as opposed to rules. While the following brief summary runs the risk of oversimplifying, it also has the advantage of clarifying.

To begin, the design of a building must be the result of a rational method rather than the articulation of a preconceived image. It must evolve from the careful statement of a functional program and the arrangement of spaces in shapes and sequences that fulfill the program. Accordingly, the procedure must start with the plan, continue with the means of covering it, and only end with the facade. In other words, the portion of the structure that is traditionally most susceptible to aesthetic elaboration should be largely predetermined by functional requirements. The result is most likely to be attractive because it is also rational. While a rational design is not necessarily beautiful, a beautiful building is necessarily rational. Thus asymmetry in facade design and irregularity in massing should be accepted without qualm.

The means for realizing a design, the structural scheme, should be devised to fit the plan rather than the other way around. The way the structure fits together should be apparent and structural members should be allowed to show. A structure should be composed to fulfill its purpose with economy, that is, in a simple and straightforward manner. The materials employed should be those that best suit the structural needs and they should be used in a manner consonant with their inherent qualities. New materials, especially those produced by industrial processes, should be welcomed and encouraged. Insofar as possible, materials should be prepared for use before being brought to the building site and new methods of preparation and construction should be readily accepted and even sought. Ornament is an indispensable aspect of architecture but it should be integral with the structure and preferably should serve a functional purpose. Neither forms nor materials nor technologies should be tied to tradition; a progressive outlook should always be maintained. If all these principles are adhered to the result will necessarily have style. But the best way to harness these principles, he *implied,* is through the use of a guiding metaphor, that of either the machine or the organism. Finally, a new architecture cannot come into being unless architects are educated in a manner consonant with its character. They must be taught analytical skills at school and practical wisdom on the building site. They should know about the architecture of the past but for the purpose of learning principles rather than of imitating forms.

If today all this just sounds like common sense it is a measure of the extent to which Viollet-le-Duc's theory of architecture has become the pervasive doctrine of modern architecture. Most of his nonmedieval works had been translated into English by the mid-1880s and so were readily available to English and American as well as continental readers. It is impossible to name any modern theoretical writer on architecture whose influence was frankly, even gratefully, acknowledged by more architects of the first importance. Many of the founding fathers of art nouveau and early modernism were individually inspired by his principles, each taking from him a different creative emphasis: Antoni Gaudí in Barcelona; Victor Horta in Brussels; Hector Guimard (via

Horta), Anatole de Baudot, Auguste Perret, Auguste Choisy, and Le Corbusier in Paris; Hans Pieter Berlage in Amsterdam; Frank Furness in Philadelphia; Louis Sullivan (via Furness) in Chicago; Bernard Maybeck in San Francisco; and most of all, Frank Lloyd Wright (via Sullivan?) in Chicago. Wright, who seems to have absorbed everything by Viollet-le-Duc that was available in English, gave a copy of the *Discourses* to his son John Lloyd, with the words: "In these volumes you will find all the architectural schooling you will ever need. What you cannot learn from them, you can learn from me."[5] While Wright stressed the organic nature of his design, Le Corbusier based his work on Viollet-le-Duc's metaphor of the machine, memorably summed up in the dictum, "a house is a machine for living in."

Although it is unlikely that later generations of architects have been directly inspired by a reading of Viollet-le-Duc, the principles they have employed are simply rearrangements and magnifications of certain aspects of his theory of architecture. Hence both the new brutalism and high-tech movements of recent decades have, in different ways, emphasized the concern for honesty in the formulation and expression of structure and in the use of materials. Indeed, perhaps only postmodernism among avant-garde twentieth-century movements has been based on theory not rooted in that of Viollet-le-Duc. Significantly, it is the movement that has addressed the aspect of architecture that Viollet-le-Duc did not incorporate into his theory—namely, meaning. For the rest, most of the various strands of twentieth-century architecture have been spun out of slightly differing interpretations of his ideas.

Meanwhile, the contemporary preservation movement, prompted in part by postmodernism, has given new currency to Viollet-le-Duc's ideas concerning restoration. Despite the controversy that has always surrounded his name in this field, he was, after all, among the earliest of restorers and probably the first to enunciate principles to guide that activity. And despite his reputation for arbitrarily altering and renewing historic buildings, he was, in fact, scrupulously meticulous in procedures and usually careful in his judgments.

Recognizing that few really old buildings have survived without alter-

5. John Lloyd Wright, *My Father Who Is on Earth* (New York, 1946), 69. See also Donald Hoffmann, "Frank Lloyd Wright and Viollet-le-Duc," *Journal of the Society of Architectural Historians* 28 (1969), 173–183.

ation during the era when their purpose was still fully vital, Viollet-le-Duc proposed that a restoration must take such changes into account and usually retain them. While neutral components in structural elements, such as ashlar blocks, might require renewal or outright replacement, decorative features should generally not be recarved because it is impossible to reproduce their authentic character. In other words, an old building should not be made like new but should retain signs of wear and damage. Every building, however, poses different situations that require difficult decisions, and one of Viollet-le-Duc's cardinal principles was that there can be no hard and fast rules, except to respect the historical integrity of the building as it has come down to us. In this we see the reverence for contextual guidance that has become one of the principal tenets of present-day restoration.

All this was an unpredictable result of Viollet-le-Duc's decades of observation and work among the singular structural devices and the exotic ornaments of an architecture constructed in the dim, distant past of the Middle Ages. While his cohorts in England became enamored of the medieval forms themselves, thereby fostering a Gothic revival, he perceived in these forms the principles of a strikingly new theory of architecture. He had, in truth, become a visionary while working among the gargoyles.

SOURCES OF THE READINGS

Viollet-le-Duc wrote eleven books (some multivolumed), of which seven deal with architecture and one with drawing. Among those eight titles five deal with topics that touch on the theory of architecture, and it is from them that the readings in this volume are taken. While these excerpts are readily comprehensible in the framework of the commentaries, the reader may want to know something of their original context. Toward this end a brief account of each work and its English translation follows, set out in chronological order. In addition, an early letter has been included in the readings, and a discussion of its translation is set out here.

1. "Rapport adressé à M. le Ministre de la Justice et des Cultes," 1843. This report discusses some of the specific problems to be faced in the restoration of the cathedral of Notre-Dame and the principles that would guide Viollet-le-Duc's judgments in handling these problems. As

a letter, the text never underwent any editorial treatment and so contains some tortured formulations that complicate an attempt to translate it precisely. In making this translation I have attempted to go beyond a literal rendering in order to present it in idiomatic English. I have averted some errors through the generous assistance of Professor Catherine Hebert of the Pennsylvania State University at New Kensington, but any still remaining should be imputed only to me.

2. *Dictionnaire raisonné de l'architecture française du XIe au XVIe siècle,* in ten volumes, published in Paris between 1854 and 1868; reprinted in Paris, 1967, and in Saint-Julien-du-Sancey, 1979. This work treats all aspects of Romanesque and Gothic architecture from the smallest decorative detail (e.g., *crochet, cul-de-lampe* to the broadest conceptual topic e.g., construction, style, cathedral), with entries arranged in alphabetical order. It is here that Viollet-le-Duc's obsessively rationalist interpretation of Gothic architecture is spelled out. A few articles, such as *arc boutant* (flying buttress) and *tas-de-charge* (the technique of providing a single stone to accommodate the springing of several arches from one point) have attracted particular notice in connection with the study of Gothic architecture, but the very long article on construction is the one that has contributed most to the lore of Viollet-le-Duc's theory of architecture.

While the *Dictionnaire raisonné* was translated in its entirety by Nathan Ricker, as a Ph.D. dissertation for the University of Illinois, *circa* 1917, this translation has never been published. The article on construction, however, was translated by G. M. Huss, an architect, and published in New York in 1895 under the title *Rational Building.* Much earlier, the article on restoration was translated by Charles Wethered, an English architect, and published in London, in 1875, as *On Restoration.* The readings from the *Dictionnaire raisonné* are drawn from these two published versions.

3. *Entretiens sur l'architecture* was published in Paris in two volumes, the first in 1863 and the second in 1872. The work began as a series of four essays on the applicable principles to be learned from ancient Greek and Roman architecture, prepared for Viollet-le-Duc's teaching atelier in 1857. When that venture did not continue he published the essays in 1858. Thereafter, six additional essays were issued singly between 1860 and 1863, the year when they were collected as Volume I. Probably a second volume was already foreseen, but once again six of

the essays were published individually as they were written: numbers eleven through fourteen had appeared by 1868 and the next two by 1870. The remaining four were composed shortly after the Franco-Prussian War (1870–71) and were collected with the others for publication in 1872 as Volume II.

Volume I was translated by Henry Van Brunt, an America architect, and published in Boston in 1875, while a second translation by Benjamin Bucknall, an English architect, appeared in London in 1877. Van Brunt's Volume II followed in 1881 and Bucknall's in 1882; Bucknall brought out a revised edition of the whole in 1889 (reprinted in London, 1959, and New York, 1987). Of the two translations Van Brunt's might be considered livelier reading but Bucknall's is much closer to Viollet-le-Duc's actual wording, so the quotations in this volume are taken from the text (1889 edition). Very possibly Bucknall's could be considered an "official" translation, because he was in Lausanne in 1876 to consult with the author about it. The *Entretiens* have been translated as *Lectures on Architecture* (Bucknall's original edition) and as *Discourses on Architecture* (Van Brunt, and the Bucknall edition of 1889); they are identified in the text as *Discourses,* the better-known title.

The *Discourses* are Viollet-le-Duc's chief work on the theory of architecture. They treat the main principles to be discovered in the study of historical architecture in Western civilization, the flaws in French architectural education as conducted at the Ecole des Beaux-Arts in the nineteenth century, prescriptions for a revised approach to the education of the architect, and the principles that ought to be exercised in regard to methods of construction, the design of structure, the handling of materials, and the treatment of architectural ornament. They are often tendentious in character, sometimes pushing the argument to its limits and even overstating the case. On the other hand, they are generally modulated with ancillary concerns that enrich his arguments and endow them with a degree of complexity.

4. *Histoire d'une maison,* Paris, 1873. Two translations appeared in 1874: by George M. Towle in Boston, titled *The Story of a House,* and by Benjamin Bucknall, in London, titled *How to Build a House, An Architectural Novelette.* It is generally known in English as *How to Build a House* and is so identified in this volume; the readings are drawn from Bucknall's text. Bucknall relates that Viollet-le-Duc wrote

and illustrated the text during the evenings of a few summer weeks when he was engaged in surveying the French Alps (actually Mont Blanc).

In the story, a schoolboy, Paul de Gandelau conceives the notion of designing a house for his sister, recently departed with her husband on their honeymoon, during the school interruption occasioned by the Franco-Prussian War. The intended gift of their father, the house is to be built in the country, near the family estate. Under the supervision of his architect-cousin, significantly named Eugene, Paul designs the house and supervises its fabrication. The story is a pretext for setting out a detailed method both for the design process and for the stages of construction.

5. *Histoire de l'habitation humaine depuis les temps préhistoriques,* published in Paris, 1875, and reprinted in Paris, 1978, and Brussels, 1978. It was translated into English by Benjamin Bucknall as *The Habitations of Man in All Ages,* published in London, 1876, and reprinted in New York, 1971.

Viollet-le-Duc fabricates a continuous narrative in which two characters, Doxius and Epergos, systematically wander around the world through millenia, observing and discussing domestic architecture. Doxius is a dyed-in-the-wool conservative who continually opposes change. Epergos, on the other hand, is always for progress and so frequently intervenes in order to promote change. The real struggle is between an urge to maintain existing cultural values and an opposing one to seek improvement wherever it might come, accepting the consequent change in values as unavoidable. Certain cultures get a distinctly positive evaluation, especially those of the Indo-European anthropological stem, while others are regarded as generally inferior. While undoubtedly regarded by his contemporaries as factual, this interpretation now smacks of racism. In any event, though, the text provides an early example of appreciation of vernacular architecture in the context of architectural theory.

6. *Histoire d'un dessinateur, comment on apprend à dessiner,* Paris, 1879, reissued in Paris, 1978. A second edition, published in Paris, 1903, was reprinted in Brussels, 1979. It was Viollet-le-Duc's last work, published only a short time before his death. The English translation of the first edition, by Virginia Champlin, appeared in New York, 1881, under the title *Learning to Draw, or the Story of a Young Designer.*

In this novelette, a little peasant boy, Jean, is educated by a kindly engineer, M. Majorin, who was attracted to the child's natural tendency to make drawings based on careful observation. The central theme is that drawing requires one to analyze what one sees and, through analysis, helps one to solve problems in design situations—and in life as well. Drawing promotes an active mentality, a scientific outlook, and a liberal spirit and could profitably be regarded as the central discipline in a modern education. In the course of events, Jean succeeds in a design career while his comfortable bourgeois friend, André, who was schooled in a passive academic regimen, becomes an inept mediocrity. This book could justly be regarded as the broadest and most philosophical expression of Viollet-le-Duc's views; indeed, it might be admitted to the literature of the ideal education, in the company of such classics as Quintilian's *Institutes of Oratory* and Rousseau's *Emile*.

I   LEARNING FROM THE PAST

1 The Origins and Development of Architecture

THE PRIMITIVE HUT

Like other writers of architectural treatises, Viollet-le-Duc addressed the matter of the origin of architecture by surmising how the earliest structures were formulated. The importance of such an exercise was to discern the first principles of architecture. For the ancient Roman, Vitruvius—and later writers in the Vitruvian tradition—the purpose had been to hypothesize a structural prototype (however it might have been conceived) for the monumental architecture of the Greeks and other early cultures. For the eighteenth-century rationalists, such as Laugier and Chambers, it was to discover in structural tradition an absolute necessity, a pure and unadorned response to the laws of nature, employing material forms readily available in nature. For Viollet-le-Duc it was to demonstrate that architecture began when rational planning and procedure were applied to the problem of the need for shelter. Because primitive man could not have approached this problem with a developed intelligence, Viollet-le-Duc implied that the scheme for the first building was revealed, coming as a gift from a higher intelligence, much as fire had been the gift of Prometheus.

A dozen creatures are grouped together beneath a bushy tree whose lower branches have been pulled downward and secured to the ground by clods of earth. The wind is blowing violently and driving the rain

1. The first shelter.

right through this shelter. Rush mats and skins of beasts afford a scanty protection to the limbs of these creatures, who with their nails tear portions of animals and quickly devour them (fig. 1).

Night comes on and the rain increases. The strongest collect dead branches and long grasses, and pluck ferns and reeds, and heap them up against the wind; then, with sticks and with their hands, they try to make the water that invades their retreat run off by throwing soil on the piled-up branches. . . .

Not far off, Epergos, seized with compassion at sight of this misery, selects two young trees a few paces apart. Climbing one of these, he bends it down by the weight of his body, pulls toward him the top of the other with the help of a hooked stick, and thus joining the branches of the two trees, ties them together with rushes. The creatures that have gathered round him look on wondering. But Epergos does not mean them to remain idle, and makes them understand that they must go and find other young trees in the neighborhood. With their hands and with the help of sticks they uproot and drag them to Epergos, who then shows them how they should be inclined in a circle by resting their tops against the first two trees that had been fastened together. Then he shows them how to fill in the spaces with rushes, branches, and long grass interlaced; then how their roots should be covered with clay, and the whole structure successively (fig. 2); leaving an opening on the side opposite to the wind that brings the rain. On the floor he has dead branches and reeds spread, and mud trodden down with the feet.

By the end of the day the hut is finished, and each family among the Nairriti wishes to have one like it. (*Habitations of Man*, pp. 4–7)

THE EVOLUTION OF PROGRAMMATIC PLANNING

For Viollet-le-Duc, the conception of a building necessarily proceeds from a statement of the functional requirements. The design then evolves as the statement is progressively clarified, taking into consideration also the materials to be used and the environmental factors of site and climate. Thus when he imagines the earliest stages of architecture, he sees progress as resulting from improvement and refinement of the program.

"Hom!" said Doxius. "Just now you spoke wisely; you said that you wished to have your father's house restored; rebuild it then just as it was—just as your father left it you."

"But," returned Epergos, "who has told you that the house destroyed yesterday was in every respect like that which was probably erected in the same place before it?"

"It was not like it," said the Aryan; "for my father told me that his father's dwelling was smaller, and was covered with dry grass."

"Then," said Epergos, "we can make the new one more spacious and strong than the last was."

"Where will you limit your desires?" murmured Doxius.

"Why should I limit them? Let us set to work, that will be better than talking." . . .

"Woman," continued Epergos, addressing his hostess, "tell us, you who have always lived in the house and have taken care of the things it contained, whether the ruined dwelling suited you in all respects;

2. The first hut.

whether you found it wide enough, high enough, and sufficiently weatherproof?"

"It is true," answered the woman, "the children were cramped for space; in high winds the smoke often annoyed us, and we were scarcely sheltered from the north wind or the heat. Still, such as it was, we lived happily and peacefully in it." And she began to weep.

"No useless tears!" said the Aryan. "Let us set to work before the sun disappears behind the mountain. Come with us, mother, and tell this stranger what you want in addition to what we had before, since he shows a desire to help us."

The wife then pointed out, on the site of the cleared ruins, the space she proposed to allot to the children, the common apartment, and the room intended for herself and her husband. And it was not without shedding fresh tears that she thus designated each part of the house.

"You see," said Doxius, "this woman thinks only of her ruined dwelling; and all that your knowledge enables you to build will never make her forget that old habitation where she brought up her family. Be satisfied, therefore, with the building such as it was; our hosts will be happy and will bless you."

"Leave me to act," replied Epergos. "Present good makes us forget what is past: the fruit makes us forget the flower." *(Habitations of Man,* pp. 16–17).

AN OVERVIEW OF ARCHITECTURAL HISTORY

The panoply of period styles and the variety of structural types can, according to Viollet-le-Duc, be reduced to three basic conceptions, all of them fostered by the basic materials employed—wood, stone, earth. The pattern of their origin and dissemination conforms to a notion of cultural history that had recently been established in the fledgling disciplines of anthropology and linguistics. In it, he contends, all valid architecture is the result of a rational response to the materials available, the climate, the means of construction available (including labor), and the cultural requirements. He also imputes certain cultural impulses to racial groups in a manner characteristic of the nineteenth century.

The same phenomenon is always recurring; the world is not so varied as you think; in the moral and material order of things, as far as humanity is concerned, three or four principles reappear everywhere, and always independently of the time, environment, and circumstances. . . . Did men first build with wood, or with stone, or with earth? This question is not simple. If men are born in a wooded region, they will naturally employ timber to make themselves shelters; but if they find themselves in a country where timber is scarce and where stone or clay abounds, they will try to make themselves dwellings of these materials. But when men born in a thickly wooded region, and who have consequently acquired the habit of building with timber, betake themselves to a land that is devoid of those large vegetable growths, they find themselves somewhat embarrassed. Still they must have houses. In this case, although they employ the novel material at their disposal, they are naturally disposed to preserve the form and appearance of the wooden structures to which they had been accustomed.

Now, whether it was the result of natural predisposition or of the environment by which the various races of mankind were surrounded at the outset, [they] adopted certain methods of construction—methods whose original elements are handed down from age to age, and make their appearance at the present day as manifestly as do the roots of each of the languages spoken by those primitive races. To illustrate this by example: the Aryans, whose original abode was a mountainous and wooded region extending from the Upper Indus to the Brahmaputra, and stretching northward into Upper Tibet and as far as the Altai chain toward its western extremity, evidently made use of the timber that those mountains afforded them in abundance, to erect their dwellings.

When they quitted those elevated regions and descended first into Hindustan, then toward ancient Media and Persia, then toward the Euxine, subsequently in a westerly direction toward our own continent, Europe, they came sometimes to wooded countries, and in that case continued to build according to their original methods, sometimes to countries where the timber was scarce, and then they built—or, more correctly, made others build for them—with pise or with stone; but these dwellings reproduce, in innumerable details, the appearance of a structure in wood. Witness those Indian buildings that are of a comparatively recent period, since they only date from the commencement of Buddhism, and which, although erected with stone, or even hewn in the rock, figure timber constructions.

The buildings found in Cambodia . . . that are posterior to the Christian era, although built entirely of sandstone—the roofs included—

preserve the appearance of timber structures in so striking a manner that at a distance they might be taken for wooden buildings.

Does it follow that these Cambodian edifices, any more than others of the same class, are to be attributed to the Aryan race? By no means. Those of Cambodia, as we judge from the numerous designs sculptured on their walls, are the product of the Mongolian race; but whence had the influences here manifest reached the Mongolian race?

They are traced to Aryan traditions, and that is why this art at second hand, mingled in its details with very various elements, exhibits all the marks of an art in its decadence. This is never the case with the unmixed or nearly unmixed productions of that Aryan race; they are not obscured by a confused mass of adventitious elements; they maintain their identity through successive ages. . . . The chalets of the Swiss mountains are exactly like the dwellings that are to be seen on the slopes of the Himalayas and in the valleys of Kashmir. You will find the same construction, the same general appearance (fig. 3) . . . in those two parts of the globe that have no connection with each other.

Thousands of years ago, the Swiss chalets, as well as those of Tibet and of the valley of Kashmir, were built in the same manner by sections of one and the same race separated long ages since.

A good deal has been said of late about certain recent discoveries— "lake dwellings." These lake dwellings—dwellings, that is to say, built in the still waters of lakes, but far enough from the shores to make their isolation in the midst of waters a means of safety for the inhabitants— are attributable to special circumstances and are not characteristic of one race more than another. There are lake dwellings erected by the yellow race—the Chinese and Turanians—and there are and were some erected by Aryans. Both alike preserve, though built under similar conditions, the modes of building peculiar to the Aryans and Turanians respectively.

Here is another sketch (fig. 4) that shows some of those habitations built in Burma, which are made almost entirely of bamboos; for that country produces them in abundance.

There the influence of the Aryan and that of the yellow race—for while the high castes are descended from the Aryans, the common people are of Turanian blood—are both apparent. We observe combinations of timber framing that belong to the Aryans; on the other hand, the use of those mattings and of that bamboo work in the building that

3. Himalayan dwelling of the
Aryan tradition.

4. Lacustrine dwelling representing mixed traditions.

more especially characterize the yellow race. The lacustrine dwellings of the lake of Bienne must have greatly resembled these, with the exception of the bamboos, for which were substituted trunks of trees or even branches interlaced, and mud. . . . The same phenomena recur again and again, or, to speak more correctly . . . in every nation we invariably find the elements that betray their origin.

Look at the Semites, who, in their infancy, did not build with wood, since it pleased the Creator to place them in countries where building timber has always been scarce. They must employ stone, or what is easier, river mud. Some of them have neither mud nor timber nor stone suitable for building. They live under tents; but as the spots where they feed their flocks are successively depastured, they must be constantly on the lookout for new ground, which seems to recede before them: from the earliest times they have thus transported their tents from one place to another.

Are we thence to conclude that these men have no conception of any other kind of shelter than that furnished by a few skins or coarse woollen stuffs sewn together? Certainly not: and the proof is that when these pastoral people were able to settle anywhere, as in Egypt and Syria in the most remote times, they built or set others to build not in the way the Aryans did, but like their Semitic kindred.

Now, while principles are invariable, and the vestiges of parent stocks are indelible, the results produced by the mingling of these stocks are infinite in variety, and their aesthetic quality must be pronounced feebler in proportion to the complication of these intermixtures.

I have no great liking for formulas that, in questions such as this, may lead to misconception. I give you these, therefore, only as a very summary outline, which will render my explanations clearer by imparting to them the precision of a chemical process. Left to the guidance of their own instincts, the Aryans always build in the same manner, and they have such a marked predilection for timber construction that they seek by preference countries that are wooded, and have a veneration for trees. All nations of Aryan origin are attached to forests, delight in them, live among them, and have certain woods that they regard as consecrated. The yellow race, following their natural disposition, and having perhaps originally settled in vast regions abundantly watered and marshy, are in the habit of building with reeds; at an early date they discovered the use of lime, the manufacture of bricks, enameling and painting, the use of glues—in fact, everything required by an industrial development of a primitive order, but in which they make rapid advances. The Semites either live, as a matter of necessity, in tents or in natural or artificial grottoes; or they make themselves grottoes with clay, that is, they erect concrete masses of mud or clay—hollow tumuli in which they are sheltered from the heat and from insects: for their settlements are in hot regions, thinly wooded, and where streams are infrequent. It was they who first supplied unconsciously the rudiments of vaulting.

I leave out of sight certain races that have either continued in a state of evident inferiority, or are not clearly marked; for it is evident that nature does not approve of those sharply defined classifications that are convenient for our purposes, but to which she is indifferent. It would not be right, however, to overlook what are called the Hamites—an important race, divided into two sections, black and white, which appear to have had, from the earliest times, a special aptitude for works in stone: stone without the interposition of mortar; stone superimposed, close-jointed and hewn. Very early mingled with the Semites, the mixture derived from that race a peculiar character—a predilection for buildings of colossal dimensions and striking appearance, and for materials of great durability.

This explains the fact that in certain countries of Africa and of Syria, and in Egypt and Phoenicia, might be seen side by side with the clay and mud huts of the poor those magnificent buildings erected with the aid of appliances, whose strength excites our astonishment.

If, therefore, these elements being known, we mingle them in different proportions, we obtain various results, but in which, nevertheless, each of those elements can be discerned, however small in quantity.

Accordingly, when the Aryans are found in contact with the Semites already mingled with Hamites, there results from this union an art of a high degree of perfection. The moral sense of the Aryan leads him to reject those exaggerations of which the Hamites are so fond; but for the structure in wood he substitutes a structure in stone, and he adopts the forms that are appropriate to the latter, although traces of the first are still perceptible. This is the phenomenon whose highest expression is presented to us in Greek art. The Greek, who is perfectly acquainted with the use of lime and employs it for plastering, does not use mortar in dressed stonework; it is set dry, with close joints, after the manner of the Phoenician buildings; but to these constructions built according to the Phoenician method he gives forms that remind one of a structure in wood. The result, therefore, is an order of art whose productions are wonderful, but in whose composition the elements from which it sprang are nonetheless observable.

If we go to Egypt we find that while the products of art are various and their origin is enveloped in obscurity, analysis is nevertheless possible, and the elements to which they must have owed their origin can be brought to light. We observe the coexistence of a Semitic method of construction, an Aryan influence, and a very conspicuous Hamite element.

If we turn to Rome, we see the construction testifying to origins not less diverse, but which remain, so to speak, in juxtaposition without being intimately blended. The Roman constructs vaulting, which was not adopted by the Greeks, but of which the Etruscans made use; he employs mortar in his buildings, but it is with brick, concrete, or rubble work, never with dressed stone. He employs the latter as the Greeks do, namely, laid dry with close joints, and he does so to the end of the Empire.

In Roman art there is therefore a Phoenician, that is Etruscan and consequently Semitic element, mixed with one of Hamite origin, as well as an indubitable Aryan element; for the Roman also, when occasion suggests it, builds with timber, and loves and venerates the forests.

In his composition there is even a tincture of the yellow race; for he has a predilection for structures in adhesive materials, and employs mortars without stint.

And observe how ineffaceable is this influence of race. Look at the English cottage; we have still the Aryan's house, not only in construction but arrangement. There you invariably see the living room (hall) where the family assemble; the parlor—reception room—place of assembly; and next that separation of the domestic life from the public life; the gynaeceum of the Greeks and the nursery of the English are pretty much the same place; for the gynaeceum must not be confounded with the harem; the one is the sanctum of the family, the other a sort of aviary shut in from the gaze of strangers. Go to Sweden or Denmark, and you will find in the private houses those arrangements that date from the primitive times of the Aryan race—the hall and the place reserved for the life of the family; a place inviolable. Your old French chateaux exhibited the same arrangement before Gallo-Roman influences predominated over the Indo-Germanic; i.e., derived from what we call the Franks. In its structure, the true English cottage (villa) is still the timber house of the Aryan, and even when built of stone the forms are suggested by the timber structure. Similarly, if you go to Damascus, to Cairo, to Isfahan, as also in Algeria or Tunis and even in Spain, you find one and the same plan, adopted from a remote antiquity and adhered to down to the present day. The court, surrounded by porticoes, the patio with its little chambers, and the upper room opening out of this patio, with its divans, and receiving only a borrowed light— a cool and quiet place for the family gathering. Well! this very arrangement was to be found in a rudimentary form, and is still to be seen in some almost deserted cities of southern Syria. . . .

Let us visit China. It is easy for you to satisfy yourselves that the houses built four hundred years ago were exactly like those that are built there at the present day, since faithful representations of those habitations are extant; and if you go further back or search more widely, you will still find the same structure; for this reason, that it is the result of an elementary method, which is neither the consequence of a mixture, nor a deduction from principles already existing.

Let us go to Mexico and Yucatán; there indeed, in the large edifices of Uxmal, Chichén Itzá, of Isamal, Palanque, and Mitla, the mixture of elements is manifest. We find the trace of original elements transferred thither at second hand, construction in wood portrayed, but simulated unconsciously even in stone; adhesive methods, masonry with mortar for example; stone worked in disregard of its natural qualities and the requirements of its setting, the traces of ornamentation derived from woven stuffs and lacework; consequently an art already very old, in unmistakable decadence; and with these decrepit forms a singular primitive barbarism in the plans and arrangements determined by the habits of those for whom the dwellings are built. Whence we may conclude that the nation by which those buildings were constructed sprang from very diverse origins, or that they were a degenerate issue, subjected to influences from powerful races that had long cultivated the arts but which that nation had only imperfectly and rudely assimilated—had badly digested, so to speak—and that they were, in especial, incapable of coordinating those influences and choosing such elements as should be adapted to the climate and conditions in which circumstances had placed them.

But I will not fatigue you by an enumeration of all the consequences resulting from those origins. It is sufficient to have noticed the chief bearings of the question, and it is time to bring my remarks to a close.

It is then certain that in the course of ages those original elements have approached each other, have separated, and have been intermingled. For a long time it was very easy to distinguish them, because the fusions were recent or incomplex. As time went on they became more extensive and complicated. Nevertheless, analysis will even now enable us to discover those original elements, however complex their combination, just as we may always ascertain the origin of a language by its roots and reconstruct it as soon as we have discovered some of those roots. The century in which we live has made great progress in the path of analysis, but the goal is still far off. In regard to human habitations the result of the inquiry will be that each will become acquainted with the elementary characteristics of his race or of the races from which he is descended; and such knowledge will enable him to improve his dwelling in accordance with his natural proclivities and aptitudes. The Renaissance movement, which was a veritable intellectual revolution, by bringing into notice a very considerable and most important period of the past of which Europe was entirely ignorant; this movement, I say, by the enthusiasm it excited in favor of classical antiquity among all cultivated minds, turned this part of the globe for a time out of its normal path of progress. Classical antiquity appeared so beautiful and perfect that it seemed desirable to stop at this point in human development, and to contract an indissoluble union with it. And admiration for that period of the past was at first confined to its form.

Thus it was that the very considerable amount of valuable work that had been accomplished during the Middle Ages came to be disregarded, or even reckoned utterly worthless. This was a mistake; more than this, it took for granted an impossibility. It is no more in the power of a period or of an individual or of a corporate body, however influential, to cancel a page in the book of human development, than to remove one of the geological formations on the plea that it is a coarse one. What has been once acquired is a possession for ever.

But this enthusiasm for classical antiquity is now producing results of a more valuable character. It has given an impulse to the investigation of the entire past, to a thorough scrutiny, analysis, and classification of all available data; and one of the earliest results of this investigation has been that there is no such subject of study as an antiquity isolated from the series of human records; that all the cycles of historical evolution are linked together and assume new forms through a succession of phases and blended influences; that here, as in geology, we cannot understand a particular deposit without knowing what is below and what is above it. Those enthusiasts for Greek and Roman forms—for in their naive admiration they were accustomed to confound them, utterly different though they are in their principle and in its expression—have succeeded in misleading Europe for two or three centuries, a mere moment, however, compared with the life of humanity; and we have been inundated with neo-Greek and neo-Roman—such indeed as would make Greeks and Romans laugh—without the slightest regard for origins, natural aptitudes, climate, materials, or the novel conditions of social life. In Paris and in Rome, in Madrid and in St. Petersburg, in Vienna and in Stockholm, so-called Greek and Roman palaces have been erected.

Nevertheless, a generation of inquiries has arisen who have had no difficulty in demonstrating that humanity is not thus homogeneously constituted; that because a Pompeian house was charming under a Neapolitan sky and admirably suited to the requirements of people who lived two thousand years ago, it by no means follows that such a house suits our time and climate. A dedicated tendency toward a reaction is therefore manifest. Every civilized nation has begun to inquire—and the inquiry will be prosecuted with increasing ardour—whence it comes, and what are its elements; and it is consequently endeavoring to adopt those original forms in art that are adapted to the genius and requirements of the race to which it belongs. This movement is already very apparent in England, in Germany, in Sweden, and in Russia, and it is becoming daily more marked. From a conservative point of view, this is, I am well aware, the culmination of moral disorder; for it prefers a unity produced by authority, and has never been willing to admit that human beings have aptitudes varying according to the diversity of their origin. I think, on the contrary, that in the development of these ideas there is a fresh source of prosperity and greatness for mankind.

The Philosopher said to man: "Know thyself"; and this is in fact the foundation of all wisdom. The time has come for us to say to humanity: "Investigate your beginnings: you will thus learn your aptitudes, and will be able to pursue that path of true Progress to which your destiny calls you." *(Habitations of Man,* pp. 380–94)

2   The Great Traditions: Greek, Roman, Gothic

Viollet-le-Duc developed most of his ideas about architecture during the middle third of the nineteenth century. He was, for that time, extraordinarily well informed about the history of world architecture and he nurtured a wide-ranging appreciation for the architectural accomplishments of many centuries. Yet for him the issues of central importance were incorporated in the works of the Greek, Roman, and French Gothic builders. With the exception of a few brief passages treating other traditions, which will be quoted in other contexts, his discovery of the central principles of architecture was posited in the discussion of those three periods.

For Viollet-le-Duc, the main concern of Greek builders was to establish an ideal structure, reflecting a rational formulation and assembly of parts, appropriate to the materials employed. He saw this concern manifested primarily in the Doric peripteral temple, which was taken to represent the Greek tradition as a whole. Roman architecture, on the other hand, was seen as addressing a preoccupation with the functional requirements of a given building, emphasizing the arrangement of spaces in the plan. The formulation of structure, then, was the means to an end rather than an end in itself, in consequence of which it was both more flexible and less cerebral in its composition than that of the Greeks. Neither principle was regarded as superior to the other but together they were taken to represent the two possible approaches to the design of buildings.

The great virtue of the Gothic tradition was that it provided a synthe-

sis of these disparate principles. *Although prompted by a functional program, the structure was perceived as the rational solution to a logical problem. Representing the most sophisticated level of inventiveness yet evidenced in the history of architecture, the Gothic tradition was held up as the most apt source of inspiration for a modern architecture. Although Viollet-le-Duc did see merit in the functional programs of French Renaissance chateaux, in general he judged the classicizing architecture of the Renaissance and its progeny in later centuries as decadent and corrupt. For this reason his theory of architecture was addressed to a rejection of the established order—epitomized by the Ecole des Beaux-Arts—and a revolutionary reformulation employing principles from a more distant past.*

GREEK ARCHITECTURE

For Viollet-le-Duc, the rationality of Greek architecture resided not in the composition of structural elements as an abstract statement but in the sense that the composition made as a construction of large stones, situated in a sunny climate. Although he earnestly pleaded the case for the formulation of all the features of the Doric order according to their functional role, it should be noted that some of them, such as the angle contraction in intercolumniations, do not serve the function he attributed and that others, such as the triglyph frieze, may be only metaphorically functional. Contrary to the Vitruvian tradition that the Doric temple represented a translation into stone of a structural system originally formulated in wood, he maintained that it had been thought out in stone from the very beginning.

Many authors and professors have asserted that the stone and marble temples of Greece exhibit in their structure the tradition of a wooden construction. This hypothesis may be ingenious, but it does not appear to me to be based on an attentive examination of these monuments. . . . At first sight the theory appears plausible; one difficulty, however, meets us at the onset, which is this: The primitive timber edifices were circular in form; they were composed of trunks of trees whose lower ends were planted in a circle and their tops brought together in a cone. Vitruvius himself . . . speaking of the primitive wooden cabin, is far from ascribing to it the forms adopted by the Grecian Doric temples. . . .

Let us imagine that a man unacquainted with the resources of the art of building desires to place pieces of timber across the tops of wooden posts or uprights. Let us suppose that this man is intelligent, as the native tribes or aborigines of Greece undoubtedly were; and that he had already invented the axe at least, if not the saw and the mortising tool. The first idea that will occur to him with the view of getting the posts in line—which is essential if he means to connect them by a crosspiece—will be to square them; for it is not easy to place the trunks of trees in a straight line while in their natural form, which always presents some twist or inequality. Our intelligent workman then (for we must not forget that he *is* intelligent) has remarked that timbers bearing on their extremities, in a horizontal position, bend under their own weight, and still more if they are loaded; he therefore inserts an intermediate piece between the top of his upright and the horizontal piece, the beam or lintel, to lessen its bearing. Will he employ for this purpose a square parallelepiped of wood, such as is shown at figure 5—a block of wood very difficult to procure, from its width being greater than the diameter of the uprights, and especially difficult to cut and fashion without the aid of the saw? Certainly not; for in addition to other objections, this capital, this square parallelepiped, will give but very little aid in supporting the bearing of the beams. He will not take so much trouble to obtain such an insignificant result; he will succeed in effectually supporting the bearing of the beam by means of the two considerable projections, as indicated in figure 6. This is veritably a timber construction, and is such as we see imitated in stone in the ancient monuments of India, and even in those recently discovered at Nineveh. The square upright presents four awkward angles; the primitive constructor cuts them away and ultimately forms an octagonal prism. The cylindrical form is the very last a carpenter adopts for vertical supports, since it is that which requires the longest process, the squaring of the wood being of primary necessity in timber framing. An ordinary working carpenter would tell us this; and we may observe in passing that it is always desirable, when endeavoring to establish theories respecting the origin of particular forms in art, to consult the crafts whose ordinary methods recall primitive modes of proceeding.

The primitive architecture of the nations of the remote East (the common source of all the arts) presents to us more than any other, both in its general configuration and in its details, veritable imitations in stone of a wooden structure; and these imitations are carried so far that even in monuments hewn in the rock, the Hindu architects have made the ceilings simulate planks and joists. Many of the Chinese houses, to take another example, have wooden porticoes, the eave plates of which are carried on posts accompanied by struts formed of curved timber, as shown in figure 7.

Now, in the crypts of Ganesa, at Cuttack in India, may be seen pillars left in the solid rock that are of this form (fig. 8).

Others again, in one of the temples of Ajunta, present another form of structure (fig. 9).

In both these examples the curved struts and the projecting caps that carry the beam, all hewn out of the solid rock, are evidently the tradition of a timber framing. The transition from the square of the base to an octagon, and then, in figure 9, to a sixteen-sided polygon, with the return near the top to the octagon and the square, is far more suggestive of processes applicable to fashioning and framing timber than of those employed in working stone. This is evident to all who have endeavored to contrive a timber support that shall be at the same time stiff, firm on its base, and as much lightened as the nature of the material will admit.

We all know the capitals of the ruins of Persepolis: many of these affect the form indicated in figure 10. Now, in the same country—in Assyria and Persia—peasants' huts of modern date may be seen whose ceilings are carried on forked posts such as are shown in figure 11, which beyond all doubt represent the origin of that form of the stone capitals of Persepolis. This forked shape has a double advantage; it not only supports the beam or lintel in front, but it also affords a resting place between the two branches of the fork for a piece of timber at right angles to the front, serving as a beam for the support of the floor joists, which thus find their place in the depth of the lintel. Figure 12 illustrates this primitive disposition of a wooden structure in which the constructor had sought to do without the framing by mortise and tenon, which came into use when tools and the other appliances for construction were improved. These are the wooden buildings that must have been imitated in stone by the tribes of Asia. The remains of their monuments, whether built of masonry or hewn in the rock, prove this fact in the clearest manner possible. But these methods of procedure have no connection with the Greek temple. Shall we seek yet more striking examples, if such are possible? Let us consider those tombs in Asia Minor

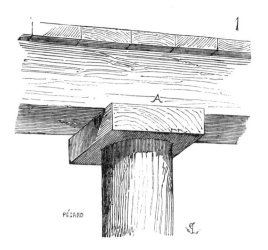

5. Improbable primitive timber construction.

6. Probable primitive timber construction.

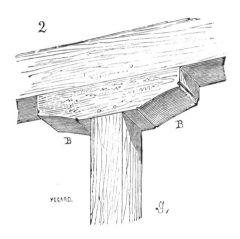

7. Chinese timber construction.

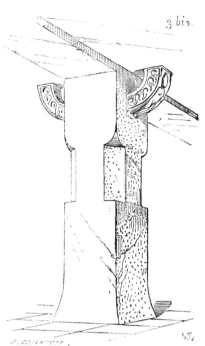

8. Stone pillar in imitation of timber construction, Cuttack, India.

9. Stone pillar in imitation of a second type of timber construction, Cuttack, India.

10. Stone capital from the ruins of Persepolis.

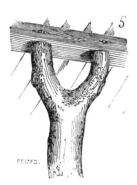

11. Forked post.

12. Ancient timber construction of Asia.

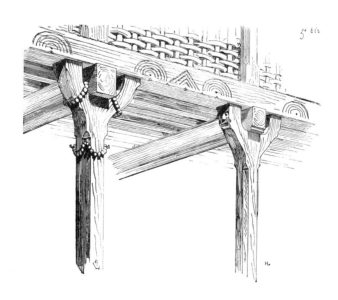

hewn in the living rock, and of which any one may form an idea by referring to the engravings of them executed from the drawings of M. Texier—those cryptlike sepulchres whose portals represent and might be taken for timber constructions. The primitive edifices of Central America present to the attentive eye the very same peculiarities; for all civilizations in their commencement proceed in the same manner.

The imitation of construction in wood appears even in the minutest details of these primitive edifices of the East: for instance we frequently see at the tops of pillars a succession of rolls one over the other presenting a decoration of the character shown in figure 13.

Is it not evident that these rolls are nothing more than the curled chips cut from the wooden post by the carpenter in the process of squaring it? The ornaments represent strings of berries and a variety of those gravings that are so easy to execute upon wood, and of which all primitive peoples, who have abundant leisure, are so prodigal. Passing from details to the examination of complete buildings, we find in India certain sacred edifices of stone that are singularly suggestive of the wooden pyramid described by Vitruvius; a collection, namely, of tree trunks or of bamboos placed horizontally one upon another, and set back in steps from the base to the summit. Others nearly resemble in shape immense baskets formed of bamboo interlaced, and adorned with garlands of berries, little figures, loops, and rings.

In India houses are still constructed with bamboo latticework placed upright, plastered with temperd clay, and covered also with latticework thatched with leaves, straw, or rushes (fig. 14). In the same country this very form is found reproduced in stone buildings of extreme antiquity.

As a conclusion to this general review of timber constructions, let us look at that Lycian sarcophagus in the British Museum, which is a reproduction in a lasting material of a form of monument such as was undoubtedly made of wood in that country, at a very remote period. Is it not plainly an immense shrine of carpentry work of which the pieces, the joinings, and the notchings are apparent—and even the very bearers by which it was to be carried? Let us attentively examine the drawing of this curious monument (fig. 15), cut in three blocks of stone. Would not anyone suppose it to be a production of carpentry, composed of posts, rails, spars, and panels? Is it not evidently a wooden cover placed upon a sarcophagus hewn out of a block of marble? If this tomb is not of an extremely early period, as the sculpture upon it would lead us to be-

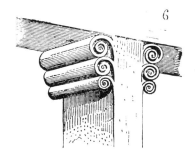

13. Form of ancient stone capital suggested by carpenter's work.

14. Lattice work construction of India.

15. Stone sarcophagus in imitation of wooden construction.

lieve, it only demonstrates more clearly that when the populations of Asia Minor and of Greece did imitate wooden constructions in stone they expressed those constructions most frankly. Here the modillions or mutules are not returned round the ends as in the Greek temple; the uprights are square instead of cylindrical; the roofs are veritable framed gables supporting the purlins that carry the roofing, which is curved and not slanting, quite in conformity with the primitive notion of a wooden building. The ridge itself represents two planks sculptured upon the sides that are exposed to view. The spars that form the intermediate floor are made to clasp the longitudinal rail to prevent any giving; the spars of the upper floor are fixed between two clips. The feet of the four uprights are held on the two bearers by means of keys conspicuously indicated. This monument reveals to us a very curious fact: in the first place, we see that in the early days of these nations the dead were placed in a sarcophagus of stone or marble, which was covered with a coffer or shrine of wood; and next it shows us that the Greek temple is a stone construction, and not the imitation of a construction in wood.

Here let me observe that although the immense eastern continent, extending from China to the Caspian, the Black Sea, and the Persian Gulf, owing to its lofty mountains, its noble rivers, the wonderful fertility of its valleys, its extensive marshes and favoring climate, furnished at all times a considerable quantity of every kind of timber, such could never have been the case with Greece. I willingly admit that its soil, barren at present, may once have produced forests. But what were these woods compared with those that grew so luxuriantly on the continent of India? Did Greece ever possess those gigantic bamboo canes so well adapted for constructive purposes? If there ever existed in Greece forests of timber fit for building, they must have been quickly destroyed. Let us then look at the Greek temple.

In the first place, what is the program? It is required to build a cella— an enclosed chamber—and to surround it with porticoes, as well for its protection as to afford shelter. Nothing can be simpler. Four walls with openings for doorways, and a succession of vertical supports surrounding them, carrying lintels that are sheltered by a projecting cornice; over all, sloping roofs to throw off the rain on the two sides that have no doorways. Reason alone has dictated this disposition. What, then, are the means of execution?

The architect seeks for a quarry in the immediate neighborhood; and he will find one at hand, for Greece and Sicily abound in materials of a calcareous nature, and the Greek cities are generally built on plateaus or the slopes of hills, and possess an Acropolis—that is to say, a rock naturally or artificially escarped—around which the habitations and public buildings are grouped. Mountains and promontories that furnish abundant materials exist in close proximity. Having secured his quarry, however, the architect has none of those powerful appliances that mechanical science has rendered familiar to us; the arms of his slaves are his only force; he therefore endeavors to avoid as much as possible the difficulties that accompany the transport of very heavy blocks. Nevertheless, the employment of materials of considerable dimensions is just what is prescribed to him by the traditions of the art in the form in which he is acquainted with it, the art as he has received it from Egypt and the East: the only system he recognizes is that of the column and lintel; he is therefore obliged to seek some method by which he may reconcile the exigencies of this form of art with the means of execution placed at his disposal. This is how he proceeds. The difficulties by which he is surrounded will not discourage him; on the contrary, they will become the most effective stimuli to his artistic genius. Art will profit by them. The Greek architect thinks, and with reason, that the cella of his temple may be built with materials of small dimensions; it is merely a wall with two apparent faces, one in the interior, the other on the exterior of the temple. Two faces—consequently, from his point of view, two stones. The construction of a wall of ordinary strength, with materials that do not constitute its whole thickness, but are composed of ashlar slabs having only one external face, like two thick paving stones set back to back, would be wrong from the point of view of the constructor, though right from that of the logician. Now the Greek is above all things a logician; he therefore prepares in the quarry slabs of ashlar, or stones intended to have only one external face. With these ashlar slabs he will build his cella. But he is aware that these two faces form two unconnected walls; so at regular intervals, to tie them together, he inserts bonders, that is, long stones forming parpaings. He requires vertical supports—in other words, columns; he perceives that these isolated piers, to present the appearance of perfect stability, should be composed of blocks as large as possible. The quarries and the means of transport at his disposal rarely enable him to erect monolithic columns. He selects in the quarry the thickest beds he can find, near to a declivity where the calcareous strata crop out. Upon the upper surface of these beds he traces a circle whose diameter is that of his intended columns: around it he sinks a deep trench wide enough for the stonecutter to stand in; and thus from the rock itself he detaches a cylinder. Having reached the lower surface of the bed and completely worked out the excavation on the side of the declivity, he upsets the cylinder, that is, turns it over on its side, and then rolls it down as a huge disk to the foot of the escarpment. There he sinks a square hole in the center of each circular face of the disk, and in these holes he fixes two pivots or axles; then by means of a timber frame and cables he rolls the column drums to the site of the temple.

Thus it was the difficulties attendant on the obtaining of his material that first obliged him to adopt the cylindrical form for the largest-sized blocks as being the most easy of transport. This is no hypothetical description; for any one may see the quarries near Selinuntum in Sicily, which were used by the inhabitants of that Greek colony. In this place, which even now goes by the name of Cava di Casa (building-stone quarry), are exhibited all these successive operations. Here may be seen, still unmoved from their calcareous bed, cylinders of enormous size, no less than twelve feet in diameter and from seven to ten feet in height; others that have rolled by their own weight to the foot of the hill; others again on the road to their destination, with the square holes sunk in the center of their circular faces. The cruel destruction of the populous city of Selinuntum by the Carthaginian invaders caused these blocks to be left in the very act of transportation; and no ruin can excite a more lively emotion than these still fresh and vivid traces of human labor, interrupted, as it were, but yesterday.

But it is not only the columns of the temple that require blocks of great bulk. The lintels that will bear from column to column must also be of considerable size if the temple is of large dimensions. In the extraction of these blocks the Greek architect will proceed in the same manner as when he was preparing to build the walls of the cella; he will compose them of two long stones placed side by side, leaving a vertical joint between the two, with their faces one on the exterior, the other on the interior of the portico. Experience soon shows him that this method presents an advantage independent of the facilities it affords to the transport of the blocks. It must be observed that all calcareous stones, marble included, are liable to have flaws, or ruptures across the bed, which are invisible at the time of extraction, but which discover themselves under the strain of superincumbent weight, and occasion a fracture that in a lintel is irremediable; whereas two lintels placed side by side have two chances to one in favor of resistance, for if one of them is defective, its twin brother may withstand the strain and thus prevent an immediate fall. And in point of fact this method is employed without exception by the Greek architect whenever he employs calcareous stones whose strength is not very considerable, such as those of Sicily. The materials for his temple being all brought to the site, the architect will elevate and place them in position by means of very ingenious contrivances. Thus, for the cylindrical drums of the columns he will make use of the square hole cut in the center of one of the beds, and, giving it a dovetail section, he will suspend them by means of the lewis; or, working back the rounded surface a little, he will leave two projecting tenons that will serve him as a catch for the rope, by whose aid the stones will be lifted one upon another; for as these blocks are laid close fitting, without either wedges or mortar, they will reach the place of their destination in a suspended position—and when once set, it will be no longer possible to displace them. All the means of suspension must then be so contrived as to leave their bed joints entirely free. The capitals will be easily raised vertically by means of the projecting corners of the abacus. As to the blocks composing the lintels that are laid end to end—which are long and not very thick and have two joints necessarily hidden, one or two faces in view, and an under bed or soffit also in view—they must be secured and hoisted by the two ends; the architect will prepare for the suspension of these by sinking in the two vertical end joints of each block a channel deep enough for a strong rope to pass freely through it as shown in figure 16. When the stone is raised to its place he will withdraw the rope from its groove. The Greeks attained wonderful perfection in the setting of close-jointed masonry. In this kind of masonry the blocks could not be wheeled on stages of scaffolding at different heights, and let down upon wedges with the crowbar, according to our method; they had to be brought exactly over their intended position, in order to be lowered gently and carefully into place. Had they rested awry on their bed, the hoisting engines would not have been strong enough to detach them again, by reason of the close adhesion of the two horizontal perfectly plane and

16. Greek mode of hoisting the
lintel stones.

close-fitting surfaces. The only means by which it was possible at that time to secure this accuracy in setting was the use of immense cranes, which were successively brought and stayed first over each column and then—when all these were erected—over the spaces between the columns, in order to hoist the lintels, triglyphs, metopes, cornices, etc. We must remember, a propos of this, that the Greeks are a maritime people, and that, as such, they must have very early possessed engines of construction that were intelligently, simply, and perfectly combined.

Having briefly described the material means of its execution, let us now proceed to the examination of the building itself; let us watch the construction of a Greek temple. The walls of the cella being built, and the columns raised, the architect perceives that the horizontal blocks— the lintels that have to bear from one column to another—may on account of their length give way under the weight they carry; so, upon the summit of the columns he places projecting blocks—in a word, capitals.

The abacus of the Grecian Doric capital is square; two of its fronts, by their wide projection, support in an equal degree the bearing of the architrave; but the two others—those that face outside and inside— support nothing. If the Grecian Doric capital had been designed in imitation of a wooden capping, these two interior and exterior projections, extending beyond the face of the beam, would have had neither object nor meaning, as I have previously explained. In a stone construction, however, these projections are amply justified. In fact, the largest blocks composing the Grecian Doric order are necessarily the architraves or lintels, bearing from column to column; for if the columns can be raised in drums more or less numerous, it is quite otherwise with the architraves, which must have a length equal to the distance between the centers of the columns, and a height sufficient to present a great resistance. But we have just seen that these blocks are lifted by their two concealed ends and laid with close joints. To lower such weighty blocks exactly upon their resting places, that is, upon the abaci of the capitals, it was essential that the operation should be performed with skill, precision, and certainty, so as not to risk a deviation of the column from the perpendicular. The interior and exterior projections of the capital then became extremely serviceable; they afforded means for placing balks of timber along the back and front, which kept the columns in line and rendered them mutually supporting; they also enabled the stonesetters to stand on either side of the lintel, without need of other scaffolding, to guide the blocks and lower them gently onto the capitals without danger of mistake, because the two balks had left between them just the space of those lintels.

We should observe that all the primitive builders are chary of scaffolding; they do not like, and the Greeks least of all, to perform labor that is to all appearances useless, that is to say, which is to leave no trace. Some of the Greek temples remain unfinished and may still be seen as they were left in course of being dressed down, that of Segesta for example; and it will readily be perceived, even by those who are but little versed in the practice of our art, that the materials that compose these buildings were raised by the simplest means as regards their suspension and setting, and that the builders have endeavored as far as possible to make the building itself serve as a scaffolding, by providing projections as resting places for timbers laid longitudinally or transversely as the case required. Moreover, these builders take good care never to elevate large blocks when they can avoid it. Above the lintels or architraves there are no longer found any but stones of comparatively small dimensions; and it is evident that to avoid too great expense and difficulty, the architecture itself cedes to the means of execution. The frieze that surrounds the architrave is merely a succession of small blocks, between which are placed slabs on edge, with a filling in at the back, often in several layers. The cornice projects but little and does not bond over the whole thickness of the frieze; it has only just tail sufficient to prevent its overbalancing (see fig. 17). But the builder, while economizing his materials, compensates by his intelligence for any defect they may present in point of strength or durability; for instance, he observes that according to a physical law, the rain water follows the under horizontal surface of the cornice projection; he therefore makes it a drip, that is, he gives a slant to this under surface in order to oblige the water to drop the moment it reaches the edge.

These are improvements in which man's faculty of reasoning only has taken part. It might be supposed that he would rest content here. Not so. Art intervenes in its turn. The building is erected beneath a clear sky, through which, during ten months of the year, a brilliant sun pours down its light. The artist quickly observes that the cylindrical pillars of his temple appear, by an optical delusion, larger at their summit than at their base. This is as shocking to his reason as it is to his sight; he converts these cylinders into truncated cones. The requirement of stability had, perhaps, already obliged him to adopt this diminution of the shafts. He further observes that the intermediate blocks—the capitals supporting the lintel—seem to crush the column by their mass; he leaves them their square form in the upper part, where it answers to a requirement of stability, and works away the under part in such a manner as to pass from the shaft of the column to the square abacus with a curve.

The artist, however, is not yet satisfied with his work: the columns appear flat when in full light, faint and ill defined when in shade. He therefore reworks the surface of the shaft in a series of vertical facets; and it is not long before he decides to hollow out these facets so as to form flutings sufficiently deep to catch the oblique rays of light on their edges, yet not deep enough for these edges to be inconvenient or dangerous to persons passing. And thus the sun's rays, by repeating on each of the shafts a series of vertical lights and shadows, restore to them the importance that they lacked while they were merely cylindrical. The artist's own feeling, moreover, tells him that to impress the eye with the value that a particular form should assume, the principal lines of that form should be repeated; just as the musician feels that if he would impress the ear with a particular phrase, it must be repeated several times in the course of his composition. Now the vertical line of the column increases in importance in proportion to the number of times this line is reproduced upon its surface. The artist, however, also knows that nothing more is needed than to make himself understood, and that he must not fatigue the senses by a too frequent repetition: he therefore sinks in the shaft of his column only the number of flutings required by the effect contemplated.

The columns, their capitals, and the lintels being now in place, the architect, as I have just observed, is no longer compelled to employ materials of large dimensions: he may place on the architrave of his temple blocks of moderate size; and this he does not fail to do. First, over each joint of this architrave crowned by a fillet and over the center of each intercolumniation he places blocks at some distance apart so as to weigh on the architrave as lightly as possible. But the artist is a Greek; he is anxious that his judicious combination should be manifest—comprehended by every one. On the external face, therefore, of each of these stones, which stand between the architrave and the cornice, and form, as it were, so many small detached pillars, he cuts a triglyph: in other words, he sinks on their visible surface upright flutings that express, as he feels, something that supports weight; and his feeling is the more correct, and his reasoning the more just, inasmuch as he proceeded in a precisely similar manner when he sought to express the function of vertical support in the columns. The triglyph is also a vertical support, and this he distinctly indicates.

The Greek architect possesses the merits and the failings of the reasoner: he insists upon making it apparent to every eye that the various parts of his edifice have each a useful and necessary function; he will not have it said that he has sacrificed anything to caprice; he is not content with knowing that his building is solid—he must make it appear such. But though he never conceals the means he employs, his artistic instinct leads him to invest each part of his edifice with a form admirably adapted both to the place it occupies and the effect it is designed to produce: his good taste forbids that pedantic repetition that wearies the public and gives it a disgust for reason by the very abuse or excess of reasoning.

To close the openings that remain between the triglyphs, the architrave, and the cornice, he inserts therein slabs set on edge and recessed back; previously requesting his brother, the statuary, to sculpture bas-reliefs upon these stones thus unframed between the triglyphs, architrave, and cornice. Figure 17 illustrates the general arrangement of this so truthful construction—which is not, as I judge, the tradition of the timber framing of some remotely distant age, as some have contended, but a veritable stone construction. The columns, by their cylindrico-conical form, the capitals with their square abacus, the entablature with its triglyphs, its inserted metopes, and its throated cornice, and the way in which all these members rest upon one another, indicate stone throughout—quarried, worked, hoisted, and made manifest by reason of its nature and of the function that it fulfils. Wood also plays its part in the Greek temple; but it is a part altogether secondary—quite distinct from the stone construction. The Greeks had too much good sense ever to have placed upon the architrave, or the beams—admitting that the architraves were primitively beams of wood—joists whose scantling would be given by the triglyphs, merely to cover—what? A portico of seven or ten feet in width.

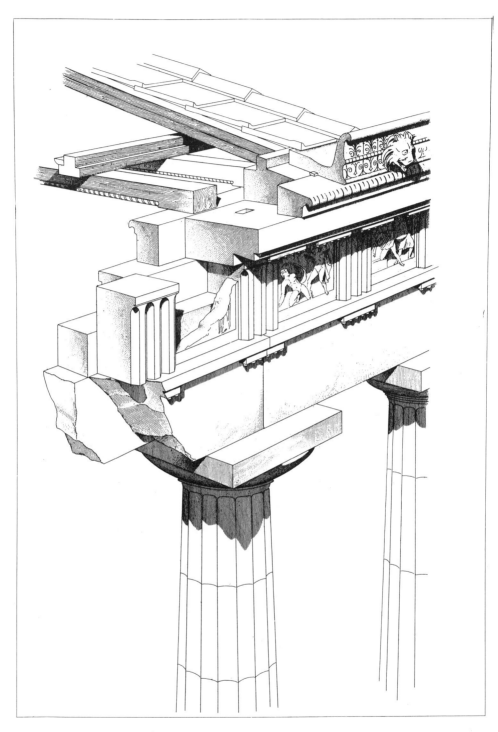

17. Analytical diagram of the
Doric order.

Every fact, moreover, without exception, comes in to disprove this supposed origin. The joists of the wooden ceiling of the portico, or the lintels and marble slabs intended for its covering, and which form a ceiling, are never placed on the architrave, but invariably on the frieze—that is to say, above the triglyphs; the space reserved for them and the projection on which they rested are still to be seen in every existing temple. This space indicates only timbers of a scantling proportionate to their bearing—namely, from six to nine inches square, or a resting place just sufficient to receive the horizontal slabs of marble when that material takes the place of timberwork.

Just as the triglyphs are taken for the ends of joists, so the rain-drip of the cornice is supposed to represent the rafter ends. But even if this hypothesis has a semblance of probability on the two lateral sides of the temple, what possible signification could rafter ends have on the fronts below the pediments? We have too high an opinion of the good judgment of the Greek artists to allow that they could ever have committed so flagrant an offense against reason and common sense. If the rain-drip did indicate the projection of the rafters beyond the frieze, they would not have put a similar drip at the base of the pediment. And beneath the projections of the cornice of this pediment they would have placed indications of the ends of the purlins; since, according to the belief in question, they so scrupulously represented in their stone construction each single piece of timber. Figure 15, representing a Lycian tomb, which is really an imitation of a wooden construction, exhibits no such absurdity: the purlins are plainly indicated on the gable ends, and the joists of the ceiling that supports the roof are not returned along the fronts of these gables; they only exist on the lateral faces.

The Greek temples are buildings of stone in which the system of the lintel is worked out in accordance with reason and taste: why not take them simply for what they are? why contend that Greeks, the inventors of logic—men gifted with refined aesthetic sensibility—amused themselves with simulating in stone a construction of wood—a thing essentially monstrous? That such imitations have occurred among the Hindus, that they have influenced the architecture of the Assyrians and of the inhabitants of Asia Minor, is possible; but to suppose it among the western Greeks is to misunderstand their genius altogether.

It is by explanations such as these of the derivations of ancient and medieval architecture—more ingenious than well-considered—that the course of architectural study has come to be misdirected, and consequently the mind of the architect perverted. In explaining buildings we think it a commendable principle to take them for what they really are, and not for what we should wish them to be. This supposition that the Greek temple is an imitation in stone of a wooden hut is of the same order as that which refers the architecture of our Gothic churches to the forest avenues of Gaul and Germany. Both are fictions well adapted to amuse the fancy of dreamers, but very hurtful, or at best useless, when we are called upon to explain the derivations of an art to those whose vocation it is to practice it.

The triglyphs fulfill the purpose over the architraves of a clerestory. They are uprights of stone, relieving the pressure on the architrave, as we have said, by their separation and the space intervening between them. It would even appear that originally the intervals between the triglyphs were often left open.

In the tragedy of *Iphigenia in Tauris,* Orestes and Pylades wish to gain an entrance into the temple of Diana to carry off the statue of the goddess. Pylades proposes to penetrate into the cella through the openings left between the triglyphs. "Look," he says to Orestes, "into the interval of the triglyphs, where there is space enough for the body to pass through." This translation word for word from the Greek text does not say "between the triglyphs;" but the speakers are not architects, and in common parlance we might say "in the triglyphs," or "in the interval of the triglyphs," as we now say "in the balusters," meaning "between the balusters of a balustrade." This passage of Euripides possesses a double interest for us: for the reference here cannot be to the intervals left between the triglyphs placed over the columns, as through these the two heroes would only have gained entrance into the open portico, and it was easier to pass between the columns than through the holes left between the triglyphs: evidently the text must refer to the triglyphs placed on the wall of the cella, where indeed they are often to be found. May not these openings left between the triglyphs placed at the top of the cella wall have been intended to admit light and air into the inner enclosure? This hypothesis would favor the supposition that the cella was completely covered in.

Let us revert to the structure of the Greek temple. The Greek architect recognizes the necessity of symmetry: it is an instinct of the human mind; but he does not allow that this instinct should override reason. In building his temple he began with the cella—the enclosure reserved for the divinity—making it an independent construction, a walled enclosure of inconsiderable dimensions, around which he placed the columns of his portico, leaving between this enclosure and the columns a space for perambulation wide in proportion to the size of the cella. He troubles himself little as to whether the centers of the pilasters at the corners of the cella (the antae) correspond with those of the columns of the portico. He has perceived that practically this coincidence of centers cannot be appreciated. His sole concern is so to arrange his columns that the wooden ceiling may rest upon the wall of the cella and the internal friezes of the portico. This consideration is his only guide. His reason leads him still further to disregard what are called the rules of symmetry; the angles of his portico engross his attention, he sees their isolated columns, which have to support a heavier weight than the rest, he foresees that if one of the architraves bearing on this angle should happen to break, it will have the effect of forcing the column outwards. Reason suggests to him the prudence of allowing a lesser space between the angle column and the two neighboring ones that he has allowed between the other columns of the portico, and of increasing the diameter of this angle column; and what his reason suggests, that he follows, in spite of the rules of symmetry. This difference between the centers of the columns enables him to put a triglyph at the angle of the frieze (which is equally accordant with reason, since the triglyph is a point of support, and if points of support are anywhere necessary they are especially so at the corners of a building), without thereby sensibly increasing the spaces between the three last triglyphs.

These difficulties in the general arrangement being solved, the architect proceeds to the consideration of details: he has observed that when it rains, the water trickles down the vertical face of the external cornice, and, mingling with the dust, leaves brown stains that darken the crown of his edifice, whose extreme verge he desires to see stand out lustrous against the azure of the sky. He lays on this cornice a gutter of marble or terra-cotta, furnished at regular intervals with projecting gargoyles, and thus succeeds in throwing the water off from the face of the cornice: but this gutter, itself exposed to the rain, soon becomes weather-stained, and he overlays it with carving or painting to render this defect less apparent. The more the born artist observes, the wider does the field of observation extend itself before him. Now the observation of the artist and that of the savant differ in their results. The savant observes in order to compare, to draw conclusions, in a word, to know. The artist observes, but he does not stop at conclusions: his conclusions lead him on to augment, modify, or neutralize the effects produced by physical laws—to struggle in concert with or in opposition to them. The artist observes that a cylinder brightly illumined presents only one light and one shade: he modifies this effect by distributing the light and shade by means of flutings; and thus compels the natural light to round his columns. He observes that the wide abacus of his capital casts, during the greater part of the day, a lengthened shadow over the top of the column, and that this shadow, rendered very transparent by the direct reflection of the light on the ground below, is so luminous that the junction of the capital with the column can no longer be distinguished; that this effect gives an appearance of weakness and indefiniteness that deprives this member of the architecture of the appearance of solidity it ought to preserve above the vertical lines of light and shadow produced by the flutings; he then sinks several deep lines at the point of junction of the capitals with the columns; and to give these lines greater vigor of effect he paints them a dark tone, and so destroys an effect of shade that shocks his artistic sense. He observes that the reflected lights in shadows produced by a vivid light are themselves luminous. He has observed that the shadow under the abacus whose faces suddenly arrest the light is hard—that the transition is abrupt—that the summit of the column is lost to the eye, and that the architrave has the appearance of resting, not upon a substantial form, but upon a void; still he must maintain for the capital a very dedicated projection; his constructive reason requires it. How then does he proceed? He seeks and discovers that profoundly considered and delicately rendered form, the circular torus supporting the abacus; he curves this torus sharply inward at its junction with the abacus, in such a manner that at the points of the tangent the rounded edge of the torus shall catch a strong light, which, reproducing that of the abacus, fades away in graduated half tints toward the neck. In this way he blends the overly vivid light of the abacus with the too complete shadow that is cast by it: again, unsatisfied with the first result, he gives his curve an inclined, almost conical, form, as far as the neck, in order that its surface may receive as much as possible the lights reflected from the ground on the neighboring walls illuminated by the sun. And thus by means of a delicate observance of light, of shadows, and of reflections, he utilizes these natural effects with incomparable intelligence, to satisfy the requirements of his eye and to preserve, even in appearance, the forms that his reason has led him to adopt as the best and the most solid.

Every student of architecture is more or less familiar with the Grecian Doric order and can easily verify the justness of the observation of the Greek architect. With regard to the forms adopted in Greek architecture for the exterior of the building, it is evident that their generating principle was the sun. The Greek artist perceives that, seen from a certain distance, the columns of his temple, though fluted, do not stand out distinctly against the wall of the cella when they are illuminated from a direction perpendicular to it; that their lights merge into the light that falls upon the cella, and that the shadows cast by the columns on the upright wall behind them completely derange, in appearance, the harmonious distribution of the solids and voids—that is to say, of the columns and the spaces between them. The architect then calls to his aid the painter and bids him overlay this posterior wall with some strong color that absorbs the light, a brown or a red; and to avoid any contradiction, even in appearance, with the actual structure of his edifice, he requires him to trace on this wall, at even distances, and with a light color, fine horizontal lines—which recall to the eye the fact that the wall is built in horizontal courses, and, seen between the columns, whose bright lines are all vertical, serve to distinguish very clearly the posterior construction from the anterior supports. So necessary was this application of color to the exterior of buildings in a country where the atmosphere is of marvelous transparency, that if we view the temple of Theseus at Athens (for instance) in full sunshine, now that it has lost its paintings, we shall find it impossible to distinguish the lights of the column from those shed on the walls of the cella; these lights on different planes mingle together and appear as if thrown upon one single surface.

If we take separately all the members of a Greek temple and study them individually, as well as in their direct relation to the whole, we shall invariably perceive the influence of those intelligent and delicate observations that attest the presence of art—that exquisite sentiment that subordinates every form to reason, not indeed to the dry and pedantic reason of the geometrician, but to reason as directed by the senses and by observation of the laws of nature.

This very brief review of the modes of procedure among the Greek artists makes it sufficiently evident that if the Parthenon is in its place at Athens, it is but an absurdity in Edinburgh, where the sun prevails over the mists only for some days in the year; it sufficiently proves to us, we believe, that had the inhabitants of Edinburgh been gifted by nature with senses as acute as those with which the Greeks were endowed, they would have proceeded in a manner quite different from that in which the latter proceeded on the shores of the Aegean or the Mediterranean. Art does not therefore reside in this or that form, but in a principle, a logical method. Consequently no reason can be alleged for maintaining that one particular form of art is Art, and that apart from this form all is barbarism; and we are justified in contending that the art of the Iroquois Indians or that of the French in the Middle Ages may not have been barbarous. What is desirable to ascertain is, not whether the Indian or the Frenchman has more or less nearly approached the forms of Greek art, but whether they have proceeded in the same manner as the Greeks; and whether, being in a different climate, having other wants and other customs, they have not necessarily, for the very reason that they did proceed like the Greeks, departed as far from the forms adopted by the latter as their climate, their requirements, and their customs differed from the climate, requirements, and customs of the Greeks. No one in the present day seriously recommends the imitation of the forms of Greek art in the province of architecture; does it therefore follow that the study of these forms is useless? Certainly not. To the architect that study is indispensable; but indispensable with the condition that it shall not confine itself to the forms, but advance to the discovery of the principle—the principle common to all the arts. It is barbarism to reproduce the Greek temple in the streets of London or Paris, for the transplanted imitation of this building denotes an ignorance of the principle that guided its erection, and ignorance is barbarism. It is barbarous to neglect the thorough and careful study of Greek art; for Greek art is that which most perfectly subordinated form to the modes of thought and feelings recognized by the people among whom it originated—principles not invented by it, but which it fully comprehended and unerringly pursued. It is also barbarous to ignore in modes of art foreign to the Greek mode the true principles that they exhibit. . . .

One essential quality of Greek art is clearness; that is to say, speaking only of architecture, the distinct expression of the purpose, the requirements, and the means of execution. Clearness, the inseparable companion of taste, pervades not only the structure of Greek buildings, which is invariably simple, easy to understand, and free from everything that is doubtful or untruthful, but likewise the details—the monumental sculptures or paintings that seem to combine with the architecture, not for the purpose of dissimulating, but of rendering its forms more evident. . . .

In the present day, we admire the various manifestations of art among the Greeks; but the reproduction of those manifestations is beyond our power; we live a different life. But their principles, embodying eternal truth, we may appropriate to ourselves; we may, in a word, reason as they did, though we do not speak the same language. (*Discourses*, II)

WHY THE GREEKS DID NOT EMPLOY THE ARCH OR ARCHED VAULTS

"Allow me to ask you one more question," said Epergos. "I saw among the Medes, and formerly in Assyria, as also among the Tyrrhenians and even the Etruscans, vaultings made of brick, unburnt or burnt, and likewise of stone; and here I have often recommended this kind of construction, which has the advantage of protecting buildings from fire and preserving the interior effectually from heat and cold. Now both the Hellenes and the Dorians of Sicily and of Magna Graecia have often seen vaultings among the neighboring peoples; why do they decline to adopt them?"

"There are two principal reasons why they do not," replied Eicos; "the first, that the Greeks do not like to adopt the methods of barbarians; or, if they do adopt them, it is with very considerable modifications. The second is that Greek artisans make a point of doing honor to their labor, and vaultings require a coarse kind of toil that is not to their taste. Whether they are built of brick or of stone, recourse must be had to a great combination of appliances and a multitude of workmen; thickwalls must be built, the vaults must be turned, and the haunches filled in. Now you must observe that we do not use lime or mortar in our masonry, as is the custom in Media and in Egypt, but only to make plastering; and vaults cannot be built without mortar. We might certainly compel slaves to perform this work, which requires more sweat than intelligence, but we are averse to doing so. Our workmen are organized in jealous corporations, who do not like to see barbarians engaged in works that they take a pride in accomplishing themselves. Thus slaves are employed only for carting, for work requiring brute force, or for bringing materials to the ground. Our carpenters and stone-cutters, our sculptors and painters are free men, endowed moreover with an excessive amount of amour-propre: they desire that their labor should be appreciated; and I have often seen common workmen take their friends along a building newly finished, to show them the stones they had cut or the timbers they had framed.

"The capitals of the portico in this residence were turned and cut by four skillful workmen; if one of them should chance to be summoned into the house, you may be quite sure he will cast a loving look at the parts wrought by him. He knows thoroughly well whether they are on the right or the left side. It is owing to this feeling of pride, which is sometimes beyond bearing, that we are able to secure work whose execution is perfect. It is quite sufficient to tell one of our artisans that the work of one of his comrades is more careful than his, to make him surpass himself. But we have great difficulty in getting even tolerable work, if it is not destined to attract observation; everyone tries to shirk it. In such cases we are obliged to have recourse to slaves. This too is the reason why you do not see among us enormous edifices such as those of Egypt. No one could be found to cut the crowning stones, the work in which—on account of the height—can only be appreciated by the birds."

"There is matter for reflection here," said Epergos, after a moment's silence. . . . "I see how the matter stands . . . and this explains antagonisms whose motives I did not perceive. . . . You love the arts so well that you make a point of keeping their various expressions within easy grasp. If your edifices are small compared with those of many other nations, it is because you wish to enjoy all their parts at a glance—to embrace their ensemble easily. Hellas has no such palaces to show as those of Babylon, which are too vast for one day's exploration."

"You are right. Not only have we no taste for edifices of too vast a size, and which, consisting of many parts in juxtaposition, do not possess that stamp of unity that we require in every work of art; but you will observe that the Greeks, in contradistinction to other nations, avoid a multiplicity of architectural features in their buildings. Whether it be a temple, a public building, or a private house, moderation is the supreme law; and it is by the judicious arrangement of the structure and the study of the proportions that these edifices seek to please, rather than by the profusion of the ornaments and the accumulation of those striking details that gratify barbarians. It must not be forgotten that we are a free people, jealous and sensitive to excess; inclined to criticism, and sparing of expense. Citizens, therefore, who are so fortunate as to possess large property must be careful not to make a public display of it, and not offend the democratic sentiments of the nation by a show of luxury. Athens has many citizens, like our host, who might make a display of their riches; but what purpose would that serve except to excite envy and malevolent suspicions? A stranger passing through the streets of Athens might suppose that all its inhabitants lived in dwellings nearly equal in style. To mention only one example, the house of Clito, which is next to this, presents to the public road an entrance greatly resembling that of Chremylus. Yet Clito is a poor fellow who lives on chickpeas. The dwellings of the Athenians are distinguished from each other only by the luxury or poverty of the interiors, into which intimate friends alone are admitted. Besides, we have not the resources either in gold or labor that the kings of Egypt and Persia can command; we have not armies of slaves or a plebs subservient to our orders; it would be impossible for us to equal or to surpass in extent or riches the public monuments of those countries. It is, therefore, in beauty and excellence of form that the Greeks have attained that superiority that is conceded to them in works of art." (*Habitations of Man*, pp. 215–18)

ROMAN ARCHITECTURE

When Viollet-le-Duc discussed Roman architecture he mainly had in mind that of the later imperial era, from the second through the fourth centuries. He was particularly drawn to the vast buildings that combined daring engineering with complex spatial schemes, especially the great baths of Caracalla and Diocletian. The aspect that interested him most was this architecture's flexible response to functional needs, representing a design process that began with a detailed program. It represented, then, an approach to building that was conceptually the opposite of Greek architecture, which began with a structural formulation.

Among the Greeks construction and art are one and the same thing; the form and the structure are intimately connected: among the Romans we have the construction, and we have the form that clothes that construction, and is often independent of it. . . .

Greek architecture always proceeds by the combination of vertical and horizontal lines and surfaces. Roman architecture adds to these two elementary principles the arch and the vault—the curved line and concave surface. From the times of the Republic we find it making use of this new element, which soon becomes the dominant principle, and which ends by subordinating the other two. . . .

The Romans very early adopted two distinct modes of construction, which nevertheless were subsequently combined in their buildings; these are construction with masonry and construction with rubble and brick. The first is only employed by them as a thick casing of large stones laid close-jointed without mortar, tied together with dowels and cramps of metal, or even sometimes of wood; behind which are thrown in masses of small stone embedded in excellent mortar. The vaultings are likewise formed in the same manner by means of principal arches of worked stone or brick maintaining a filling-in of concrete.

This system of construction obliges the Roman architect to adopt arrangements in plan that are peculiarly his. There are massive piers forming points of support destined to carry the weight of the vaultings. In these constructions there are no walls, properly speaking, but separate points of strength, connected by partitions that are comparatively thin, as they have nothing to carry. From this principle result dispositions that are admirably adapted to the arrangements required in edifices of vast size containing a great many different services; for instance, large chambers surrounded by small ones, a number of rooms varying in form, surface, and height, passages and staircases, etc. . . .

Little as the Roman cares about cost of labor, he nevertheless possesses a mind too well regulated, has too much good sense, is too good an economist, to waste anything in unnecessary work. As a builder his calculations soon convince him that the piers supporting the vaulting of the large chambers and the arching of the four small ones would present the same strength with less material; he hollows the piers as shown in figure 18, by leaving on two of the sides next the small rooms recesses semicircular in plan and vaulted in form of quarter sphere, beneath the springing of the barrel vaults. Thus he adds to the space of the four small rooms. A construction of this sort, which in fact is merely composed of rubble work with brick facings, does not admit either within or without of any decoration resulting from the structure. But the Roman would be magnificent; he is not content with having rigorously satisfied the requirements of a program, but would embellish his construction; he will, for example, set up a portico against one of the fronts of the building. This portico certainly has a use; but it forms no part of the original conception of his work. He will therefore call in artists and will procure monolithic columns—blocks of immense size; for his appliances are powerful, and when he desires to appear wealthy, he spares no cost. The structure of the building we have just described is his— it is his own art; the adventitious decoration he will borrow from the Greek. . . .

He will take the Ionic order, or rather the Corinthian; for the last, despite its elegance, presents more numerous reliefs and profiles, striking effects and lively contrasts that will throw it out more clearly against the solid mass of the building. Within, the Roman will have the vaulting overlaid with fine stucco and divide it into compartments, in order to make its real size apparent. This stucco will be carved, but in a manner appropriate to the materials; that is to say, it will only admit of a flat ornamentation, adapted to receive painting and render it effective. He will cover the lower part of the wall with slabs of colored marble divided by slightly projecting moldings; for he is unwilling to destroy the aspect of unity that an interior illumined by a diffused light should preserve. While desirous that the external dress of his building should present striking projections that will throw broad shadows in due proportion to the magnitude of his construction, he will prefer for its interior garniture an effect of quiet and unbroken richness. . . .

The attention of the Roman architect is directed first of all to the arrangement of the plan; as becomes a people that must and will impose determinate arrangements in accordance with its social and political state.

In fact, if we look at buildings veritably Roman, such as the baths, palaces, villas, and other great public works, what first strikes us is the

18. Roman system of rubble and
brick construction.

purely original dispositions of plan. These buildings present an agglomeration of chambers that have each their due dimensions; their points of support have an importance merely relative to these dimensions; and this collection of different services forms a whole whose parts stay each other—the smallest supporting the largest, advantage being ingeniously taken of the openings between the points of support. It is desirable to note how in these vast establishments space is economized, how the constructive masses are hollowed when this can be done without sacrifice of solidity, and how the interior configuration of the plan is adapted to its destination. If from the plan we proceed to examine the sections and elevations, we see that the heights of the chambers are in due relation to their perimeters; and yet the whole together forms but one building, like a hive composed of cells of various sizes. Here it is that the Roman genius exhibits itself; here the Roman is himself and borrows from no one; from these productions it is that we should seek instruction that will be serious, profitable, and eminently fruitful, and not from those architectural forms that the Romans merely borrowed from the Greeks when they wanted to build temples to the gods. . . .

Let us select from among the Thermae of Rome those that have been most thoroughly studied and contain all the services we have just specified. Let us take the Thermae of Antoninus Caracalla . . . and let us examine the ground plan of this establishment (fig. 19). Profiting by the disposition of the ground, the architect has formed an immense plateau, ABCD. At the front, on the entrance side G, are the cells for separate baths, with porticoes and easy stairs. These bathrooms present a succession of barrel vaults in two stories, recalling the arrangement of the rooms in the Pretorian barracks; each one includes an anteroom described in the program and a basin large enough to contain several persons. The enclosure of the Thermae is entered by a large principal opening in the center at G, and by several secondary openings along the palaestrae. Passing within the entrance one may perceive, amidst an immense space divided into gardens, walks, etc., the group of buildings constituting the principal services of the establishment. This group presents a symmetrical mass; in fact, the architect concluded that in order to avoid crowding, the secondary services should be repeated, and that the principal services, requiring immense halls, could be single, since crowding cannot occur in very large spaces, however great the multitude. Now, what are these principal services? (1) the cold-water bath;

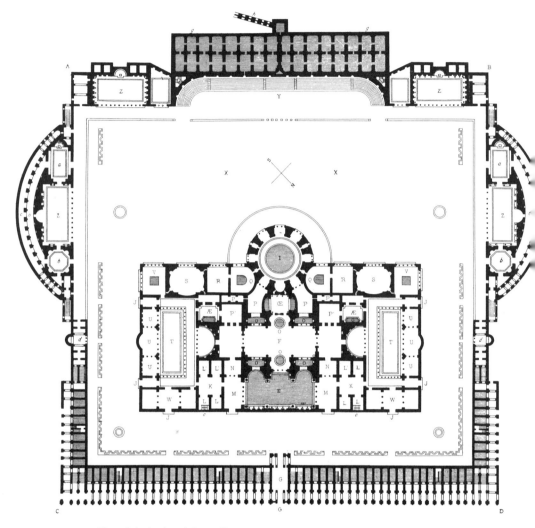

19. Plan of the baths of Caracalla.

(2) the tepid bath; (3) the warm bath with its heated vestibule. At E the architect placed the cold bath; at F the tepid bath and temperate chamber; at I the warm bath with its vestibule. The three great services are thus well marked; they occupy the center of the edifice and guide the distribution of the whole; for it is evident that the architect first considered the relative dimensions that must be given to these halls—both as to extent and height beneath the vaulting—to accommodate the number of persons they were designed to hold.

The other services are grouped around these three great principal divisions. The architect remarks with excellent reason that a building that is liable to be crowded at certain times should, to avoid confusion, present several entrances. At J he provides two entrances; he plans two halls, K, for persons to undress in, with the annexes, L—vestiaries for the custody of the clothes, rooms for the slaves who have charge of them outside the passageway, and rooms for anointing and for stowing the sand intended for the wrestlers. From these two halls K, those who wished to plunge into the cold water basin, or only to be spectators of the swimming exercises, could enter the covered spaces M. The cold-water basin K is open to the sky; for cold water in a covered place is insalubrious; besides, it is not necessary to shelter from the rain people who are bathing in cold water. Rooms intended for persons wishing to repose or converse are contrived at N. Hence the bathers enter the tepid hall F (tepidarium), likewise divided into three sections; one, the principal, for exercises; and the two others, the lateral ones, for the spectators.

Smaller basins are placed in the recesses O, and in the middle of the two lateral sections. At P are reserved two courts for the furnaces and reservoirs of warm water. In the middle of the hall F you enter the second tepidarium OE, which serves as vestibule to the warm-water bath (caldarium). The two passages that give entrance from the vestibule into the caldarium are comparatively narrow and indirect, in order to prevent the entrance of the external air and of drafts. The warm-water bath is an immense circular hall covered by a very lofty hemispherical dome, so that the warm-water vapor may not be condensed on the basin. In the recesses left in the wall of the circular hall are placed smaller basins for solitary bathers. Openings furnished with glazed lattice work admit light to the lower and upper story of the caldarium. The bathers who wish to make their way out find at Q the temperate rooms with basins of tepid water, which serve for a transition between the temperature of the caldarium and that of the external air. And thus those who go out cannot inconvenience those who enter. Next follow cold rooms, R, opening into the outer gardens. From these cold rooms there is an entrance through the open spaces, S, used for exercises, and by narrow passages into the small rooms that precede the sudatorium AE. Reservoirs for the caldrons are contrived in the spaces P'P'. At the extremities are planned vast peristyles, T, with exedrae for those who desire to walk, discuss, or listen to the rhetoricians; then come the spaces U, intended for the instruction of the pupils in gymnastics. Two special vestibules with libraries are disposed at W. In the angles, at V, are placed cold-water basins for the service of those who practice exercises in the xystus, X, which is terminated by a wide range of rising seats, Y, for the spectators of the games.

On each side of the xystus are the palaestrae, Z, with the academical halls, a, and those intended for discussions, b; the portico for the gymnastic masters is at c. Apart in a quiet place are the rooms, d, in which the professors of philosophy and rhetoric meet for their conferences. Lastly, rooms for the slaves—the bath servants—are at e, with apartments above. Immense reservoirs in two stories are disposed at g; at h is shown the aqueduct that supplies the water.

It may be objected that if the program is exactly observed, it is because that program has been suggested by the building itself. This remark would not be just; for if we examine the plans of the Thermae of Agrippa, of Titus, of Diocletian, or of Constantine, we shall find this program equally well observed, with noteworthy differences in the laying out.

Besides, that is not the question; what we would examine is the admirable distribution of this plan, whose general and minor dispositions I have been describing. Observe how ingeniously these various services are distributed in the general block of the plan; look at this plan—notice the orientation; see how the architect has placed all the warm rooms in a southwest aspect; how he has projected the vast rotunda of the caldarium beyond the line of the plan by more than half its diameter, in order that it may get the sun's rays at all hours of the day. See again how in such a large space the architect economizes his ground; how cleverly he fits the rooms into each other, making use of all the spaces afforded by the construction; how he stays and supports these masses of building, sustaining the largest and highest by means of those that are less in surface and in height. See how well the thrusts of the vaultings are contrebutted; how clear and intelligible is the plan; how each part occupies just the position and the space suitable for it; how cleverly the issues are contrived—wide and numerous where the crowd is likely to gather, smaller, indirect, and deep so as to form a screen where the drafts might be uncomfortable or dangerous. From what people had the Romans learned the admirable arrangements of these plans? From themselves, by simply satisfying their own requirements. How did they set about constructing this assemblage of buildings combined to form a single whole? In the simplest manner, and that which in point of economy was most suited to their social state. The walls and the enormous piers of the buildings in question are by no means adapted to a construction in worked stone. Here the Romans have no occasion for this material, whose transport is so difficult and costly, and which requires considerable time to work, mount, and lay: they employ only brick and rubble. The faces are made with triangular bricks, with their largest edge outside; in the middle, concrete, well mingled, of large gravel and excellent mortar. At intervals, however, for the purpose of regulating the progress of the construction and insuring the levels, a course of large flat bricks is built in, 4 feet 9 inches apart. Relieving arches of brick, built into the construction, direct the pressures upon the principal points of support. In the vaulting, the band arches are of large bricks, usually in two rings, and the filling-in of concrete, composed of mortar and pumice stone. But in order safely to ram this concrete on the planking of the centers, the builders began by laying upon these planks two courses of wide bricks flatways, breaking joint, like an arching of quarry work under the vaulting. This construction—at once so simple, so economical, and so ready of execution—being conceived and executed, the architects erected their porticoes with columns and entablatures of marble; the walls and piers are everywhere—in the interior at least—covered with slabs of marble up to a certain height; as to the vaultings, the tympanum, and the back of the niches, they are overlaid with stucco and mosaics. And thus this enormous mass of concrete and brick is clothed in a splendid dress of precious materials, paintings and surfaces of mosaics, composed of vitrified pastes of various colors. In all the rooms, pavements of marble mosaic are laid upon an isolated bed, resting on ranges of small pillars connected by a flooring of large bricks laid double; these marble pavements are not only dry and perfectly healthy, but they can be warmed underneath by means of hot currents produced by furnaces.

Our costly means of construction—the quarries of useless stone we accumulate in our buildings, and, side by side with this prodigality, the extreme poverty of the details of the interior construction, the plaster and composition work—these are, it must be admitted, very barbarous modes of procedure, if we compare them with those of the Romans, at once so simple, truthful, and rational. At enormous cost we pile up in our edifices stone upon stone; we expand all our resources in working and carving them. We draw upon our quarries as if they were inexhaustible, to erect buildings of limited size; and when we have made such efforts, with such a useless expenditure of strength, and have raised walls that in our climate are always damp (stone being only too good a conductor of moisture), we have not sufficient means left to clothe and adorn these expensive buildings with beautiful and lasting material. We therefore call to our aid plaster, composition, ornaments, and deal; and thus we cover with rags a body precious in itself, but whose value is concealed from all and rendered useless. If we affect to be Romans, profess to owe our arts to the Romans, and call our architecture the offspring of theirs, we should at least imitate them in what they did that was wise and rational—not erect with stone blocks buildings such as they judiciously constructed with concrete and brick; seek less the form of their architecture than its structure, which was so well adapted to that form; be sincere like them, and not dupe ourselves by aping their architecture if we no longer adopt their means of execution. It must not be imagined that this substitution of materials merely entails useless expenditure, that its only inconvenience is the disregard of a principle; it presents disadvantages appreciable by all. These great Roman buildings, constructed as we have described—composed so ingeniously of groups of different services judiciously brought together within a narrow compass, the smaller rooms profiting by the intervals left between the points of support necessitated by the elevation and extent of the larger—possess an advantage of which I have not yet spoken: these great buildings, I say, preserve in their interior an equal and agreeable temperature that would be very advantageous in a climate like our own. There exists at Rome an immense edifice whose general plan and system of construction recall the great halls of the

Thermae; I mean St. Peter's. Now, in this building, which exceeds in content other celebrated buildings, the temperature is nearly the same in summer and in winter; soft and cool in summer without being damp, and mild and dry in winter. That is a consequence not only of the disposition of the plan, which is Roman in character, but of the nature of the construction—thick walls of concrete and brick, which transmit neither the heat nor the damp cold from without; they serve as a nonconductor to the external temperature.

In France our stone buildings are dangerous in summer on account of the coolness that their surfaces preserve; in winter they are icy cold.

If we examine the sections and elevations of the Thermae of Caracalla, we find immense openings formerly furnished with frames of bronze, enclosing panes of glass, alabaster, or simply lattice work. But we also observe that these lights open toward the most favorable points of the compass, making the most of the sun's heat and avoiding the cold and damp aspects. In fact, the Romans attached great importance to the orientation of their buildings. Vitruvius touches several times upon this subject in the course of his treatise; he even indicates the way to lay out the streets of a town so as to render the dwellings convenient and to avoid great drafts of air. He says (book VI, chap. i): "That a building may be well designed, regard should first be had to the climate (the region, the latitude, as we should say), for the same arrangement will not suit in Egypt and in Spain; it must be different in Pontus and in Rome. In northern countries the buildings should be vaulted, well closed in, and their openings small, facing a warm aspect. On the other hand, in southern countries, subject to the burning heat of the sun, the openings should be large and face the north and northeast, to avoid the heat: thus the inconvenience resulting from natural extremes will be obviated by Art." The Romans, however, when they became masters of the world, adopted everywhere the same mode of construction, because, in fact, their methods were applicable everywhere; but they were careful to dispose their rooms and the openings for admitting light, heat, or coolness, according to the locality.

In their vaulted buildings the Romans seem to have particularly preferred two especial dispositions: the circular arrangement, closed in by a hemispherical dome, and the arrangement in bays, which we see adopted for the great central tepid hall of the Baths of Caracalla (fig. 20), in the baths of Titus and of Diocletian, and in the building

20. Tepidarium of the baths of
Caracalla.

21. Groined vaults of the basilica
of Maxentius.

known as the Basilica of Maximus or of Constantine. The Romans invented only two kinds of vaulting: the hemispherical vault, and the cradle or semicylindrical vault; the intersection of two cradle vaults suggested to them the groined vault (fig. 21). These three systems sufficed for everything; and the combinations of their plans are simply the necessary result of these methods. If they build a circular hall, they cover it with a hemisphere; if a semicircular hall, they cover it with a quarter sphere; if an oblong hall, the lateral walls of whose longer sides are thick or well abutted by contiguous buildings, they cover it with a cradle vault, which is nothing more than a longitudinal half cylinder; if a square hall whose angles only present a perfect resistance, they cover it with a groined vault. If the oblong hall is very wide, if its side walls have to be pierced by large openings, thereby presenting only isolated points of support, they divide it into square bays (generally three, in order to get a central bay); and they cover it with three groined vaults— that is to say, a longitudinal half cylinder intersected by three half cylinders of equal diameter with the first. . . .

If Roman architecture varies little in the decorative envelope with which it clothes its construction, none is more fertile as regards the arrangement of plan or the structure.

The various programs of Roman edifices as rendered by the architect present clearly marked and distinct arrangements. Is it impossible to mistake Thermae for a theater, a theater for a basilica, or a basilica for a temple. The exterior aspect of their buildings never presents anything but the envelope of the actual content; their plans are simply the expression of the requirements of the case, and they never sacrifice these principles to what is nowadays called "architectural effect." The first consideration is to find the simplest and most exact rendering of the scheme, the second, to invest the forms dictated by utility with the outward show of power and riches. If the schemes are vague, if the requirements are not defined with sufficient rigor, as in the basilica, for example—a building of a miscellaneous order, promenade, market hall, exchange, tribunal, debating hall, and antechamber—then we see architects varying their plans and differing in the manner of interpreting the program; but if, on the contrary, the program is perfectly definite, if it is imperative both as regards the whole and the details of the disposition in question, then we see the edifices designed to respond to them reproducing with very little variation the forms that experience has pronounced the best. Such, for instance, are the amphitheaters, the circuses, and the theaters. Look at the Coliseum of Rome, the amphitheater of Verona, and the arenas of Nîmes and of Arles. In general arrangement, in plan, and in exterior aspect these buildings are identical. *(Discourses, IV)*

THE DIFFERENCES BETWEEN GREEK AND ROMAN ARCHITECTURE

Viollet-le-Duc loved to draw comparisons between Greek and Roman architecture because, despite their shared formal vocabulary of the columnar orders, he interpreted these traditions as representing the antipodes of architectural conception; that is, architecture designed to reveal how it is put together versus architecture designed to provide a structural envelope around functionally determined spaces. He admired both types, although he regarded the Greek system as inherently the more artistic. Moreover, in terms of decoration, he saw in much of Roman architecture a basic flaw of dishonesty and bad taste, for which he reserved special contempt.

I cannot too frequently repeat it: Art is unique. Its essential characteristic is the harmony it presents with national manners, institutions, and genius. If it assumes different forms, it is because this genius, those manners and institutions vary; if, in the course of time, it seems to return to the point whence it set out, it is because an analogous phenomenon presents itself in the national institutions, manners, and genius. . . .

The genius of a people is none other than the mode in which it expresses its physical and moral requirements. The genius of the Greek people leads it to give prominence to its conceptions and to clothe them with a rational form. The genius of the Roman people leads it to subject everything to considerations of public interest, to what we call the government. The Greek subordinates his institutions to his genius, while the very genius of the Roman nation is submission to its institutions. . . . Athens had its Socrates; Rome could not have had such a man. Socrates is an Athenian at Athens; he is listened to, he is dangerous, he undermines beliefs by subjecting them to discussion; he is put to death: he would not have been a Roman at Rome, would not have been listened to, would not have been dangerous. . . . It was not philosophers, it was reformers of the social constitution, or those who put themselves in opposition to the civil law, that were regarded as dangerous at Rome.

The architectural orders invented by the Greeks composed the structure itself; that is to say, in the architecture that accorded with these orders there was only one mode of structure; therefore the structure of the Greek edifices and their appearance were essentially united. It would not be possible to despoil a Greek building of the order that forms its principal decoration without destroying the building itself. A glance at the remains of Greek edifices suffices to show us that the Doric or Ionic orders adopted by the architects constitute these buildings. The Greek orders are none other than the structure itself, to which that form was given that was most appropriate to its function. In the orders adopted from the Greeks the Romans saw only a decoration that might be removed, omitted, displaced, or replaced by something else, without the structure to which the decoration was applied being thereby seriously affected. . . . Accordingly, in many buildings, such as theaters, amphitheaters, and palaces, they engaged the orders in the building itself; that is to say, they made use of columns as buttresses to give greater footing to the parts that were weighted, while they also thus obtained an external or internal decoration. It must not however be supposed that the Romans were the first to discover this application of the orders; the Greeks made use of engaged orders. . . . But I do not suppose the idea ever occurred to the Greeks of superimposing engaged orders, in the Roman fashion—as on the exterior of the Theater of Marcellus, the Coliseum, and many other buildings. In engaging the orders in the building the Greeks proceeded on a principle quite contrary to that which actuated the Romans on a similar occasion. The idea the Romans had was that of erecting buttresses presenting a decoration that custom had made familiar. They raised one, two, or three stories; they piled one, two, or three orders one above the other (fig. 22), like so many superimposed buttresses. They reasoned so little when it was a question of giving to an object a form suited to its nature, that they placed upon each of these orders its complete entablature, just as if each of them had to terminate the edifice. . . .

The Greeks, when they engaged the orders in the building, proceeded on a true principle. Since in their view the order was nothing other than

22. Applied orders on the theater
of Marcellus, Rome.

the expression of the structure—the means of support—when they deemed it necessary in certain cases to form a solid enclosure between the columns, as had been done before them by the Egyptians and Assyrians, this wall, this enclosure, was merely a thick partition. . . . But to take the voids for the solids, the partitions for the part of strength, and the buttresses for a mere decoration, as the Romans did at a later day, was—with all due respect for the Romans, and for those who copy them without serious examination—to reason barbarously. Having departed so far from the path of reason, the Romans went still farther; they made arches beneath the projecting entablatures of the engaged orders (see fig. 22). This, as I have already remarked, would seem to a Greek the last degree of aberration; it would show an utter ignorance of the forms of Greek architecture. . . .

Greek architecture may be best compared to a man stripped of his clothes, the external parts of whose body are but the consequence of his organic structure, of his wants, of the framework of his bones and the functions of his muscles. The man is so much the more beautiful as all the parts of his body are in harmony with their purpose, and, with nothing superfluous, they yet suffice for their functions.

Roman architecture, on the other hand, may be compared to a man clothed: there is the man, and there is the dress; the dress may be good or bad, rich or poor in material, well or ill cut, but it forms no part of the body; if well made and handsome it merits examination; if it restrains the man's movements, and its shape has neither reason nor grace, it is unworthy of notice. In Roman architecture we have the structure, the veritable, substantial, and useful construction devised to meet the requirements of a plan laid down by a master hand; and we have also the covering, the adornment, which is independent of the structure, as the dress is independent of the man's body. To the Roman, whose tendencies are mainly political, its form is a question of secondary importance. He demands but one thing from the appareler of his buildings, which is that the dress shall do him honor. Otherwise, it is a matter of indifference to him whether it is structurally logical, whether it exactly interprets the essential constructive forms of the edifice, whether it is the fit and true casing of those forms, and whether it explains their purposes. . . .

When the Roman has erected his building in the manner just described, if he can find capable artists and can procure marbles—even though it were at great expense and from the most distant countries—as soon as the necessary conditions of his program are fulfilled, he overlays his construction with costly material cut into thin slabs, ornaments it with string courses, and attaches to it columns and entablatures. On the vaulting he lays carved stucco work, painted and gilt: in fact, in material effect he apes the Greek as much as he can. But the Greek buildings are small, whereas the Roman buildings are large and lofty; the Roman superimposes the Greek orders; and, what is still more worthy of remark (and here the indifference of the Roman for Greek rationalism shows itself), the Greek orders support architraves only, while the Roman hardly ever employs in his public buildings anything but the arch and the vault. He builds up engaged columns against the piers of his arches, and over the archivolts he puts architraves on his columns; that is to say, he makes use of the Greek composition as a frame serving to ornament the necessary part of his construction—a strange blunder, which plainly shows how the Roman separates the construction from the decoration, regarding the latter as a mere luxury, a dress whose use or origin is of slight concern to him. It is in this application to their buildings of Greek forms in contradiction with Greek construction that the Romans should not be imitated. *(Discourses,* III)

THE MIDDLE AGES

Gothic architecture represented for Viollet-le-Duc a synthesis of the Greek genius for structural formulation and the Roman gift for programmatic planning. When he thought of Gothic architecture in a conceptual sense he had in mind the churches of the Ile de France, especially those of the twelfth and thirteenth centuries, epitomized by the High Gothic skeletal structures with flying buttresses. He interpreted this scheme as an elastic framework of disparate forces balanced in equilibrium, radically different from the inert masses of Greek and Roman architecture. As it turns out, some of his ideas about Gothic structure, especially as regards the elasticity of construction in stone and the supportive role of the diagonal arches of ribbed vaults, have been challenged by Pol Abraham and even proven wrong by Robert Mark (see bibliography for both). But before that happened these ideas had been translated into concepts for a modern architecture and put into practice—a striking example of the paradox that new truth sometimes emerges from misapprehension.

Let us imagine ourselves in France in the twelfth century: we are not absolute masters, we lack the space necessary for building; objection is made to our having it, and it is conceded only after considerable opposition; we are not supplied with immense stores of timber by vessels solely employed to transport it for our use; on the contrary, we have to go and seek our framing spar by spar, among twenty proprietors, from each of whom we shall only get a few pieces; or, on the other hand, we must buy it, and if it is known that we want it, since there is no fixed market price we shall have to pay dearly for the timber. Suppose again that we cannot have stone brought to us by means of requisitions, by disciplined soldiers or by slaves, but that it must be sought for in various quarries from different proprietors, be transported at our own expense or by voluntary aid; that the lime is supplied at intervals and in small quantities; that our workmen are forced laborers who do as little as possible, or men to whom wages must be paid, and that every now and then the lord of the manor takes away these men to go and fight against his neighbors. Should we, under these circumstances, build an edifice such as the Basilica of Constantine? or, if we commenced it, could we finish it? Should we not fall short of timber and lime before the work was half done? or if after many delays we finally succeeded in erecting it, would it possess the qualities necessary for its perfect stability? Under conditions such as I have mentioned, should we not, on the contrary, if we were prudent and well advised, subdivide our work, avoid encumbering the site, apportion the labor so that it may be suspended or recommenced without imperiling the whole? try to economize our materials, since they are difficult to procure, and endeavor to obtain great results by means of limited resources? Let us see then how we should proceed to erect a hall analogous to the Basilica of Constantine. Our quarries afford us abundance of freestone; so we shall not waste our time in making and burning bricks. Stone, however, is an expensive material; we shall therefore be economical with it and shall only use the quantity necessary. Instead of raising a buttress of brick and rubble work, pierced at its base by an archway, we shall put two stone columns AA′ and an exterior buttress B (fig. 23). Instead of turning a barrel vault of rubble work at right angles to the nave, we

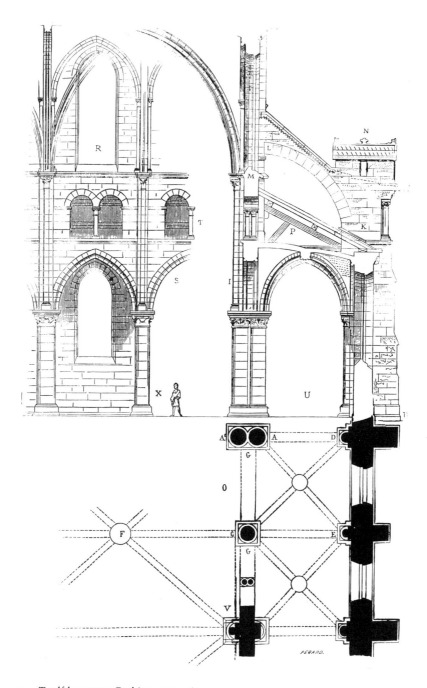

23. Twelfth-century Gothic construction.

shall put an intermediate column, C, and build two groined vaults AD, EC over each bay of the aisle. Raising a wall GG astride on the coupled columns, the remaining outward part of the double capital A will serve as support to the springer of the transverse rib AD, and that of the capital A will receive the attached shafts I running up the wall to carry the central vaulting, which will be groined but divided by a transverse rib CF. Instead of raising solid buttresses to abut the thrusts of the central groined vaulting, we shall only erect a pier K on each buttress B, and throw over a half arch, KL, replacing the inert resistance that the solid wall would have afforded by an active resistance—active inasmuch as it acts by pushing against a wall M that tends to depart from the perpendicular by the thrust of the central vault. But as we are not satisfied of the sufficiency of the abutment K to resist the combined action of the vault thrusts directed against the flying buttresses, we surmount the pier K with a weight N, which insures its stability. Our climate scarcely admits of those concrete terraced roofs, cemented or paved, such as the Romans formed in Italy; we shall therefore elevate the central vaulting sufficiently to allow of a roof P beneath the upper windows R; and with a view to relieving the arches S as well as lighting and ventilating the timber roofing P, we shall pierce openings at T over the arches. We shall soon perceive that the coupled columns AA′ are useless, and that we may replace them by a single cylindrical pillar, since the pressures—if the structure is as it should be—fall between these two columns. But we are well aware that this construction, consisting of props from the ground and thrusts met by active counterthrusts, cannot have the firmness of base, the inertia of the Roman structure; that movements may occur, and that consequently the vaulting should not consist of a concrete and homogeneous mass, but should have a certain elasticity to enable it to yield to the strain without rending. Moreover, we have not at our command either the quantity of timber required for the centering of Roman vaults, nor the materials suitable for their construction. We content ourselves with forming the transverse and diagonal ribs on centers; and these arches themselves become permanent centers enabling us to turn portions of concave vaulting from one to another according to every required curve without making use for this purpose of intermediate centering. If circumstances render it necessary, we can, on this plan, suspend our works, recommence them, execute them all at once or in parts without disadvantage to the edifice.

We reflect deeply on what we are doing, and consult our reason only without concerning ourselves about traditions or time-hallowed forms. The diagonal ribs being naturally the longest—those whose diameter is the greatest—we retain the semicircle for these; and with a view both to lessen the thrust of the other ribs and to raise their apex nearly to the level of the keystone of the diagonal ribs, we trace the transverse ribs, the arches, and the wall ribs, with two portions of arcs, which intersect at the height we desire to give them. Thus we are no longer restrained by the necessity of making groined vaults on a square plan—that is, vaulting resulting from the intersection of two equal or nearly equal cylinders. Every plan, whether drawn on a parallelogram, a quadrilateral, a triangle, a regular or irregular octagon, can be vaulted by our method. We have freed ourselves from the rules imposed by the Romans and more or less adhered to by the Romanesque architects. I can readily conceive that there should be those who prefer the section of the Basilica of Constantine to that of an analogous hall built at the end of the twelfth century. The later conception is more complicated, demands more skillful combinations and a larger amount of reflection; but is it on that account more barbarous? From the section of the Basilica of Constantine we can never produce anything but the section of the Basilica of Constantine. We have here an art matured—perfect, if you will—but unalterable; this is its final expression; whereas the combinations presented in the section shown in figure 23 are capable of endless developments; for this reason, that the equilibrium of balanced forces affords us every variety of combination and opens before us ever new paths.

Among the early Gothic architects we find the arch absolutely determining the support; the arch determines not only the structure but the form; the architecture is dictated solely by the arch. The Romans did in numerous instances subordinate their structures to the arch, to the vault; but, I observe once more, in their architecture every support is an inert mass, and their vaulted buildings are, as it were, hollowed out in a single block; they are enormous castings; whereas the architects of the twelfth century assign a function to each part. The column is a real support; if its capital is expanded, it is to sustain a load; if the moldings and ornaments of this capital are developed, it is because such development is necessary. If the vaults are divided by ribs, it is because these ribs are so many sinews performing a function. Each vertical support depends for its stability on being stayed and weighted; every arch-thrust meets another that counteracts it. Walls, as supports, no longer appear: they have become mere enclosures. The entire system consists of a framework that maintains itself, not by its mass, but by the combination of oblique forces neutralizing each other. The vault ceases to be a crust—a shell in one piece; it is an ingenious combination of pressures that are really in action and are directed on certain points of support disposed so as to receive them and transmit them to the ground. The moldings and ornaments are shaped with a view to manifest this mechanism. The moldings fullfil exactly a useful function; externally they protect the architectural members by throwing off the rain water, the simplest form of section being adopted for that purpose; internally they are few, only indicating the different levels or frankly jutting out for the purpose of corbeling or footing. The ornaments are designed solely from the local flora, for the architects wish everything to be of home production and borrow nothing either from a foreign art or from the past; they are moreover adapted to their place, always apparent and easy to understand; they are subordinated to the architectural form and the construction; they are worked before they are set in place, and take their position as members essential to the whole. . . .

The architects of the secular school of the Middle Ages, notwithstanding the penchant we have always manifested for appearances, subjected form, and, in fact, appearance generally, to the processes and materials employed. They never gave to the hall of a castle the form of a church, to a hospital the aspect of a palace, or to a city mansion the semblance of a country manor: everything is in its appropriate place and exhibits the character suitable to it. If an interior is spacious the windows are large; if an apartment is small, the openings are proportioned to the space they are intended to illuminate; if a building is divided into stories, this is indicated on the exterior—in fact, sincerity is one of the most striking excellencies of primitive Gothic architecture; and it must be observed that sincerity is one of the conditions essential to style in the arts. . . .

The architecture of the secular school of the thirteenth century is a real architecture; it is applicable to all purposes, because its principles proceed rather from a course of reasoning than from a form. Form never shackled those architects who, in the thirteenth century, erected that vast number of churches, palaces, chateaux, and civil and military edifices; yet the least fragment of a structure of that period indicates its origin, is stamped with the seal of its time.

It is desirable to show at the outset that it is impossible to separate the form of the architecture of the thirteenth century from its structure; every member of this architecture is the result of a necessity of that structure, as in the vegetable and the animal kingdom there is not a form or a process that is not produced by a necessity of the organism: amid the multitude of genera, species, and varieties, the botanist and the anatomist are not mistaken as regards the function, the place, the age, the origin of each of the organs that they separately examine. A Roman building may be stripped of all its decorations or deprived of its external form without prejudice to the construction; or (as has been the case with the Pantheon at Rome, for example) a Roman edifice may be clothed with a form that has no necessary or intimate connection with the structure. It is impossible to remove decorative forms from an edifice of the thirteenth century or attach any to it without detriment to its solidity—its organism, if I may so express myself. . . .

In architecture art does not consist in the employment of costly marbles, or the accumulation of ornaments, but in distinction of form and the truthful expression of the requirements; for it costs no more to cut a molding according to a judicious principle and a good design than to work it without regard to its position or the effect it should produce. (*Discourses*, VII)

TWO CLASSIC EXAMPLES OF VIOLLET-LE-DUC'S ANALYSIS OF THE RATIONALE OF GOTHIC STRUCTURE

Although Viollet-le-Duc focused his interpretation of Gothic structure on High Gothic examples, the detailed analyses that are most characteristic of his rationalist approach are addressed to the more highly refined and less orthodox regional tradition of Burgundy with its double-shell walls. The two most memorable ones concern the church of Notre-Dame at Dijon and the cathedral of Auxerre. For him, every piece of these structures was formed to play a particular functional role in the composition as a whole and no piece is superfluous. Even the decorations, he maintained, have practical value.

Notre-Dame at Dijon

At Dijon there exists a church of moderate size, under the name of Notre-Dame; it was built about 1220 and is a masterpiece of reasoning, in which the science of the builder is hidden under an apparent simplicity. We shall begin by giving an idea of the structure of this edifice. The apse, without any aisle, opens upon the transept; it is flanked by two chapels or smaller apses facing the east like the chancel and opening into the transepts in the prolongation of the aisles of the nave.

The apse of Notre-Dame at Dijon is composed, in the interior, only of a thick basement, not very high, carrying isolated piers connected in every direction, and having for the exterior enclosure only a sort of partition of stone pierced by windows. Naturally the piers are designed to support the vaults; as to the partitions, they support nothing, for they are only a means of enclosure. On the outside the building consists only of plain buttresses.

Figure 24 gives a perspective view of this apse; since it has no aisles, the buttresses support the vaults directly, without flying buttresses. These buttresses are thick and solid and in them alone dwells the stability of the edifice. Nothing is simpler in appearance and in reality than this building. Thin walls pierced by windows close all the space left between the supports. An exterior passage is left at A, to facilitate repairs on the large glass windows. All the facings are well protected from the rain by sloping roofs without offsets and by cornices or copings. Clearly, this is only a solid envelope, a screen.

Let us now enter the church of Notre-Dame at Dijon. Just as the exterior is simple, solid, covered and screened, so the interior presents light and elegant arrangements. This edifice was built and still is situated in a populous quarter, surrounded by narrow streets, and the architect has felt it his duty to sacrifice everything to the interior effect. We recognize, moreover, that he must have been limited in expense and must have avoided useless expenditure. He was chary of the materials and did not use one stone too many. The apse, accordingly, on the inside (fig. 25) is composed of a thick basement, A, built in courses and ornamented by an independent arcade inlaid in the wall. From this basement the pillars B start and rise to the extremities of the arches of the great vault. These pillars are set against the stratum from the base to the tablet C, which connects them in a molding to the outer structure. Over this basement is a passage or gallery, designed to facilitate access

24. Apse exterior of Notre-Dame, Dijon.

76

A'

E. COILLAUMOT.

25. Apse interior of Notre-Dame,
Dijon.

to the glass windows D and to decorate the church, if necessary, on holy days. The piers E are detached; they consist of four columns set against the cleavage from base to capitals, a large one (37 centimeters in diameter), and three slender ones (from 12 to 15 centimeters in diameter).

In A' we give the section of these piers. The large column and the two at its side are each in one piece as far as F, the course of the capitals, while the pillar starting from the ground is in one piece as far as the tablet G. This tablet forms a ceiling over the lower gallery, and connects the large arcade with the outer walls. At the height of the gallery on the third row (the triforium) there is the same arrangement of the piers and the same section A', only with an intermediate pillar, H, bearing an arcade composed itself of large, thin pieces of stone, like slabs (flags) set upright. Above the triforium, a second flagging, I, serves as a ceiling for this triforium and attaches the arcade to the outer building; next comes the starting point of the arches of the large vault, supported by the exterior buttresses. The high windows then open above the archway of the triforium and are no longer in a recess, as below, in order to give all the light possible and to leave on the outside the passage of which we have spoken before. Thus the thrust of the arches is transmitted obliquely to these exterior buttresses, which are built in courses, and the inner piers are only rigid points of support, incompressible because consisting of large stones set against the cleavage, but presenting, because of their small impost, only a frame capable of bending, at need, to one side or the other, without or within, without danger, should any settling occur.

As to the walls K, they are, as we have seen, only partitions 20 centimeters thick at the utmost. Now let us take away from this structure everything not essential to it, let us take its skeleton and this is what we shall find (fig. 26): A, a buttress, built up and a passive mass; B, a column, slender but rigid and resisting like cast iron, thanks to the quality of limestone used; C, courses at the height of the arches and, consequently, flexible at need; D, the connection between interior and exterior; E, a second column, but shorter than the one below, for, since it is higher up, any movement taking place there would have more effect; F, a second course joining interior and exterior; G, the skewbacks of the arches; H, simple walls that support nothing and serve only to enclose the building; I, the abutment placed only at the point where the thrust of the arch acts. There is nothing too much, but everything

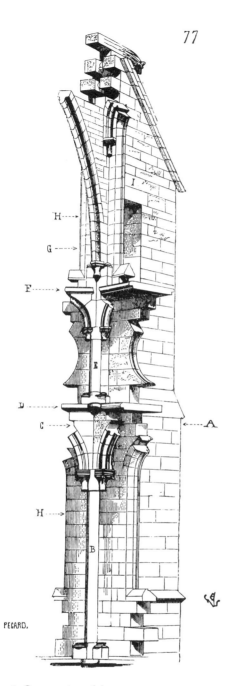

77

PEGARD.

26. Construction of the apse,
Notre-Dame, Dijon.

that is necessary, for this construction has stood for more than six centuries and does not yet seem near its fall.

It is not necessary to recall here what we have said about the function of the monolithic pillars that accompany the columns B and E, and which we have supposed removed in figure 26. They are only accessory supports that give firmness and stability to the principal columns, without being absolutely indispensable. The weight of the vaults rests far more upon the buttresses, because of the action of the thrust, than upon the cylinders B and E. As the interior clusters of pillars carry only a very slight weight, there was no need of giving them great resistance. But if we had an aisle, if the buttresses, instead of being immediately opposed to the action of the vaults, were removed by the whole width of this aisle, then the vertical piers should have a larger impost, for they really would carry the weight of the vaults. The nave of this church is vaulted according to the early Gothic method. The diagonal arches are on a square plan and are cut by a transverse arch. The lower piers are cylindrical, built in drums and of equal diameter. Still, each pair of capitals differs somewhat, for they carry alternately either a transverse and two diagonal arches or one transverse arch only.

We give the view of an inner division of the nave of Notre-Dame at Dijon (fig. 27). At A' we have drawn the section of the impost A, in B' the section of the impost B, with the horizontal projection of the abaci of the capitals. These capitals jut out farther on the side of the nave, to receive the pillars that rise to the beginning of the vaults, always in accordance with the principle that consists in moving back the vertical supports so as to draw off a part of the thrusts. In C' we give the horizontal section of the piers C, and in D' that of the piers D, at the level of the triforium, at E' the horizontal section of the skewbacks E, and at F' that of the skewbacks F, on a level with the abaci receiving the great vaults.

This general sketch having been given, let us examine with care the structure of this nave. We have already said that the architect of Notre-Dame at Dijon had at his disposal a limited area crowded in between narrow streets; so he could not give to the buttresses of the nave supporting the whole system a great projection beyond the perimeter of the aisles. If he had followed the methods adopted in his time, if he had remained submissive to routine, or, to be more accurate, to the rules

27. The nave of Notre-Dame,
Dijon.

already established by experience, he would have designed the flying buttresses of the nave as indicated in figure 28.

The thrust of the great vault acting from A to B, he would have placed the last voussoir of the arch at A and its coping at B and he would have moved the front of the buttress from C in such a way that the oblique line of the thrusts should not pass the point G. But he cannot go beyond the point I, since the width reserved for the public road does not allow it; and, on the other hand, on the interior he cannot pass the point K, which is on the vertical of the engaged pier L, without causing a false bearing and breaking the transverse arch M, whose curve it is important to keep; for if a too considerable weight acts upon the haunches of that arch at N, that arch will push the detached pier on the interior in the direction OP. Hence the architect must fix the pier of his flying buttress in the space included between K and I'. But we know that this pier must be passive, immovable, for it is the true point of support for the whole system; and it can evidently acquire that immovability (its narrow base being taken into consideration) only by a particular arrangement, a supplementary vertical resistance. Accordingly, the constructor solves the problem as follows: he builds the pier between the two points desired (fig. 29); he loads heavily the summit of the flying buttress at A; he slopes the coping BC so as to make it tangent to the extrados of the arch; then he brings the rear surface of the pinnacle D over to the point E out of the vertical of the wall F, so that the space PF may be a little less than a third of the space FG. Thus the thrust of the great vault is strongly opposed, in the first place, by the weight A and is neutralized by that pressure; so that now only the flying buttress itself acts upon the pier K, so far as it is loaded at A. Accordingly, if that arch were to be put out of shape, it would be in accordance with the drawing R; it would break at S and the pier K would bend.

But the architect moves back his pinnacle and loads the pier outside of its perpendicular as far as the point E, that is to say, as far as the point where the rupture of the flying buttress might take place; he thus checks that rupture, for under its load the point S' of the flying buttress cannot be displaced; but the pinnacle D only presses against the arch, while it does not weight it, since the space CO is greater than the space OP; hence the weight of the pinnacle, which is a well-built, homogeneous construction of large stones, rests on OC, the center of gravity of the pinnacle being between O and C; consequently if the arch were torn

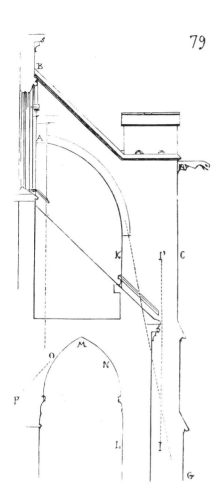

28. Diagram of a conventional
flying buttress.

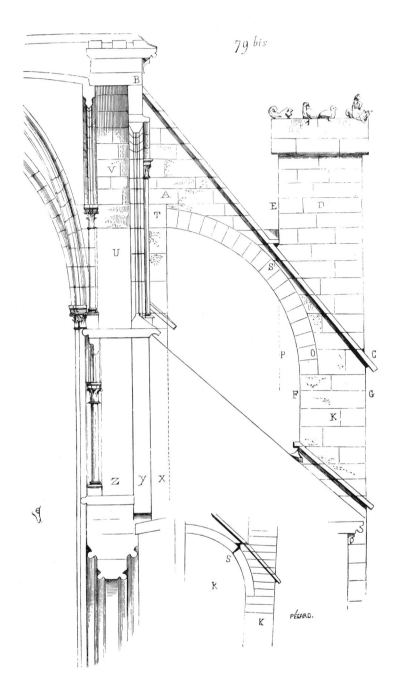

29. Section of nave wall and
flying buttress, Notre-Dame,
Dijon.

down, this pinnacle would remain upright; thus it loads the pier K with a greater weight than that of a pinnacle having only FG in breadth, and hence assures in this way the stability of the pier FG, too feeble by itself to resist the thrust without the addition of this weight, while, at the same time, he compresses the haunches of the flying buttress at the point where that arch would tend to break if thrust out of place.

Fact is more conclusive than all logical deductions; the construction of the nave of Notre-Dame at Dijon, in spite of slightness of its exterior supports, has not undergone the least deformation. Let us not lose sight of the interior; let us notice that the vaults do not push directly upon the tops of the flying buttresses and that between the tops of these arches and the skewback of the vault there exists, above the triforium U, an interior support V just at the height of that thrust, neutralizing its action in a singular manner. Let us study the details: the block of stone T, against which the last voussoir of the flying buttress rests, is no other than the lintel carrying the support of which we were just speaking and at the same height as this lintel are fixed the two capitals that carry the wall arches of the vault (see fig. 27). This lintel is set just on the level of the action of the thrust from the great vault.

Let us analyze this construction piece by piece (fig. 30). We see at A the column, the principal support of the triforium at the height of the piers carrying the extremities of one transverse and two diagonal arches, a support flanked by the two lesser columns B. At C are the large pillars set against the stratum upon the abacus of the large capital on the ground floor and passing in front of the group BAB in order to arrive under the course M of the capitals of the arches of the great vault; a course consisting of a single stone. At D is the capital of the triforium. At E is the skewback of the arcade of the triforium, also consisting of one stone. At F are the two blocks closing the arcade. At G is the course forming the ceiling of the triforium and connecting the arcade and the course of the capitals M to the exterior support, under the roof, a support whose courses are drawn at H. At G' is one of the slabs, placed next to that at G and connecting the rest of the arcade to the partition built under the upper windows, of which I is the sill. These slabs G' carry the fillet K, projecting over the roof of the aisle. At L is the first section of the exterior buttress seen above the roof. At M is the course of the capitals of the great vaults, carrying the bases of the two pillars, set against the stratum, that sustain the wall-arches. At N is the skew-

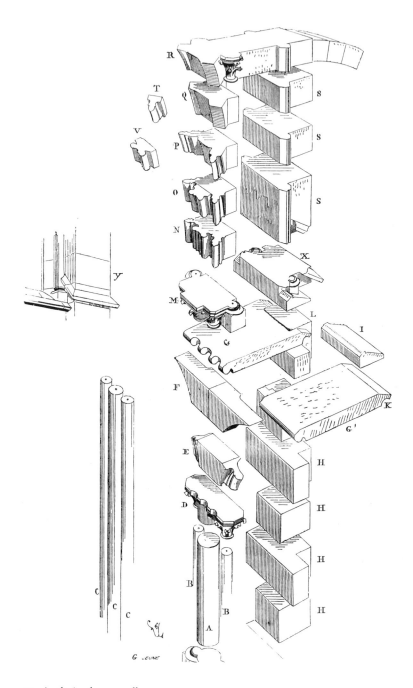

30. Analysis of nave wall construction, Notre-Dame, Dijon.

back of the great vaults, whose upper bed is horizontal and which carries the extremities of the two diagonal and the transverse arches. At O is the second skewback carrying the two diagonal arches and the transverse arch, the upper bed of the latter being now normal to the curve, while the beds of the two diagonal arches are still horizontal. At P is the third skewback, no longer carrying the transverse arch, which is henceforth independent, but still carrying the two diagonal arches whose beds are horizontal. At Q is the fourth skewback, carrying nothing but the shoulder piece behind the diagonal arches, for laying the first filling stones. At R is the lintel, of which we were just speaking and which connects the skewbacks with the pier whose courses are at S; this lintel carries the shoulder pieces behind the diagonal arches, for it is important to give firm support to these now independent diagonal arches whose voussoirs are represented at T, while one of the voussoirs of the transverse arch is given at V. At X is the course of the exterior buttress carrying the ledges of the windows, the bases of the exterior pillars of these windows, and the fillet passing above the list (or fillet ridge) of the roof, as the perspective detail Y indicates. The terminus of the voussoirs of the flying buttresses then rests against the lintel R, and, beginning with the lintel, the interval between the pier and the vault is filled (see the interior view, fig. 27).

If we examine the section (fig. 29), we see that the buttress X, the wall of the triforium Y, the passage Z, and the inner pier present a considerable thickness; for the passage is quite wide and the wall and buttress together measure about 60 centimeters and the group of columns forming the inner pier about 30 centimeters. Now, all this must rest upon a single capital, crowning a cylindrical column. There will be evidently an imperfect balance, and if the buttress X bears upon the haunches of the transverse arch of the aisle, the pressure that it will exert will push the column inward and make it lose its upright position and, the upright position once lost, the whole equilibrium of the building is destroyed.

The builder has at first given to the capital (fig. 31) the form A; that is, he has moved the axis of the column into the vertical plane passing through the middle of the archivolt B. Upon this capital he has placed the two skewback stones C and D, with their beds horizontal: the first skewback C carrying the bases of the pillars set against the stratum and rising to the beginning of the great vaults, while the third skewback E has its sections normal to the curves of the transverse arch and the

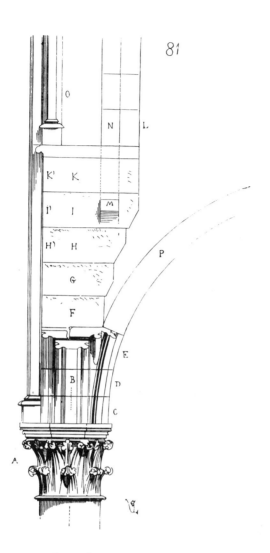

31. Weighting of nave pier,
Notre-Dame, Dijon.

diagonal arches and archivolts, for starting from this skewback the arches detach themselves from one another. Having set free the arches, which henceforth are laid in independent voussoirs, the builder has erected a pier, having projections to the right and left, F, G, H, I, K, in corbels, up to the vertical of the buttress L; and in the course I, he has taken care to reserve two skewbacks M to receive the arches sustaining the wall of the triforium N.

The interior pier O, composed, as we have said before, of a cluster of pillars, set against the stratum, rests upon the inner part of that pier. It is understood that its courses F, G, H, I, K, are each in one piece and strong. The heaviest weight and the most stubborn resistance are those of the pier O, since it carries vertically the buttressed vaults; for the buttress L carries almost nothing, since the summit of the flying buttress does not weigh upon it (see fig. 29), and it merely keeps the structure in equilibrium. Accordingly the stones K, I, H, being weighted at the ends K' I' H', cannot sway; hence the buttress is held firm. As to the thrust of the transverse arch P and that of the diagonal arches of the aisle, it is wholly neutralized by the weight that presses downward in the vertical of the pier O. It is now understood how essential it is that the pier O be composed of large stones set upon end and not of courses, for this pier supports a twofold pressure: that from above downward, caused by the weight of the vaults, and that from below upward, in consequence of the tendency to tip, produced by the buttress L upon the ends of the stones K, I. If, then, these piers O were built in courses, it might happen that the mortar joints, if strongly compressed by that twofold action, would diminish in thickness; now the least settling in height of the piers O would result in deranging the equilibrium of the entire system. On the contrary, the leverage produced by the courses I and K under the pier O has the result (those pillars being perfectly rigid and incompressible) of sustaining very firmly the starting point of the great vaults.

We shall the better understand this system of building by supposing, for example, that in order to execute it, cast iron, stone and wood have been employed (fig. 32.) Let the column A and its capital of cast iron be set upon a pedestal of stone and let them support the stone skewback B. The builder gives a broader projection to the capital toward the interior of the nave than on the side of the aisle. Upon this capital he raises the courses B, C, D, E, F, G, etc., in the form of corbels. He sets three iron columns H along the inner wall and augments them by three other

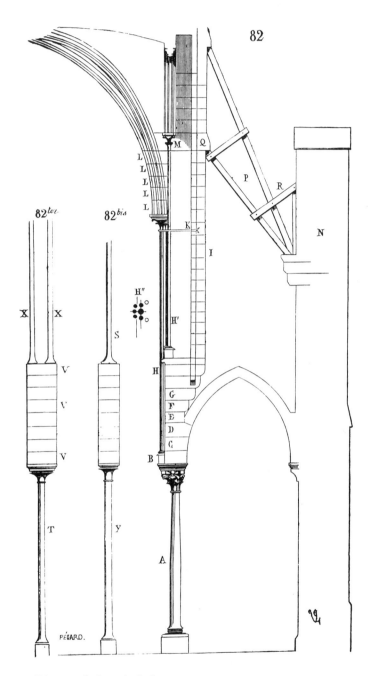

32. Diagram of a hypothetical
wall section and flying buttress, as
if constructed of cast iron, stone,
and wood.

columns H′ (see section H″); these columns HH′ are attached to the buttress I by rings and a cramp iron K, in order to make the buttress fast to the pier and to hinder the rounding outward of either. The buttress I is built of courses of stone. Upon the columns HH′, the architect places the skewbacks L of the great vault; the two side columns OO continue alone up to the lintel M that buttresses the arches of the great vaults. On the outside he raises a pier N of stone, in order to be able to keep the interior structure in the vertical, by means of the prop P, strengthened to prevent its displacement by the crosspieces R.

There is no inconvenience, on the contrary, in case the buttress I, built in courses, should be compressed, or should settle; for the lower the point Q falls, the more rigid will be the prop P against the back of the lintel M. Nevertheless, this buttress I is needed to keep the back of the lintel M in a horizontal plane, but most of all to give stability to the column A. In fact, one need not be very well versed in the knowledge of the laws of equilibrium to know that if, between a column Y and a column S, both slender (fig. 32b) we place several horizontal courses, it will be impossible, however well loaded the column S may be and however well propped may be the course, in one sense, to keep these two columns in a vertical plane, parallel to the plane of the props; while, placing on the column T (fig. 32c) horizontal courses V propped in one direction and upon these courses two pillars XX′ passing through a vertical plane perpendicular to the plane of the props (always supposing the two pillars X,X′ to be loaded) we shall be able to keep the columns XX′ and T in planes parallel to the props. In this consists the entire system of construction of Gothic naves set upon columns.

That is the explanation of the galleries set one above another in Burgundian architecture, a sort of hollow buttress whose inner wall is rigid and its outer wall compressible, thus giving great strength of resistance and of impost to the spingings of the high vaults, avoiding enormous abutments to support the flying buttresses and destroying, by its equilibrium and its pressure upon two distant points, the effect of the thrusts from the vaults of the aisles.

In truth, all this may well appear complicated, subtle, and labored; but it will certainly be conceded us that it is ingenious, very skillful, and scientific, and that the authors of this system have made no confusion of Grecian art with the art of the North; of the Roman with the Oriental;

that they have not put caprice in the place of reason and that there is in these constructions more than appearance of a logical system. . . .

The church of Notre-Dame at Dijon is a small edifice and one might suppose that the Burgundian architects of the first half of the thirteenth century did not permit themselves similar hardihood in monuments with broad extent of surface and very high. It is the contrary that takes place; it seems that working on a large scale these builders gather more assurance and develop with still more boldness their means of execution.

Auxerre Cathedral

The choir of the Cathedral of St. Stephen at Auxerre was rebuilt from 1215 to 1230, over a Romanesque crypt that led to the adoption of certain arrangements unusual in the large churches of that period. Thus the chancel is surrounded by a simple aisle with single square apsidal chapel. As to its construction . . . certain difficulties resulting from the Romanesque arrangement of the plan, which they did not wish to change, have been solved in the most ingenious manner.

We give half of the plan of the apsidal chapel (fig. 33), sacred to the Holy Virgin. This plan is taken at the height of the gallery of the ground floor, resting, as in Notre-Dame at Dijon, upon an arcade. At X, we have represented, on a smaller scale, the horizontal projection of the vault of the aisle in front of that chapel. According to the Burgundian method the wall arches are detached from the wall; they rest upon the monolithic colonnettes and spring from A to B, C to D, E to F, etc. The central colonnettes of each cluster, also monolithic, sustain the force of the pressure, and the vault consists of two diagonal arches IK and LM, one transverse arch NO, and the intermediate arches PQ and RS. These two intermediate arches fall, at the right of the aisle, upon two detached columns Q and S, set against the stratum, each in one piece and having 24 centimeters of diameter to 6.60 meters of height from base to capital. The difficulty was to neutralize so exactly the different thrusts, acting on these columns Q, S, that they could not leave the vertical. It was a problem to be solved similar to that which the builder of the chapels of Notre-Dame at Châlons-sur-Marne had set before himself, but upon a much larger scale and with points of support incomparably more slender.

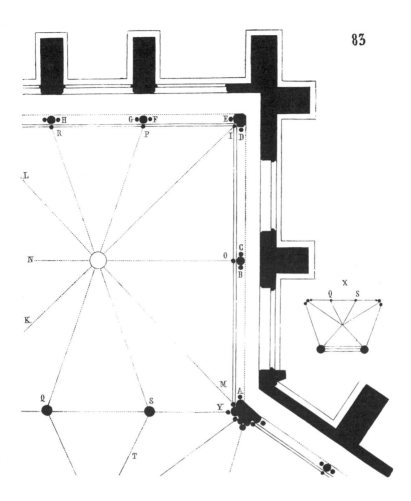

33. Plan of the axial chapel,
Auxerre Cathedral.

Let us take our stand for an instant in the aisle and look at the summit of the column S, whose diameter, as we have already said, is only 24 centimeters. Upon this column is placed a capital, whose abacus is octagonal and broad enough to receive the beginning of the two arches ST and SR and in addition two small columns carrying the transverse arches SQ and SY.

A tall skewback, whose lower bed is at A (fig. 34) and its upper bed at B, is reinforced in the angles obtained between the arches and the pillars by sheaves of foliage. Up to the level of the abacus of the capital C, the arch D of the aisle rises and curves already, by means of two other skewbacks with horizontal beds, while the arch E (the intermediate arch of the chapel) of a greater diameter is farther out of the vertical and is composed, after leaving the bed B, of independent voussoirs. The pillars, F, of the transverse arches at the entrance of the chapel are monoliths and balance these skewbacks, keep them rigid, and rest firmly upon the two faces of the abacus. Figure 35 gives the section of the beginning of the vaults at the level GH. This construction is bold, one cannot deny, but it is perfectly solid, as during six centuries and more it has undergone no alteration.

We see in this one of the most ingenious applications of the Gothic system of vaults, the unequivocal proof of the freedom of the builders, of their sureness of execution and their perfect familiarity with the resistance of materials. These pillars are made from the hard stone of Tonnerre, as also the skewbacks. As to the effect produced by this chapel and its entrance, it is surprising but does not inspire that anxiety that every too-daring attempt causes. The arches buttress one another so well, not only in reality but also in appearance, that the eye is satisfied. Even to that fourfold sheaf of foliage surmounting the capital and giving body to the lowest skewbacks, everything concurs in reassuring the observer. Someone may object to these two columns at the entrance. Why is not the architect content with throwing a transverse arch from one pier at the angle of the chapel to the other? To this there is but one reply: . . . it is necessary, because of the radiating form of the aisle, to obtain upon the outer boundary a greater number of points of support than upon the inner boundary, in order to have the transverse arches almost equal at the base and exactly equal under the key, to close the triangles of the vaults at the same level.

The vaults of the chapel of the Holy Virgin and of the aisle of the

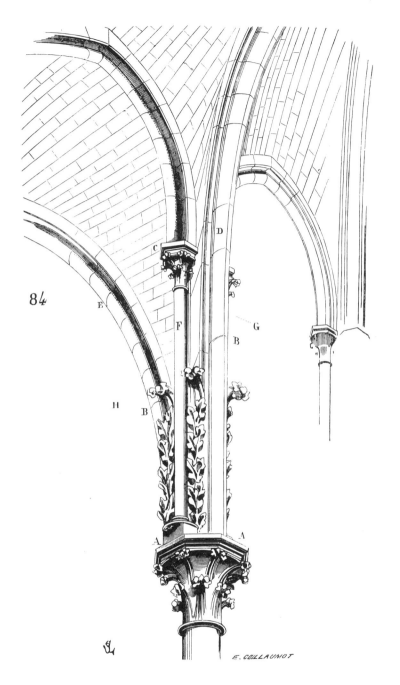

84

E. COULLAUMOT

34. Vault and pier capital of the
axial chapel, Auxerre Cathedral.

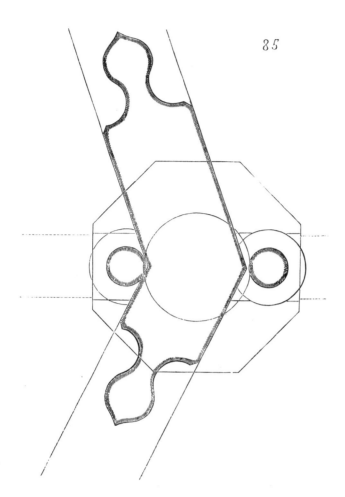

35. Plan of vault arches
above monolithic pier,
Auxerre Cathedral.

cathedral of Auxerre are arranged like the majority of Burgundian vaults of the thirteenth century, that is, . . . their wall arches are distinct from the walls and . . . a flagging supporting a water channel unites these wall arches to the tops of the walls. . . . Having admitted the principle of equilibrium, of active forces opposed one to another to produce stability, the builders of the Middle Ages . . . could not but end by exaggerating, in the successive applications of these principles, whatever they might have that was good, rational, or ingenious. . . .

Elasticity being the first of all the neccessary conditions in monuments erected on slender supports, it was still necessary to find, besides that elasticity, absolute rigidity and resistance. . . . The builders at the beginning of the thirteenth century did not pile the stones one upon another without purpose and without noticing the effects that were produced in large edifices, in accordance with the laws of weight. Their masonry lives, acts, fullfils a function, is never an inert and passive mass. . . . The Gothic building has its organs and its laws of equilibrium and each of its members cooperates with the whole by an action or a resistance. *(Rational Building* [from *Dictionnaire raisonné,* vol. 4], pp. 175–201, 217)

GOTHIC STRUCTURE AS A SOURCE OF INSPIRATION FOR MODERN ARCHITECTURE

For Viollet-le-Duc, the principles underlying Gothic structure (as he defined it) were those most appropriately applicable to a yet-to-be-invented modern architecture. In commending this example to young architects he was consciously turning his back on the Gothic Revival and the actual imitation of Gothic forms.

Now . . . Gothic construction, despite its defects, its errors, its attempts, and perhaps because of all these, is a preeminently useful study; it is the surest initiation into that modern art that does not yet exist but is struggling, because it establishes the true principles to which we ought still to submit today; because it has broken with antique traditions, and because it is fertile in applications. . . .

Beauty is not, in an art wholly conventional and logical, linked forever to one single form; it can always reside there when the form is but an expression of satisfied need, of judicious use of the material given.

Because the multitude sees in Gothic architecture only its ornamentation, and because this ornamentation no longer belongs to our time, is this a proof that the construction of these edifices can no longer find an application? One might just as well maintain that a treatise on geometry is worth nothing because it is printed in Gothic characters, and that students reading in such a book that "the angles opposite the vertex are equal to each other" are learning mere folly and are being misled. Now, if we can teach geometry with books printed yesterday, we cannot do the same in construction, and we must necessarily seek these principles where they are traced—in the monuments; and this book of stone, strange as are its type and its style, is as good as any other, in reality, as to the ideas that it has suggested.

In no other order of architecture do we find these ingenious and practical means of solving the numerous difficulties that surround the constructor living in the midst of a society whose needs are complicated to excess. Gothic construction is not, like antique construction, immutable, absolute in its means; it is supple, free, and as inquiring as the modern spirit: its principles permit the use of all the materials given by nature or industry in virtue of their own qualities; it is never stopped by a difficulty; it is ingenious: this word tells all. The Gothic builders are subtle, ardent and indefatigable workers, reasoners, full of resources, never stopping, liberal in their methods, eager to avail themselves of novelties, all qualities or defects that place them in the front rank of modern civilization. These builders are no longer monks submissive to rule or tradition; they are laymen who analyze everything and recognize no other law than that of reason. Their faculty of reasoning scarcely halts at natural laws, and if they are forced to admit these, it is in order to conquer them by opposing them one to another. . . .

We do not pretend . . . to disguise any of the defects of the systems presented; this is not a plea in favor of the Gothic construction, but a simple exposition of its principles and their consequences. If we are well understood, there is no sensible architect who, after having listened to us with some attention, will not recognize the uselessness, to say no more, of *imitations* of Gothic art, and who will not understand at the same time the advantage that one can derive from the serious study of that art, and the innumerable resources presented by that study so closely allied to our genius. *(Rational Building* [from *Dictionnaire raisonné,* vol. 4], pp. 81–82)

II ENGAGING THE CREATIVE FACULTY

3   Educating the Architect

Ever since the example of Vitruvius, writing in the late first century BC, *the education of the architect has belonged to the realm of architectural theory. According to Vitruvius, the architect should be broadly educated in all the areas of learning that touch upon the natural environment, the social and cultural context, artistic traditions, and building technology. He recommended that the architect be conversant with geometry, arithmetic, optics, history, philosophy, music (for acoustics), medicine, law, and astronomy. In the early Renaissance, Alberti, concerned to promote the architect as a scholar and gentleman distinct from the craftsman-builder, emphasized the importance of cultivating the artistic and theoretical side, such that in the ensuing periods the education of the architect became more that of a humanist-artist than of a builder. By the mid-nineteenth century, the concern for art had virtually excluded other considerations.*

Reacting against this prevailing view, Viollet-le-Duc urged an approach that was primarily scientific in outlook, more empirical than dogmatic and more practical than artistic. The rational faculties that were central to his code of architectural principles could be properly cultivated only through an education appropriately devised for that purpose. He stoutly maintained that the formalist training provided by the French state in the Ecole des Beaux-Arts was totally unsuitable and that it not only did not produce good architects but also impeded the development of a modern architecture. His remarks on this subject fall

into two categories, an indictment of the architectural education preva-
lent in his day and a prescription for a new approach.

First of all, an architect must be trained not through rote exercises,
the purposes of which (he maintained) were never explained, but
through the cultivation of the powers of reason.

There is an *école d'architecture* in France, but there is no course of
architectural lectures delivered in that school; or if by chance such a
course is given it limits itself to a few generalities concerning one phase
of the art. Respecting the carrying out of architectural works, the organization and administration of labor, the history of civilization in
France, the comparison of the various styles or groups of styles of
architecture, their relation to civilization, their development or decay,
and the causes of such growth or wane; the art of economizing resources by employing the materials peculiar to the various localities,
and the judicious application of those materials to the forms they are
adapted to receive; the importance to an architect of being ready and
able to explain and justify his design by sound reasons in a clear and
logical form of expression; and the wide and catholic principles that,
when they have free scope, must develop energetic intelligence, and
clothe those principles in new forms—not a word is said.

Amateurs can only acquire a sound taste (which in architecture especially is identical with sound reasoning) by contact with artists; but if
they would form the taste of influential patrons, architects must be able
to explain to them the reasons that lead them to adopt such or such a
method; if these conceptions are to be admitted or defended, they must
be defensible. *(Discourses,* IX)

In How to Build a House, *Viollet-le-Duc has the tyro Paul ask his*
architect cousin (significantly named Eugene) how he came to acquire
his rational method. The reply is an account of a misspent traditional
education corrected through a combination of happy circumstances and
self-conscious initiative. The process of correction approximates the
combination of practical education and on-the-job training that Viollet-
le-Duc espoused.

"When I left college I was articled to an architect for two years, who
set me to copy drawings of buildings, of which I was not told either the
age, or the country, or the use; then to lay on tints. During this time, I
took lessons in mathematics, geometry, and drawing from models. I

was then prepared to enter the Ecole des Beaux-Arts, where not much is taught, but where they compete to obtain medals and the Grand Prix, if you can. I remained there three years, making five in all. Meantime, I was obliged to get my living, for I had no more than enough to pay for my lodging and to buy clothes. I was obliged, therefore, to get into an office—that is to say, to work for so much an hour at an architect's, who was in large practice. There I used to trace plans and nothing else, except now and then to make some detail drawings—heaven knows how, for I had never seen the smallest part of a building executed. But my employer was not exacting, and the master builders supplied by their experience what was wanting in these details. Seeing that all this would not put me in a speedy way to master my profession, and being so fortunate as to have had a few hundred pounds left me, I resolved to travel—to study architecture in actual buildings, and no longer in those shown me on paper. I set myself to observe, to compare, to see practical men at work, to examine buildings that were crumbling to pieces, that I might discover *in anima vili* the causes of their ruin.

"At the end of five more years I was sufficiently acquainted with my profession to be able to practice it. Total—ten years; and I had not built even a dog kennel. One of my patrons introduced me to an agency for government works, where I saw methods employed that scarcely agreed with the observations I had been able to make during my previous architectural studies. If at any time I allowed myself to make remarks on this discrepancy, I found they were not well received. The circumstances, and the fact that a fine opportunity offered itself for making use of what I had learned, occasioned my stay there to be of no long duration.

"A large commercial company was on the point of erecting manufacturing works on an extensive scale. They had engaged an architect who was proposing to erect buildings in the Roman style, which was not exactly what they wanted. They did not think it quite to the purpose to build in the plains of the Loire edifices recalling the splendors of ancient Rome. I was introduced to the directors; they explained to me what they wanted. I listened; I worked indefatigably to acquire what I was ignorant of, in order to satisfy my clients. I visited factories, made the acquaintance of large contractors, studied building materials, and at length furnished the draft of a plan that pleased them, but would scarcely satisfy me now. The work was begun; assiduous study and constant attendance on the ground enabled me to supply my deficiencies in point of knowledge, so that they were satisfied with my commencement. Most of these gentlemen had town and country houses. I became their architect, and this soon obtained me large practice and more work than I could execute; especially as I have come to the conclusion that it is necessary to be always studying, reasoning, and improving; so that (looking at the matter in this light) the further you advance the more difficulties you have to encounter."

"How, then, should architecture be studied?"

"Why, as I have shown you, by practicing it. In France, at any rate, no other method has been employed hitherto, and perhaps this is the best."

"But how do those learn to build who do not travel, as you did, but simply study in the usual way?"

"They do not learn to build. They only learn to imagine and design impossible structures, under the pretext of preserving the traditions of "high art", and when they are tired of putting these fancies on paper, they have a place as clerk of works given them, where they do what you are going to do; the only difference being that they feel a disgust for the work because they were expecting something very different."

"But, beginning as I am going to begin, shall I be able afterward to study the—what shall I call it?"

"The theory—the art, in short. Certainly, you will be able to study it much more easily; for the modicum of practical knowledge you will have acquired in building a house, or in seeing it built from foundation to roof, will enable you to understand many things that, without practice, are inexplicable in the study of the art. This will give you the habit of reasoning and of satisfying yourself as to the why and wherefore of certain forms and certain arrangements dictated by the necessities of practical building—forms and arrangements that appear simply fanciful in the eyes of those who have no idea of those necessities.

"How are children taught to speak? Is it by explaining to them the rules of grammar when they are only three years old? No; but by speaking to them, and inducing them to speak to express their wishes or necessities. When they have learned to speak nearly as well as you and I do, the mechanism and rules of language are explained to them, and then they can write correctly. But before learning according to what laws words ought to be placed, and how they ought to be written to compose a phrase, they had become acquainted with the signification of each of them.

"If we had not in France the most singular ideas respecting teaching, we should begin with the beginning, not with the end, in the study of architecture. We should impart to students the practical elementary methods of the art of building, before setting them to work to copy the Parthenon or the Thermae of Antoninus Caracalla, which, for want of those first practical notions, are to them mere phantoms; we should thus train their young minds to reason and to become aware of all their deficiencies, instead of exciting their youthful vanity by exercises purely theoretical or artistic at an age when they cannot clearly understand the forms that are given to them as models."

"A house such as we are going to build seems to me a very small affair. Surely such a construction can hardly supply the information necessary for erecting a great edifice."

"Do not imagine that, Paul; construction, apart from certain branches of scientific and practical knowledge, which you will be able to study at leisure, is nothing but a method—a habit of reasoning—a compliance with the rules of common sense. Of course you must possess common sense and consult it. Unfortunately, there is a school of architects that disdains this natural faculty, asserting that it fetters imagination; for we have among us idealists, as there are in literature and among painters or sculptors; though if idealism is permissible among litterateurs and artists—for there it is harmless—in architecture it is quite another thing; it is expensive, and you and I have to pay for it. We have consequently the right to consider it at least out of place. The reasoning faculties and good sense have to be called into exercise quite as much in building a house as in constructing the Louvre, in the same way as you may show tact and intellect in a letter as well as in a large volume.

"The ability of an architect is not determined by the quantity of cubic feet of stone he uses. The size of the building makes no difference."

"You maintain, then, that as much ability is required to build a moderate-sized house as to erect a vast palace?"

"I do not say that; I say that the faculties of the mind, reasoning, accuracy, the exact appreciation of the materials at our disposal, and their proper use, are manifested as well in the construction of the simplest habitation as in the erection of the most magnificent architectural monument."

"I shall then be able to learn much in observing the building of my sister's house?"

"Certainly. First, because one learns much when one has the wish to learn; secondly, because in a house, as in the largest of palaces, the entire architectural staff will have to present themselves before you, from the excavator to the decorative painter. Whether the carpenter makes twenty doors or two hundred, if you can get a clear notion of how a door is made, hinged, and hung, one alone is quite enough; you have no need to see a thousand."

"But here we shall not be making doors (for example) such as those of royal apartments?"

"No; but the principles on which they are, or ought to be, made are the same for both; and it is by departing from these principles that we fall into mere whims and follies. When you know how a wooden door is made you will see that the structure is adapted to the nature of the material employed, viz., wood, and to the purpose it has to serve. This knowledge acquired, you will be able to study how clever men have made use of these elements, and how (without departing from fundamental principles) they have produced simple or splendid works; you will be able to do as they have done, if you have talent, and to seek new applications of principles. But you must, in the first place, know how a door is made, and not imitate at hazard, while destitute of this preliminary practical knowledge, the various forms that have been adopted, be they good or bad." *(How to Build a House,* pp. 82–87)

Viollet-le-Duc maintained that one of the greatest evils that had crept into the practice of architecture was the rupture between engineering and artistic creativity. The result had been to reduce the quality of work on both sides of the division, especially impoverishing the artistic branch of building.

"What is the difference, then, between an architect and an engineer?" Paul ventured to ask.

"Upon my word, that is a question not easy to answer—I will give you an apologue:

"There were once two little twins who resembled each other so much that even their mother could not distinguish them. Not only were their features, height, and gait the same, but they had also the same tastes and abilities. They had to work with their hands, for their parents were poor. Both became masons. They acquired skill in their calling, and they worked equally well. Their father, a narrow-minded man, thought that these four hands that wrought at the same work with equal perfection would produce more and do still better by allotting separate labors to each pair. To one of the pairs, therefore, he said, 'You shall only do underground work'; and to the other, 'You shall only work aboveground.' The brothers thought this scarcely reasonable, as they had been accustomed to help each other in both sorts of work; however, as they were obedient children they complied. But whereas hitherto these workmen had agreed and had cooperated to the advantage of the work, from that time forward they did not cease to dispute with each other. The one who worked above the cellars maintained that his foundations were not suitably prepared, and the one who laid the latter asserted that the conditions of their structure were not respected. The result was that they separated, and as each had now become habituated to his particular work, he remained unfit for anything else."

"I think I see the gist of your apologue, but—"

"But it does not explain to you why a difference has been made between engineers and architects. In fact, a skillful engineer may be a good architect, as an accomplished architect ought to be a good engineer. Engineers make bridges, canals, docks, and embankments; but this does not prevent them from raising lighthouses, erecting factories, warehouses, and many other buildings. Architects ought to know how to do all these things; they actually did them formerly, because then the twin brothers were not separated, or rather, they were one and the same person. But since this individuality has been separated into two, each half follows its own direction. If the engineers build a bridge, the architects say it is ugly—and are not always wrong in saying so. If the architects build a palace, the engineers think, not without reason, that in its construction the materials have been employed unskillfully and without due economy or an exact acquaintance with their properties in point of durability and strength."

"But why do engineers build bridges that architects do not consider beautiful?"

"Because the question of art has been separated from that of science and calculation by that narrow-minded father who thought one brain could not entertain both. The architects have been told: 'You are to be artists; you are to look at nothing but form—trouble yourselves about nothing but form'; while to the engineers it has been said: 'You are to occupy yourselves only with science and its applications; form does not concern you; leave that to artists who dream with their eyes open, and are incapable of reasoning!'

"Ah! that seems strange to your young mind, I can see. It is simply absurd, because the art of architecture is only a result of the art of constructing—that is, of employing materials according to their qualities or properties; and because architectural forms are notoriously derived from this judicious employment of them." *(How to Build a House,* pp. 224–26)

The means for healing this rupture could only be an education in which the architect is taught engineering as well as art and, optimally, the engineer learns how to practice his craft with appropriate artistry.

If we take a fair and unprejudiced view of things we cannot shut our eyes to the fact that the professions of the architect and the civil engineer tend to merge one into the other as was formerly the case. If it is the instinct of self-preservation that has caused architects of late to resist what they regard as the encroachment of the engineer on their domain, or to set themselves against the methods adopted by the latter, this instinct has badly served them, and if it rules it will have no other result than gradually contracting the architect's field and limiting him to the function of decorative designer. A little reflection will show us that the interests of the two professions will be best saved by their union, for in point of fact the name is of little consequence: it is the thing that is essential, and art is that thing. Whether the engineer acquires a little of our knowledge and love for artistic form—so far as that love is rational and is something more than mere sentiment—or whether the architect enters upon the scientific studies and adopts the practical methods of the engineer; whether both thus succeed in uniting their faculties, knowledge, and appliances, and thereby realize an art truly characteristic of our times, the result cannot fail to be advantageous to the public and creditable to the age. *(Discourses,* XII)

OBSERVATION AND RATIONAL ANALYSIS AS EXERCISED THROUGH THE PRACTICE OF DRAWING

The preparation for the training of an architect necessarily includes a formal education. Viollet-le-Duc focused on the discipline of drawing as the framework for assimilating various kinds of learning experiences. For him, drawing was no less a matter of intellectual training than of artistic expression, beginning with unbiased observation, continuing through analysis, and culminating with problem solving. In Learning to Draw, *he explains this process by describing the education of a young peasant boy, Jean, under the tutelage of a kindly engineer, M. Majorin.*

Direct Observation
The value of direct observation is that it is not prejudiced by culturally acquired formulas; it permits one to discern the truth of a situation in empirical fashion.

"That's not the way to do it," said André.

"But that's the way I've seen it," answered Jean, who seemed to be no longer a pupil, but to have openly rebelled.

"We will see," said André finally, since he evidently could not convince Jean. "This is not the way to draw a cat; is it, papa?"

"Let me see it," said his father. André handed M. Mellinot a piece of crumpled paper, on which was penciled the following sketch (fig. 36).

"If it is intended for a cat, it's a cat with two paws. And what's that growing out of the top of his head?"

"That's his tail," answered Jean timidly.

"Oh!" said M. Majorin, rousing himself from his revery, "let me see it."

He looked attentively at the cat and at Jean; so that the latter blushed, and hung his head, and really did not know what to do with his hands, which embarrassed him very much.

"How old are you?" asked M. Majorin.

"Eleven years old on All Saints' Day, sir."

"Do you go to school?"

"Yes, sir, when papa does not take me to pluck weeds from the gardens of the bourgeois."

"Do they teach drawing at your school?"

36. Jean's drawing of a cat.

"No, sir. They teach us to make only rounds and squares, and those not often."

"And does it amuse you to make rounds and squares?"

"Not very much."

"You prefer to draw cats?"

"Yes, sir."

"Where did you draw this?"

"On the steps of the house, where I was sitting."

"And what was the cat doing there?"

"He was turning round like that, looking for something."

"And you begged him to stop in front of you to have his picture taken?"

"Oh, no, sir! He wouldn't have done it."

"Then, how did you manage to draw him?"

"I looked at him as he came up to me very slowly, as if he were going to ask me for something to eat, for I was taking my luncheon; and he looked so funny—oh, so funny!—just like a real person. I looked at him and didn't laugh, because cats don't like to have anyone laugh at them. I watched him, and he watched me; then I took a paper, and the pencil André gave me, out of my pocket. But when the cat saw them, he ran away. Then, remembering just how funny he looked, I drew him on the paper."

"But you know very well that cats have four paws."

Jean did not answer.

"Why did you draw only two?"

"Dear me, sir! I didn't notice, I didn't see the others."

"Come, give me a kiss."

If this abrupt conclusion surprised Jean, it astonished M. and Mme. Mellinot even more.

"Will you give me your cat?" resumed M. Majorin.

"Oh, yes, sir! I'll draw others."

M. Majorin was visibly moved. They continued their walk, and the children ran into the woods.

"If I had a boy like this little fellow!" said M. Majorin almost involuntarily, after a long silence.

"Is it because he drew a cat with two paws, and a plume on the top of its head, that you express this desire?" responded M. Mellinot.

"No: because he was born an observer, and because this quality, or faculty if you will, permits one to advance, and, above all, to avoid many foolish mistakes."

"I do not understand why, to tell you the truth, one should draw a cat with two paws."

"No, you do not understand; or rather you, like many others, have seen only with the eyes of those who do not know how to see.

"To you a cat is a feline with four paws, a tail, two prominent flexible ears, and whiskers. If one should omit to show you a part of this inventory, you would not acknowledge it to be a cat. The little fellow does not care much about that: he did not see a mass of poor images pretending to represent complete cats, but a cat in a certain position that struck him, and he seized the principal features of the position. Being seated, he did not see the back of the animal, which was hidden from him by its head, and the tail appeared without any intervening part.

"His attention was not attracted to the hind paws, which were almost entirely concealed by those in front, and he did not see either the belly or the flanks. His eye in a few seconds seized the principal lines and the appearance of the animal, and his unskilled hand rendered what his eyes communicated to his understanding." (pp. 5–9)

Rational Analysis

The act of observation should be accompanied by an analytical outlook that permits one to perceive the order, even a geometrical order, of the natural world. To perceive this order is to grasp the essential character of things and their relationship to the rest of the environment.

"Gather that ivy leaf, and tell me what you see in it."

Jean hesitated before answering.

"Do you not observe that it is composed of a support called the petiole, which is attached to the stem, and of other things besides: of a membrane, which is the skeleton of this vegetable appendage, and of a green tissue called the blade?"

"Yes, sir."

"And do not these ribs of the leaf tell you anything?"

"Yes. There are five of them; that in the middle is the longest."

"And the others?"

"The others are smaller."

"Well, keep this leaf, and do not spoil it; and we will presently see what it will tell us."

When M. Majorin entered the house, he took a graduated circle, and, placing the petiole where it joins the blade on the center of the circle (fig. 37), he showed Jean that the ribs of this leaf were so disposed that they gave with the petiole and the rib of the axis two angles of 62 degrees and one angle of 56 degrees—total, 180 degrees; and the ribs of the other part of the blade gave the same angles, within a very small fraction; that the midrib was the longest, the lower ones shorter, and the lowest of all shorter still.

Jean began to find many properties in this leaf.

"Are all the leaves of the ivy made in this way?" he asked.

"Not entirely: the midrib is more or less long, and consequently the leaf is more or less sharp or thick; but there are always these five ribs, leaving between them angles that differ but little from those we have just observed.

"But yet the ivy leaf, like all the vegetable and animal appendages, independent of the varieties that each individual presents (for there are not two leaves of the same plant that are identical), is subject to the irregularities caused by a sickly state or an excess of nourishment.

"Privation and abuse are the great causes of degeneracy or corruption. By the side of the modest ivy plant, from which you have gathered this well-formed leaf, there is another that grows to excess, perhaps because it has found a very rich soil. This other plant sends out wild shoots on every side: it is too ambitious, and I am obliged from time to time to check its advance by the aid of shears. . . .

"Well, here are two of the leaves of this luxuriant plant, which I have gathered on this side. See, they vary from the regular plan and are deformities; and, if you will examine the plant, you will find a number of leaves that in their haste to develop, have not been governed by the common principle (fig. 38). Prosperity spoils them and changes their form. This is to teach you that in nature you must select everywhere and constantly; and when you wish to reproduce the form of a crystal, plant, or animal, adhere to the rule that is imposed on each, and avoid what is unnatural. But this belongs to aesthetics. Do you know what aesthetics are?"

"Oh, no!"

"You will later, I hope, and without suspecting it.

"You understand, then, that geometry has something to do with leaves. Here is another example," continued M. Majorin, opening an album in which were fastened leaves of plants. "This leaf of a vine (fig. 39) is contained in a regular pentagon. A regular pentagon is a figure composed of five equal sides and five equal angles. You will observe that, although the two large lateral ribs are curved, they follow a symmetrical direction and end in the angles AB of the pentagon. Does this mean that all leaves of vines are exactly of this form?

"No; but all those in favorable conditions present the same character and possess their five principal ribs, that of the straight axis being longer than the other four. And this leaf of a fig tree (fig. 40) also forms, does it not, an irregular but symmetrical pentagon, the extremities of the ribs exactly meeting the angles of the geometrical figure? . . .

"But when we examine minerals we find it quite otherwise. You will see that in their formation they assume forms borrowed from what are called solids; that is, from bodies produced by geometrical figures.

37. Ivy leaf.

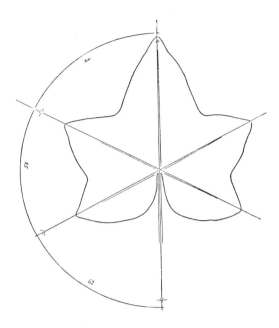

38. Deformed leaves.

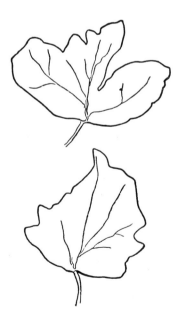

39. Vine leaf.

40. Fig leaf.

"Geometry is part of everything, and is met everywhere, and is the great mistress of nature: therefore one must learn it, if one wishes to observe and comprehend the works of creation." (pp. 27–33)

Observation and Drawing

To draw what one observes is to become fully conscious of what one looks at and to make it memorable. Having remembered it clearly one is able to reflect on it analytically and propose solutions to problems.

"In the study of drawing there are two elements—physical labor, the exercise of the eye and hand; and intellectual work, that is, the habit of observing with exactness and engraving on the memory what one has observed, so that the mind can compare and draw deductions from the comparison.

"The method that consists in placing before the eyes of the pupil graduated drawn models, and in beginning by the simplest outlines to successively reach a head or a modeled ornament, may be good to accustom the hand of the pupil to copy these models mechanically, but in what way does it exercise his understanding? In what way can it even give knowledge of the objects copied? The pupil sees in them only flat pictures, composed of white, black, and gray, which he must mechanically reproduce. Does he consider the planes and the light and shade of the figures? Hardly more than the sheet of glass in photography considers the effect of the solar rays on the substance that covers it.

"From these pupils choose the ablest, those who have obtained prizes and have succeeded in reproducing an engraved pattern with such perfection that one would take the copy for the original, and suddenly ask them to draw a bottle from memory, one of the most simple and common objects, and they will give you only an imperfect sketch.

"Then of what use is the trade you have given them? When their studies are over, it never occurs to them to take a pencil to represent an object whose form they would describe; they never think to make a sketch that will remind them of a scene, a place, a piece of furniture, or a tool. And why? Because they have never been taught to see; and one learns to see only by drawing, and not from engraved patterns but from objects themselves; and further still, only on condition of being able to explain these objects, and to describe their properties and their relations to each other."

"It seems to me you exaggerate a little, for how many can we count in the first rank among skilled observers who are unable to draw!"

"Yes; but do you know at the price of how close attention they succeeded in grouping their observations, and how long it took to draw deductions from those observations that were with difficulty fixed in the memory, on account of their inability to draw them? And, in regard to the observers of whom you speak, has not photography come just in time to give a singular development to their studies, and to the conclusions drawn from them? and do you not believe that drawing is now just as necessary, not on account of the pleasure of collecting pictures in portfolios, but because drawing accustoms the eye to see more quickly, more justly, and better, while establishing between the organ of sight and the brain a kind of joint work that facilitates deductions?

"We pass before an object a dozen times and look at it attentively because it interests us, and we think we are perfectly familiar with it in its general form as in its details. Some day we take a notion to draw it, and discover qualities that we did not suspect, though we had firmly determined to closely observe. One who has acquired the habit of drawing without fatigue, without being obliged to make an effort, as one writes, draws all that he looks at attentively; or, in other words, while looking he performs what he would do if he wished to reproduce the object on paper.

"You understand that it is not a question here of art and composition, or of producing works worthy of Raphael or Leonardo da Vinci; but of contracting a habit and establishing an intimate relation between the eye, brain, and hand, so that one of these organs can never receive an impression without the other two being able to second it.

"To return to these learned observers just spoken of: it has frequently happened to me to be brought into contact with many of them: well, although I do not pretend to be either a savant or an artist, I have often pointed out to them facts that they did not suspect, simply because, being accustomed to draw, I had looked at certain objects in the vegetable, animal, or mineral world as if it were necessary for me to draw them. Because the majority of our distinguished savants have reached high positions without being able to draw, it must not be concluded that drawing would not have facilitated many of their researches, or have enabled them to save much time.

"I hardly know a career in which drawing would not be useful, if not absolutely necessary, for the very simple reason that it teaches one to see correctly, to remember what one has seen, and to give a form to thought.

"I do not claim to be able to make an artist of Jean: he will become one if he has it in him. I propose only to teach him to see correctly; to consider what he sees, and to render it so that his observations may serve him, whatever the career he follows, whether that of a workman or a soldier, merchant or lawyer, artist or engineer. It is an experiment that cannot in any way injure his future; but taking drawing as a medium—or, as I understand it, the habit of observing, comparing, and reflecting before advancing an opinion—I intend to develop his mind, nourish his intelligence, and give him a taste for learning." . . . (pp. 66–70)

Every day M. Majorin opened a new field of study to his pupil.

His method consisted in sowing in his youthful mind all those principles of general knowledge for which the practice of drawing is necessary, in order to make him understand the usefulness of this form of language, which is too often wrongly held to be a special art, while, on the contrary, it is simply complemental like the art of writing and speaking.

He considered his pupil's natural taste for drawing, and, knowing how easily natural talent falls into a career that has for its aim only the production of the purely artistic, he believed that one should always study how to apply drawing to a direct object—to the study of a science or the exercise of a profession. . . . (pp. 174–75)

At school meanwhile, Jean did not neglect the study of drawing; although, in this institution as everywhere else at that time, the absence of method rendered instruction almost useless. But Jean had learned principles that are not soon forgotten, and his drawing teacher had the good sense to leave him to do as he pleased. Therefore, putting aside the engraved models distributed to his schoolmates, he copied the few plaster models that adorned the class tables, or any object before him. Vacation, during which M. Majorin always showed him new things, also gave him an opportunity to study nature and perfect himself in the practice of drawing. We must state that the stock of knowledge brought by Jean, when he entered the institution . . . , had singularly facilitated his understanding what was taught him. If a Latin author were to be translated, Caesar's *Commentaries* for example, he quickly understood passages that were perfectly obscure to his schoolmates. He made sketches on the margins of his versions to indicate the section of a *vallum,* the arrangement of a contravallation and its wooden towers, the form of an *agger,* or the construction of the famous bridge of the Rhine. Thanks to the liberal spirit that prevailed in this institution, the professor was not shocked at this unusual proceeding, and even willingly discussed the translator's illustrations with the pupils. But Jean's delight was to show M. Majorin, on Sundays, his illustrated interpretations of the texts; and this gave rise to conversations that deeply interested the pupil and made him particularly fond of these studies, which weary the minds of the majority of students.

How could it be otherwise, without representing the scenes that were thus made to pass before their eyes?

But we must confess that history, geography, and the mathematical and physical sciences were more particularly liked by Jean . . . because of a natural taste or on account of the habit he had acquired through M. Majorin of interesting himself in positive things, and of reasoning. . . . (pp. 218–19)

Artistic Analysis
While analytical observation helps the scientist solve problems it also assists the artist in capturing the essence of a scene, in abstracting from the totality of data those that invoke the aesthetic response.

"Volumes have been written on the beautiful in art, but all the paper that has been printed never caused a fine work to be made. It is because the beautiful, if anything is meant by the word other than a kind of conventional law or form, comes from the manner of observing nature, and not from the reproduction of an eclectic type. The beautiful is harmony, the exact agreement of form with function; and it is in this that science necessarily cooperates with art. Science proves that a certain peculiarity of the human skull, for example, necessarily leads to a certain arrangement of all the parts. Scientific observation led Cuvier to reconstruct a whole animal out of a jaw or limb, and later discoveries have confirmed his statements. The artist who seeks the beautiful, or harmony, feels a greater interest in knowing how nature proceeds, and what logical consequences are deduced from the construction of a part.

"Egyptian artists certainly did not practice anthropology; but with them delicacy of observation took the place of experimental science; and when one examines the oldest Egyptian works he will be surprised at the perfect harmony existing between typical parts of men or animals. Our modern savants, if they knew how to sculpture or draw, could not do better. But, unfortunately, our education is so defective that while our artists absolutely neglect science, our scientists are not able to use a pencil even tolerably well.

"You already draw very well and can perfect what you know; you should remember, if you purpose following a scientific career, that drawing will give you facilities that are wanting to the majority of savants; and, if you wish to be an artist, science can give you a very marked superiority over those in your profession, and, above all, originality, which is the most important quality in art. Thus, in devoting yourself to art, bear in mind that you must have recourse to science; in devoting yourself to science, do not for a moment forget to use the language of drawing, which not only describes the best, but, through practice, teaches one to see. . . .

"There is a distinction to be made between the scientific and the poetic or artistic method.

"The scientific method consists in giving the smallest results of every observation, and in making a complete analysis of the object or the subject observed preparatory to a synthesis. Art or poetry can make this analysis, and consequently advance like science; but it ought to present only the general effect or the principal impression that is indelibly fixed in the mind. In this lies its merit and difficulty; for to render this principal impression one must feel it, although but few can and many in letters and arts believe themselves poets who are only appraisers taking an inventory. Well, to return to these Japanese drawings: here is a certain scene, for example, which by the aid of a few lines and three colors represents a foam-crested wave moved by the wind; in the background are defined the outlines of trees and the summit of a volcano, Frou-Li. A flock of birds are wheeling round on a gray sky. The execution is very simple. But the lines are so happily studied and expressed, the shapes of the foam broken by the wind are so admirably interpreted, on account of an evidently close observation of details, that this sketch makes a deep impression. One can hear the shock of the waves and the crackling of the drops of water and the whistling of the wind. In a word, one is present at the scene.

"It must have been that the artist who so powerfully rendered it, although it is so fleeting, received such an impression, and, in the working of the elements that compose the subject, singled out its predominant character and the accidental union of lines that picture it with so much spirit and truthfulness. The artist was a poet in the true meaning of the word." (pp. 226–28, 232–33)

The Moral of the Story

Drawing, taught as it should be, and as M. Majorin took pains to teach it to Jean, is the best way to develop the mind and form the judgment; for thus one learns to see, and to see is to know. (p. 320)

4   Adopting a Design Method

THE NECESSITY OF METHOD

Designing a building, Viollet-le-Duc held, was not a matter of applying received prescriptions but of employing a rational procedure. For him, the treatises of the Renaissance tradition, providing formulas for the classical orders and myriad rules of proportion, were anathema. In How to Build a House, *he had the architect explain that there can be no useful code of rules because every new building represents singular circumstances and conditions. Any helpful guide, then, must be presented in terms of principles.*

"Though in morals the good is absolute and independent of circumstances, it is not the same with building. What is good here is bad elsewhere, on account of climate, habits, nature of materials, and the way in which they are affected by local circumstances. While, for instance, it is desirable to cover a roof with slates in a temperate and humid climate, this kind of roofing is objectionable in a warm, dry, and windy climate. Wooden buildings will be excellent in one situation and unsuitable in others. While it is desirable to admit the light by wide openings and to glaze large surfaces in northern climates, because the sun's glare is subdued, this would be objectionable in southern countries, where the light is intense and where it is necessary to procure shelter from the heat. A code of morals is possible, but we cannot establish absolute rules in building; experience, reasoning, and reflection must therefore always be summoned to our aid when we attempt to build. Very often young architects have asked me what treatise on building I should recommend as the best. There is none, I tell them; because a treatise cannot anticipate all contingencies, all the special circumstances that present themselves in the experience of an architect. A treatise lays down rules; but ninety-nine times out of a hundred you have to encounter the exception and cannot rely upon the rule. A treatise on building is useful in habituating the mind to devise plans and have them put into execution according to certain methods; it gives you the means of solving the problems proposed; but it does not actually solve them, or at least only solves one in a thousand. It is then for intelligence to supply in the thousand cases presented what the rule cannot provide for." *(How to Build a House,* p. 61)

The only basis for prescribing design procedure must be in the form of method, which helps to determine the sequence of steps. Every good building results from a problem-solving approach. In Learning to Draw, *the engineer Majorin explains this point to his young protegé Jean.*

"We must begin our studies with method. Do you know what method is?"

"No, good friend." (It was thus that M. Majorin wished to be addressed by Jean.)

"Well, method, little one, is to put everything in its right place, and to do everything at the right time. When Mme. Orphise makes your soup, how does she begin?"

"She puts it on the fire to warm, and then—she puts bread in it."

"And then you eat it. Is that all?"

"Dear me! no: there are carrots and cabbages in it."

"And where does this soup come from? Does she go to the spring for it?"

"Oh, no! M'ame Orphise makes it beforehand."

"Ah! of what?"

"Beef and vegetables."

"And salt?"

"Yes, and salt."

"Then, to make your soup, it was necessary to think beforehand, as you say, of every preparation for it: namely, the purchase of a piece of meat, money in the pocket to pay for it, and a basket on one's arm to put it in; to go in the garden to dig carrots, and cut a cabbage; to go to the spring to fetch water in a very clean jar, and then to boil it; next to have plenty of coal ready; then to pick over the vegetables, and, while the water is still cold, to put meat and carrots in it; to watch lest the water boil over, to skim the scum that rises to the surface, to salt the soup, and, of course, to have enough salt at hand. Then, when the meat has boiled enough to change the pure water into soup, to pour it into a soup tureen, in which one has first put pieces of bread, and then to put aside part of this soup for the next morning's meal. Method, then, consists in performing each of these operations at the proper time. Without method, you have no soup, my dear boy. Well, whatever one does in life, if he wishes it to succeed, must be done with method." (*Learning to Draw*, p. 19)

The creation of a modern architecture was hampered (in the nineteenth century) not by the lack of new materials or even new technology but by the lack of a design method that would make it possible to integrate all capabilities.

Since the French Revolution of the last century we have entered on a transitional phase; we are investigating, searching into the past, and accumulating abundance of materials, while our means and appliances have been increased. What then is wanting to enable us to give an original embodiment and form to so many various elements? Is it not simply method that is lacking? In the arts, as in the sciences, the absence of method, whether we are engaged in investigating or in attempting to apply the knowledge we have acquired, occasions an embarrassment and confusion proportional to the increase of our resources. . . . The program being satisfied and the structure determined, what have we to do in proceeding from the simple to the compound? First, we must know at the outset the nature of the materials to be employed; second, we must give these materials the function and strength required for the result, and the forms that most exactly express that function and strength; third, we must adopt a principle of unity and harmony in this expression—that is, a scale, a system of proportion, a style of ornamentation related to the destination of the structure and having a definite signification, as also the variety indicated by the diverse nature of the requirements to be complied with. . . . This is the rock on which nearly all our architects, since the sixteenth century, have made shipwreck; they have either sacrificed the requirements and the judicious employment of the materials to a form that is symmetrical without being rational, or they have not known how to give an appearance of unity, a oneness of conception to the buildings, while satisfying the program and employing the material judiciously. *(Discourses, X)*

A METHODICAL PROCEDURE

If any theoretical prescription can be made to the architect it is a methodological procedure to follow in the course of working out a design. The steps most directly related to the rational development of a design are quoted below from How to Build a House. *As it is set out, the text might appear to be limited to describing the creation of one particular house. However, the process may also be understood to represent a logical progression of steps appropriate to the designing of any building.*

Step 1: Establishing the Program
For Viollet-le-Duc, the great legacy of ancient Rome to the western tradition of architecture was what he perceived as the first step in their design procedure, namely to define the purposes of a proposed new building and to delineate its functions in a program. Nothing, he held, is more necessary to the creation of a good design than a clear notion of what is wanted and needed.

This house in prospect for Paul's sister has seized on his imagination; he figures it to himself sometimes as a palace, sometimes as a turreted manor house of the old style, sometimes as a Swiss cottage, covered with ivy and clematis, with innumerable carved balconies. He has a grown-up cousin who is an architect; he has often seen him at work at a drawing board; under his hand buildings rose as by enchantment. It did not appear very difficult work. His cousin Eugene has the necessary instruments in the room he occupies when he comes to the chateau. Paul will try to put on paper one of those plans of which his imagination has given him a glimpse. But there is a difficulty at the outset. He must know what would suit his sister best; a baronial castle with towers and battlements, a Swiss cottage, or an Italian villa. If it is to take her by surprise, the surprise must be at any rate an agreeable one. After a good hour's meditation, Paul thinks, and with some reason, that he ought to go and consult his father.

"Oh, oh! you are in a great hurry," said his father, after Paul's first words. "But we are not quite so far advanced as that. You want to draw a plan for Marie's house. Well, try then. But in the first place, we must know what your sister wants—how she would like her house arranged. After all, I am not sorry to hasten things forward a little. We will send her a telegram."

"Baveno. Italy. From X—— Mad. N——, Hotel de ———. Paul wants to build a house here for Marie. Send program."

Twenty hours afterward the following telegram reached the chateau:

"X——. From Baveno. To M. de Gandelau. Arrived this morning— all well. Paul has an excellent idea. Ground floor—entrance hall, drawing room, dining room, pantry, kitchen not underground, billiard room, study. First floor—two large bedrooms, two dressing rooms; baths; small bedroom, dressing room; linen room, closets, attic bedrooms; cupboards plenty; staircase not breakneck. MARIE N——."

Without doubting for a moment that his sister had taken in earnest the despatch addressed to her, and had replied accordingly, Paul set himself resolutely to work. . . .

"We must . . . build the house almost on the summit of the incline facing the north—sheltering it from the northwest winds under the neighboring wood. The entrance will have to front the ascending road; but we must arrange for the principal apartments to command the most favorable aspect, which is southeast; moreover, we must take advantage of the open view on the same side, and not disregard the spring of fresh water that flows on the right toward the bottom of the valley; we shall therefore approach it and locate the house in that resting place that nature has arranged so favorably to our views, some yards below the plateau. We shall thus be tolerably sheltered from the southwest winds and shall not have the dull-looking plain, which extends as fas as the eye can reach, in front of the house. This settled, let us look at the program. No dimensions of rooms are mentioned; we shall therefore have to determine this. According to what your father has told me, he intends this house to be for constant residence, habitable in summer as well as in winter, and consequently to contain all that is suitable for a large landed proprietor. He means to spend about £8,000 upon it; it is therefore a matter that demands serious study, especially as your sister and her husband make a great point of 'comfort.' . . .

"When you wish to build a house, or any edifice, you give the architect a program, i.e., a complete list of all the rooms and accessories that are wanted. But this is not enough; you say such or such a room must have such or such a width by such or such a length, or have such or such an area so as to accommodate so many persons. If it is a dining room, for instance, you will mention that it must accommodate 10, 15, 20, or 25 persons at table. If it is a bedroom, you will specify that besides the bed (which is a matter of course) it must accommodate such or such pieces of furniture or occupy an area of 300 square feet, 400 square feet, etc. Now you know that an area of 400 square feet is equivalent to a square whose side is 20 feet, or a parallelogram of about 24 feet by 16 feet 8 inches, or of 30 feet by 13 feet 4 inches. But these last dimensions would not suit a room; they are rather the proportions of a gallery. Independently, therefore, of the area of a room, its breadth and length must bear certain relations according to its purpose. A drawing room or a bedchamber may be square; but a dining room, if it is to accommodate more than ten persons at table, must be longer than it is broad, because a table increases in length but not in width, according to the number of the guests. You must therefore add 'leaves' to the dining room as you do to the table." (pp. 8–9, 14–15)

Step 2: Developing the Plan
Beginning with the portion of the scheme that is either most important or imposes the greatest number of desiderata, the plan should evolve from the arrangement of spaces into the most workable sequence. The shaping and arranging of spaces is best disciplined by the imposition of a guiding regulator, be it a grid, a module, or simply a scale. If a structure is to be of more than one story, the story that matters most will determine the spatial limitations of the others. Each successive restriction reduces the number of design decisions that have to be made, so after a certain point the plan may almost seem to design itself.

"At this point then the architect, in preparing the plan, even if it is only a sketch, adopts a scale, i.e., he divides a line drawn upon his paper into equal parts, each representing a foot. And to save time, or to simplify the work, he takes for each of these divisions the 192nd, or the 96th, or the 48th part of a foot. In the first case we call it a scale of $\frac{1}{16}$ inch to a foot, or a scale of 16 feet to an inch; in the second, a scale of $\frac{1}{8}$ inch to a foot, or a scale of 8 feet to an inch; in the third, a scale of $\frac{1}{4}$ inch to a foot, or a scale of 4 feet to an inch. Thus you prepare a plan

192, 96, or 48 times smaller than its realization will be. I need not say that we may make scales in any proportion ad infinitum—one, two, or three hundredths of an inch to a foot, or to 10, 100, or 1,000 feet, as we do for drawing maps. In the same way we may give details on a scale of 6 inches to a foot, or half the actual size; 2 inches to a foot, or a sixth of the actual size, etc. Having chosen his scale, the architect is enabled to give to each part of the plan exact relative dimensions. . . .

"Take for your sister's drawing room 18/16 on this graduated rule, which will give 18 feet on a scale of $\frac{1}{16}$ inch to a foot. Just so; that gives us the shorter side of the drawing room. Now take 27/16 on the same rule, which will give 27 feet; that will be the longer side. Now your oblong is drawn with dimensions perfectly exact. You will have to surround this room with walls, for we can scarcely give ordinary floors a greater width; you must therefore have walls to receive the joists. A rubble wall through which flues have to pass can hardly be less than 1 foot 8 inches in thickness. Your drawing room will therefore support itself. Next in importance to the drawing room is the dining room. Where are we to place it? We ought, especially in the country, to be able to enter it directly from the drawing room. Is it to be on the right, or on the left? You have not the least idea; nor I either. But chance cannot settle the question. Let us think about it a little. It would seem natural to put the kitchen near to the dining room. But the position of the kitchen is a matter presenting some difficulties. When you are not at table you don't like to have the smell of the viands, or hear the noise of those engaged in kitchen work. On the one hand, the kitchen ought not to be far from the dining room; on the other hand, it ought to be far enough from the chief rooms for its existence not to be suspected. Besides, the backyard, the outbuildings, the poultry yard, a small vegetable garden, washhouses, etc., ought to be near the kitchen. It is a matter of importance too that the kitchen should not have a south aspect. And we must nor forget that your sister, who knows how a house ought to be managed, has taken the precaution to say in her laconic program: 'Kitchen not underground.' She is right: underground kitchens are unhealthy for those who live in them, present difficulties in the way of surveillance, and diffuse their odor through the ground floor. We shall put it therefore on a level with the dining room, but without direct communication with the latter, to avoid odors and noises. Let us examine our ground, its position and aspects. The most undesirable aspect, and that which in the present case offers the least agreeable prospect, is the northwest. We shall therefore place the drawing room with its exterior angle toward the southeast; on the right we shall put the dining room; and next the kitchen, which will thus face the north. Do not be in a hurry to draw the plan of these subordinate apartments, for we must know first what position they are to occupy in relation to the drawing room and the entrance hall. We are required to provide a billiard room. It will be well to place it on the southeast, as a pendant to the dining room. The hall and your brother-in-law's study must be near the entrance. If we place the dining room and the billiard room, whose dimensions are to be nearly equal to those of the drawing room, in juxtaposition and continuation with the latter, the drawing room will be lighted only on one of its shorter sides, for we must put the entrance hall in front. The drawing room would in that case be gloomy, and would command a view of the country only in one direction. Let us then put the dining room and the billiard room at right angles to the drawing room, allowing the latter to jut out on the sides of the favorable aspect. Let us give each of these two apartments a length of 24 feet by a width of 18 feet. These are convenient dimensions. Then mark in front of the drawing room an entrance hall, whose area we shall determine presently.

"We will try next to give to the walls of those apartments the position required by the general construction. The entrance to the dining room and the billiard room—which is also a place of assembly—is to be from the drawing room. The opening from the drawing room into the billiard room must therefore be wide enough for those who may be in either of those apartments to assemble without inconvenience. But we ought to be able to reach the entrance hall from the billiard room without going through the drawing room; and so with the dining room. We observe that lateral prospects were required for the drawing room, whose length is 27 feet. If we take 8 feet for the side lights, and 1 foot 6 inches for the thickness of the wall of the billiard room or the dining room, there will remain 17 feet 6 inches to the entrance partition of the drawing room; our billiard room and dining room being 18 feet wide, these apartments will reach 8 inches beyond the entrance partition of the drawing room. That does not matter. Let us mark out the second wall, also 1 foot 6 inches thick. Thus we have the three chief apartments determined. In the central line of the billiard room we will make an opening into the drawing room of 8 feet 6 inches. On the side of the wall separating it from the dining room we will open a door of 4 feet 6 inches into the dining room, within 8 inches of the partition separating the drawing room from the entrance hall. Thus we shall enter this dining room not in the center, but on one side, which is more convenient; for you know that in going to or leaving it the gentlemen offer their arms to the ladies. It is therefore desirable that in going out or coming in there should be no obstacle in their way. The door leading from the drawing room to the dining room will be also out of the central line of the opening from the drawing room into the billiard room; but that I do not mind. This door will balance with the window on this side looking outward, and we will put the fireplace between them. We will open a central door from the entrance hall into the drawing room.

"In front, against the wall of the billiard room, let us put your brother-in-law's study, with a small anteroom, where people who have business with him can wait, so as not to be wandering about in the hall. On the dining room side of the hall we will put the pantry. The study must be at least 12 feet 6 inches wide. We will make the entrance hall jut out a little to form a projection.

"The staircase is a very important point in every house. It should be proportioned to the house, neither too spacious nor too scanty. It must not occupy space uselessly; it must give easy access to the upper stories and be sufficiently conspicuous. It we take a part of the staircase out of the entrance hall, which is very large—18 feet by 16 feet—it will be very conspicuous, and we shall gain room. The width of a staircase in a house of this style and size should be at least 4 feet. But the hall ought to communicate directly with the dining room, the pantry, and all the offices to the right of the plan. Let us reserve a passage of 4 feet and mark the first step. The height of the lower story between floor and floor should be, reckoning the size of the rooms, 15 feet; which will give them a clear height of 14 feet, reserving 1 foot for the thickness of the floor of the chamber story. The steps of an easy staircase should be about 6 inches high. To ascend 15 feet we require thirty steps. Each step should be 10 to 12 inches wide. The staircase should have an extension of 25 feet for steps of 10 inches in width, or 30 feet for steps of 12 inches, reckoning thirty steps. Let us take a mean—say 27 feet. We must find room for this extension of 27 feet at the least. We will therefore place a staircase projection at the angle of the entrance hall prominent enough to bring us, in winding round a newel (which will be in the prolongation of the wall on the right of the drawing room), to the first floor, passing out into the antechamber of this floor. . . . I mark out this staircase for you: we shall have to return to it. The first fifteen steps come into the length of the newel and the wall, and allow us to place below the last half flight of the stairs the water closet for the family on the ground floor. Opening from the passage we will next put the pantry. Then the servants' staircase in a tower; then the serving room; then the kitchen in the wing; a bakehouse and scullery, a washhouse, and a way out from the kitchen to the kitchen garden. Forming a return, we will put a stable for three horses, a coach house for two carriages, a harness room, and a small flight of stairs to reach the rooms for the coachman and groom, and the hayloft in the roof. Near the stable we will leave a way into the yard and the larder and servants' conveniences.

"We will separate all these offices from the main building by a plinth wall and trelliswork at the right of the round tower servants' staircase, which will give us a courtyard for the kitchen, stable, and coach house. In front we will reserve a space for the poultry yard, the fowl house, and the manure pit. . . .

"Now that we have traced out the general plan of our ground floor, let us try to improve it in detail.

"It would be very nice to have a bay window at the end of the drawing room looking out on the garden. Nothing prevents us from planning another at the end of the billiard room, with a divan where the gentlemen might smoke, and a third at the end of the dining room, which would allow the dishes to be passed in through a turn from the serving room and afford room for the sideboard and carving tables.

"We shall find these projections useful on the first floor.

"But we ought to have a way out from the drawing room or the billiard room into the garden. I must confess that I am not very fond of those flights of steps, which are scorching under a hot sun and very disagreeable in wind and rain; if, then, in the angle formed by the billiard room with the drawing room, and along it, we were to place a conservatory enclosing a flight of steps, I think it would be a convenient arrangement. Thus we could pass from the drawing room or the billiard room into this conservatory, and could take coffee there in wet weather and have a covered approach to the garden. Some flowers and shrubs placed along the glazed side would enliven the billiard room without darkening it. But in front of the entrance hall we will have a flight of steps in the usual style, which we shall take care to put under shelter, the position of the staircase allowing us to do so without difficulty.

"Let us draw out all this as nearly as we can; we shall have to revise it when we have studied the first floor, whose arrangements may oblige us to modify some of those on the ground floor (fig. 41).

"As the walls must rise from the bottom, you will put a piece of tracing paper over this ground plan to avoid loss of time. You will thus have beneath your eyes and pencil the walls to which you must accommodate the superstructure, and we shall presently see whether there is reason to modify some parts of this ground plan.

"Just so. Let us first trace the termination of the staircase; the last of the thirty steps we shall require is in a line with the wall on the right of the entrance hall; it is the landing that will open on the antechamber above the hall. Over the drawing room we shall place Madame N.'s room; but as this area would be too large, we shall take advantage of the space to put a second partition, which ladies never find superfluous. To give light in this space we shall glaze an upper portion of the partition next to the antechamber. These double doors will insure greater privacy in the bedroom, and prevent the passage of sounds. Besides, this second antechamber will enable us to provide a direct communication with Monsieur N.'s apartment, which we shall place in the favorable aspect, that is over the billiard room.

"As this area also is too large, we shall take out of the space thus available a lady's dressing room and a bathroom, and provide an entrance to Monsieur N.'s room direct from the antechamber through a private passage. This passage will also open into the lady's dressing room, that for your brother-in-law over the study, his bedchamber, and the closets for these apartments. Thus when the two doors leading to the antechamber are shut, these rooms will be completely cut off. With a corridor answering to that of the ground floor on the right we shall establish a communication between the antechamber, the servants' staircase, the linen room (an important matter), which we shall place over the kitchen, with a large wardrobe for your sister on the right of her bedroom, and a nursery (for we must provide for every contingency), which, as well as the wardrobe, will be over the dining room. The recess or bay window of the ground floor will afford us the means of giving a nice dressing room for the children's or guests' room on the

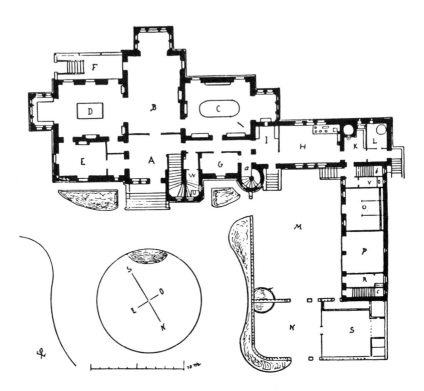

41. Plan of the ground floor of a
house. A, entrance hall; B, drawing room; C, dining room; D, billiard room; E, study; F, conservatory enclosing flight of steps;
G, butler's pantry; H, kitchen;
I, serving room; K, L, bakehouse
and washhouse; M, office yard;
N, S, poultry yard; O, stable;
P, coachhouse; R, harness room;
a, servants' staircase; b, cellar
steps; c, groom's staircase;
V, W, water closets.

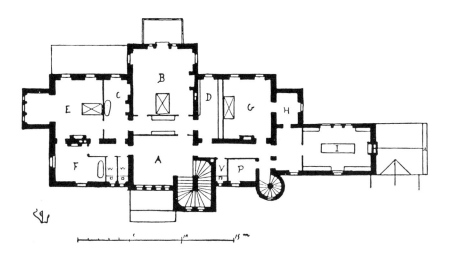

42. Plan of the first floor. A, antechamber; B, Madame N.'s bedroom; C, dressing room and bathroom; D, wardrobe; E, Monsieur N.'s bedroom; F, dressing room and bathroom; G, nursery; H, dressing room; I, linen room; P, lumber room; W, water closets.

first floor; and that of the billiard room will furnish a very agreeable addition to Monsieur N.'s room. As to the bay window in the drawing room, we will cover it with a flat roof, with a balustrade, which will give your sister's room a handsome balcony, where an awning and flowers can be placed in the summer (fig. 42).

"You see, Paul, our plan begins to assume a definite shape. . . ."

On going down to the garden, Paul began to examine the family mansion with an attention he had never yet bestowed upon it. He had never thought before of observing how its apartments were arranged. He began to calculate the space lost in those interminable passages; he perceived here and there dark and useless corners. The staircase started badly. On the ground floor it could not be found without knowing the arrangement of the house. The kitchen was at a vast distance from the dining room, and to get from the one to the other you must cross a carriage road, go down two steps and mount six. For the first time in his life this struck him as barbarous. Walking about waiting for the breakfast bell, Paul began to ask himself whether his father would not do well to pull down his old mansion and build one on a new plan devised by himself with his cousin's advice. He began to reckon up the several faults in the arrangement of the house, not forgetting its too numerous breakneck passages. He considered the somber drawing room, flanked on two sides by the two old towers that masked the side views, his father's little study lighted by a narrow window and entered by a pretty large room, generally unused, which served as a fruit room in the autumn; and many other defects besides. (pp. 16–25)

Step 3: Determining the Structural System
Once the arrangement of spaces is determined in a plan, the means for translating the scheme into a stable structure must be worked out. In the case of a nonstandardized structure, such as a house, it is necessary to delineate the geometry of the roof planes, which implies all the structural apparatus necessary to provide a shelter over the plan. Hence the structure is a response to the functional necessities rather than an a priori *system into which the functions must be accommodated.*

"When you draw a horizontal or ground plan, independently of the arrangements, you have to consider how your buildings shall be covered in. For the most important question in a building is that of the manner of roofing it, as every building intended for internal use is a shelter. That is unquestionable, is it not? Well, then, in your building, the plans of which you have now before you, what is observable in the general form of the main block? Two parallelograms intersecting—so (fig. 43). One parallelogram, abcd, intersected by another, efgh. We do not now take into account the bay windows and staircases. If then we raise gables upon the walls ac, bd, with a length of slope equal to the line ac, we shall have two equilateral triangles whose bases will be ac and bd, and the angles of inclination 60°, which is the most suitable pitch for slating, inasmuch as it gives no hold to the snow or opportunity for mischief to the wind. If in like manner we erect upon the walls ef and gh two gables having a similar inclination, these walls being less in length than those marked ab, cd, the triangles will be smaller and their summits less elevated than the first. Consequently the roof raised upon the smaller parallelogram will penetrate that raised upon the larger, and will form by its penetration internal angles that we call valleys; I draw these valleys ik, kl, mn, mo. The inclination of the two

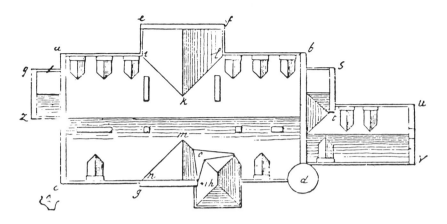

43. Roof plan.

roofs being equal, these valleys will, in plan, divide the right angle into two equal angles: you know enough of geometry to understand that.

"Here, then, we see the simplest way of roofing our building; and when roofing is in question, the simplest methods are always the best. Now, in order that our two stairs may give access to the third story, it is necessary that their walls should rise above the cornice of the building and form for them alone an additional story. We will then raise these stair walls and will give them roofs of their own. One—that of the principal stairs—shall be pyramidal; and the other—that of the small stairs—conical.

"There is no reason why we should not erect small gables upon the two walls gz, st, of the bay windows, always with the same inclination of 60°, and cover these projections with two small roofs abutting against the great gables ac, bd. As to the building appropriated on the ground floor to the kitchen and on the first floor to the linen room, we will follow the same method, and, erecting a gable on the wall uv, we shall have upon this wing a triangular roof, which will also abut against the great gable bd. We shall then have a meeting of two slopes at the bottom of the roof of the bay window st and of that of the linen room wing. We shall form a lean-to (so as to do without inner gutters), which will penetrate these two roofs and discharge the water at t. The horizontal projection, therefore, of this assemblage of roofs will be as the drawing shows in figure 43. The chimney stacks will pass through these roofs, as I indicate to you; and in order to prevent the chimneys from smoking, these stacks should rise at least to the level of the ridge, that is, a little above the topmost crest of the highest roof. With regard to the roofs of the outbuildings, as they are lower—being only one story in height—we need not trouble ourselves about them just now.

"Observe that, as these gables rise perpendicularly, we are enabled to get in the roof a third story, affording some very convenient bedrooms for guests, besides the servants' rooms (in the attics), which we must provide, and light by means of dormer windows; while we shall be able to provide for the bedrooms in the gables handsome windows with balconies, if we wish.

"That settled in principle, it will be as well to arrange the divisions of this story in the roof. Lay a piece of tracing paper upon the plan of the first floor. Good: now trace all the thick walls that must of necessity be carried up under the roof, since they contain fireplaces. Draw 3 feet 3 inches within the eave walls—i.e., those that do not carry gables—a line that indicates the space rendered useless by the slope of the roof; thus you will get the space of which you are able to make use. The principal stairs reach to this floor, as well as the servants' stairs. To the left of the thick division wall, which, from the principal staircase, goes to join the angle of the main building toward the southeast—the desirable aspect—we are going to dispose the bedrooms for guests, which will thus form a separate quarter communicating with the chief apartments by the principal stairs. We can in this part get two good bedrooms, A and B, with their dressing rooms a and b; and two smaller bedrooms C and D, all having fireplaces. We must not forget the water closet for these rooms, at W. On the other side, in immediate communication with the servants' stairs, we can easily get four servants' bedrooms, E, F, G, H, a lumber room I, and a water closet L for the servants (fig. 44).

"In the upper part of the coach house and stable building and over the washhouse, we shall also be able in the roofs to arrange three or four bedrooms for the coachman, groom, etc." (pp. 32–35)

Step 4: Deriving the Design from the Structural Necessities
Only after the structural system necessary to provide spaces over the plan has been devised is it feasible to formulate the elevations. While the elevations are visually the most conspicuous aspect of the building and

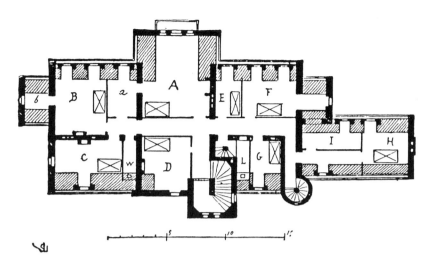

44. Plan of the second floor. A, B, good bedrooms; a, b, dressing rooms; C, D, smaller bedrooms; W, water closet; E, F, G, H, servants' bedrooms; I, lumber room; L, servants' water closet.

the most susceptible to artistic embellishment, they must be derived from the structural composition and not based on a preconceived scheme. If they are asymmetrical and irregular in form, so be it; elevations that are a natural outgrowth of the structure will have a formal integrity that is visually pleasing. In other words, a building that is produced by a rational design process is likely also to be beautiful.

"And now for the elevations.

"We will raise the ground floor 4 feet above the exterior ground level, in order to give air to our cellars and to preserve the ground floor from the moisture of the earth. We will give the lower rooms a height of 14 feet to the ceiling. Draw at this level a horizontal stringcourse 12 inches deep, which will be the thickness of the floor. To the rooms of the first floor, which are smaller than those of the ground floor, we will give a height of 12 feet in the clear. Now, mark the thickness of the cornice, with its tabling, 1 foot 9 inches. Then will begin the roofs, whose height will be fixed by that of the gables. Taking the entrance front we project the angles of the building, the doors and the windows from the plan.

Here, then, we have the outline of the facade arranged (fig. 45)."
(pp. 36–37)

It was time to think about studying the details of the elevations. That overlooking the garden was only roughly sketched out. Paul was hoping that it would present a more regular appearance than that of the entrance side. He made a remark to that effect, for Paul had seen many country houses in the environs of Paris that seemed to him charming, with their four pepperboxes at the angles, their porch in the very center of the facade, and zinc cresting on the roof. He had too high an opinion of his cousin's ability to allow himself to criticize the facade of his sister's house, as designed for the entrance side; but in his heart he would have preferred something more conformable to the laws of symmetry. Those windows of all forms and dimensions shocked his taste a little. When the facade on the garden side (fig. 46) was sketched—a frontage that, this time, presented a symmetrical aspect—Paul declared himself satisfied with it; and in the evening, the family being assembled, he asked why the entrance front did not present the symmetrical arrangements that delighted him on the garden side.

"Because," said Eugene, "on the garden side our plan gives us rooms that are the counterparts of each other, of equal dimensions and corresponding purposes; while on the entrance side we have very diverse services in juxtaposition. The question you raise, Paul, is a very large one. Two methods may be followed. On the one hand, you may plan a symmetrical architectural casing, in which you try, as best you can, to accommodate the services required by a habitation. Or, on the other hand, you may arrange these services in plan, according to their importance, their respective place, and the relations that are to be established between them, and erect the casing so as to suit these services, without troubling yourself to obtain a symmetrical appearance. When it is proposed to erect an edifice whose exterior aspect is destined to exhibit a grand unity of design, it is desirable to endeavor to satisfy the rules of symmetry, and to take care that the building shall not present the appearance of having been built piecemeal. In a private habitation it is imperative first to satisfy the requirements of its inhabitants, and not to incur needless expense. The habitations of the ancients were not symmetrical, any more than those of the Middle Ages. Symmetry strictly applied to domestic architecture is a modern conceit—an affectation—

45. The entrance front.

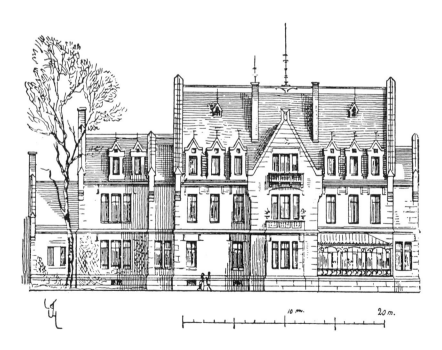

46. The garden front.

a false interpretation of the rules observed during the best periods of art. The houses of Pompeii are not symmetrical: the country house—the villa—of which Pliny has left us a complete description, did not present a symmetrical ensemble. The castles, manors, and houses built during the Middle Ages are anything but symmetrical. Lastly, in England, in Holland, in Sweden, in Hanover, and in a large part of Germany, you may see numbers of dwellings wonderfully appropriate to the needs of their inhabitants, which are constructed without regard to symmetry but are nevertheless very convenient and elegant in appearance, from the simple fact that they clearly indicate their purpose.

"I know that there are many persons quite disposed to put themselves to inconvenience every day, in order to have the vain pleasure of exhibiting regular and monumental facades outside; but I think your sister is not one of those persons, and therefore I have not hesitated to proceed according to what I conceive to be the law of common sense in making the designs for her habitation. I can fancy her asking me, with her quiet and slightly ironical smile—

"Why, my dear cousin, did you make me so large a window in this small room? We shall have to stop up half of it.' . . . Or, 'Why did you not give me a window on this side, where the view is so pretty?'

"If I replied that it was to satisfy the laws of symmetry, she would perhaps have laughed outright, and, *in petto,* might probably have thought that her respected cousin was after all a fool, with his 'laws of symmetry.'"

"Alas!" said M. de Gandelau, "there are too many people in our country with whom considerations of vanity take precedence of everything else, and that is one of the causes of our misfortunes. Appearance is the great object. Every retired bourgeois who has a country house built wishes to have his turrets regularly disposed at the corners of a building, symmetrical, indeed, but in which he is very indifferently lodged—satisfied if this inconvenient erection is called the chateau, internal comfort being sacrificed to the gratification of exhibiting outside bad stucco carvings, zinc ornaments on the roof, and a quantity of nonsensical decorations that have to be renewed every spring. Build us then, cousin, a good house, well sheltered from the sun and rain, thoroughly dry within, and in which nothing is sacrificed to that debased luxury that is a thousand times more offensive in our country districts than it is in the city." (pp. 104–5)

"Construction . . . is an art requiring foresight. The good builder is he who leaves nothing to chance, who does not put off the solution of any problem, and who knows how to give each function its place and value with respect to the whole, and that at the right moment. We have drawn plans for the several stories; we have given the details necessary for constructing the lower parts of the house; now we must draw the working elevations. The first thing is to make an exact section of the front walls giving the height of the floors, the levels of the tie bars, and the base of the roof."

Eugene, who, as we may suppose, had previously realized to himself, if not drawn, all the parts of the building, had soon sketched out this section for Paul, who did not cease to wonder at the promptitude with which his master succeeded in drawing on paper any detail required. He could not help remarking it again.

"How do you manage to indicate the arrangement of all these parts of the building without hesitating a moment?" said he.

"Because I have thought about them, and have represented to myself all these parts while drawing or setting you to draw their combinations. If they are not on the paper they are in my head; and when I have to render them intelligible to those who are commissioned to execute them, I have only to write, so to speak, what I know by heart already. And thus it is always desirable to proceed. Look at this section, and these few details (fig. 47); let us examine the drawing together; you will soon observe that you have already seen all that the sheet of paper contains, and that with a little attention you would be able to arrange these different parts in their due order. You see the thickness of the wall on the ground floor figured, and with its central line dotted; the height of the window sill, A, and its support; the arrangement of the window casing and its lintel; the height of the floor and its thickness. The string-course, B, had to be determined; it should have the thickness of this floor; it indicates it externally. Then, reducing the outside walls to 1 foot 8 inches on the first floor, we put a setoff course at C; window sills like those of the ground floor. The height of the first story from floor to floor has already been settled. The under member, D, of the cornice indicates the thickness of the second floor; lastly comes the cornice table of hard stone, which receives the eaves gutter. As regards the first-floor windows, they are formed like those of the ground floor, excepting that the inside reveal is less deep by 4 inches, since the wall is 4 inches less in

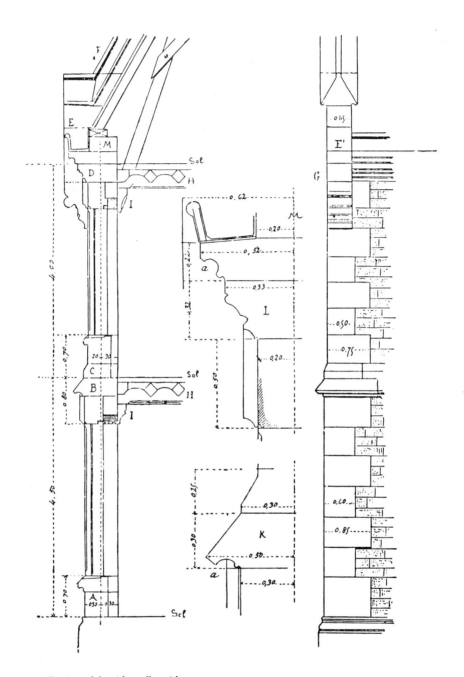

47. Section of the side walls, with details.

thickness. Their lintels are similar, as well as the casing that has to take the sheet-iron jalousies, and the tie bars come underneath these lintels. As we have gables, the cornices cannot return and must stop against a projection, E, which, rising above the roof, receives the coping F, which will have a projecting fillet to cover the junction of the slating with the gable. At G, then, I draw the angle of the building with this projection, E, and the coping we have spoken of. As I foresee that the joists will have too long a bearing in some places, I suppose the intermediate beams, H, to carry them and the corbels, I, for the support of these joists.

"At K I have drawn the stringcourse of the first floor, with the projections figured from the center of the wall, and the setoff course above; also at L, the cornice and its table course. You will observe that this table course slopes toward the outer edge, beneath the gutter, so that, in the event of an overflow the water may run off outside, and not find its way into the wall. This table course has a throat, a, as well as the stringcourse, to prevent the water from running down the wall. These moldings will have to be drawn to their full size for the stonemason. On the course, M, behind the gutter will stand the dormer gables, which will admit light to the second floor in the roof. As to the roofing, of which I merely indicate here the base, I will show you what it is to be. Take these sketches, then, and make from them figured drawings to a scale of half an inch to a foot, so that they may be worked from." (pp. 161–62)

Step 5: Determining Ornamentation

Ornament is inherently desirable in architecture, but it should grow out of the way a building is put together or be attuned to the shape or material qualities of a structural member. Often a decorative effect can be produced through an imaginative structural solution. In any event, decoration should never be arbitrarily applied to surfaces and should never pretend to be something it is not. Simple treatments, usually just enhancing the natural properties of the building materials, are preferable.

"We must construct the floors with wood. But I have already told you that timbers that have not been soaked for some time and have been cut scarcely two years, decay very rapidly when enclosed, chiefly in their bearings, that is their extremities built in the walls. To prevent our

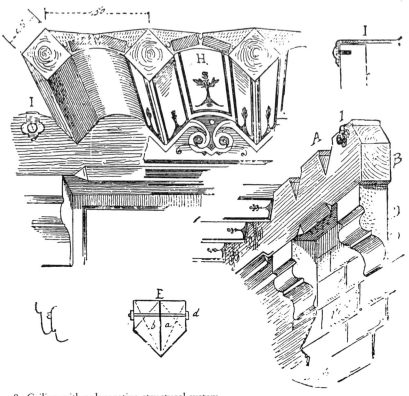

48. Ceiling with a decorative structural system.

floors giving us anxiety respecting their durability, we must leave the timbers visible and not build them in the walls. We will, therefore, adopt the system of bearers attached to the walls to receive the bearings of the joists; and as we have small oak trunks, we will content ourselves with squaring them on two faces and place them diagonally, as I show you here (fig. 48). For bearings of 16 to 20 feet, which are the largest we have, timbers 7 inches square will be sufficient. If we think them insufficient we will put an intermediate beam; that remains to be seen. These joists, diagonally placed, present moreover their maximum of resistance to deflection. We will place them at 20 inches from center to center. Their bearings will be in the notches made in the bearers, as marked at A, and the soffits—which are the spaces between the joists—will be made with bricks placed flatways, overlaid with mortar and plastered beneath. We may decorate these ceilings with line painting, which renders them light and agreeable to the sight, as at H. Joists thus placed do not present internal angles difficult to keep clean, and among which spiders spin their webs. A dust with a soft brush readily cleans these soffits.

The interior, though simple, according to M. de Gandelau's express instructions, was in good taste; there was nothing to be seen in the way of plaster ornament or gilding. The entrance hall was surrounded by a low oak wainscot, forming part with the doorcases. The wood of the latter and of the wainscot had preserved its natural colour, and was simply dressed with linseed oil and wax. Above the wainscot, the walls, painted stone color, set off by a few red lines, gave a neat and inviting aspect to the entrance. The drawing room was surrounded by a wainscot five feet high, painted white; the fireplace, wide and lofty, could warm a numerous circle. The jambs of the fireplace were cased with wood, and on the lofty mantelpiece, in an oaken frame, was prettily painted a bird's-eye view of M. de Gandelau's estate. The ceiling, with its two beams and joists, painted in light tones set off by black and white lines, seemed to enlarge the apartment and gave it a warm and habitable appearance, presenting on hot days lights and shades of an amber tint. The wall between the ceiling and the wainscot was hung with painted canvas. The chimneypiece stood out in bold relief on this background. The entrance end of the drawing room would have been rather somber if the wide opening into the billiard room had not flooded it with light, softened by the verdure of the plants within the little conservatory. But what gave the drawing room a character that fascinated Paul at once was the bay window, all brilliant with light and furnished with a chintz-covered divan. The billiard room, also, was surrounded by a wainscoting of unpainted oak, and the same painted hangings. A portier closing over the bay window made it serve the purpose of a little boudoir, whence there was a charming view on three sides. The plants placed in the conservatory transmitted on the south side only a softened and tranquil light into the billiard room. The dining room had been decorated almost in the same style as the billiard room, and two large oaken sideboards formed part with the wainscoting in the two recesses reserved for them.

Paul was eager to run upstairs to see his sister's rooms. Hung entirely with Indian chintz, with a plain brown dado, this apartment exhibited great simplicity. The ceiling, however, treated like those of the ground floor, gave it an original and pleasing aspect. (pp. 249–50)

The similarity between this method and that enunciated by Frank Lloyd Wright throughout his life and most explicitly in The Natural House *(1954) indicates that Wright almost certainly read Viollet-le-Duc's book (translated into English by 1874) and assimilated it into his own philosophy and practice.*

III ANTICIPATING A MODERN ARCHITECTURE

5   Handling Materials

Viollet-le-Duc's principles for the use of materials were shaped by his enthusiasm for employing new, industrially produced materials in combinations that would permit the exploitation of their inherent qualities. Such a concern implied a moral attitude also, one that promoted honesty in the use of materials, or truth to the medium. In this respect he paralleled John Ruskin, whose The Seven Lamps of Architecture—*published much earlier, in 1848—may have been an unacknowledged source of inspiration. However he acquired this concern, it became one of the central doctrines of his theory of architecture, along with honesty in the expression of structure.*

No one will deny in theory that the various properties of the materials ought to be considered in the form given to them when employed in building. Stone, marble, wood, cast or wrought iron, and the various forms of baked clay have widely different properties: in view of this variety and even opposition of character in the several materials, the form that suits one of them cannot suit another. This being regarded as indisputable, it must, I think, be granted that many forms habitually adopted in our edifices take no account of the properties of the materials, and can only be referred to certain traditions that show a want of accurate knowledge of those properties.

We might seem justified in supposing that since modern science has carried the knowledge of the various properties of the material employed to a high degree of perfection, our builders would take advantage of its researches to give to the materials forms bearing a due relation to those properties: but it has not been so; or at any rate the attempts made in this direction have been but timid, and exhibit a constant anxiety to introduce no alteration into the traditional forms bequeathed by anterior phases of art. Civil engineers themselves, who had been among the foremost to extend the domain of science in that direction, were less disposed than others, perhaps to make the forms that they gave to the material harmonize with its properties. This has arisen from the false direction given to the teaching of art—a teaching that only gives examples borrowed from former civilizations, without ever explaining the reason why the forms and the materials in which they were produced were originally adopted.

The teaching of architecture as carried on in France, instead of allying itself intimately with science and criticism, seems inclined to look askance at both of them, encouraging them only on the condition of their not encroaching on what it is pleased to call the traditions of "high art"; as if the chief condition of art in architecture as well as in every other department was not conformity to truth in adopting forms suggested by the harmonious concurrence of all knowledge relating to the department in question. And so we hear it maintained in the present day, as it was formerly, that iron cannot be employed in our edifices without dissembling its use, because this material is not suited to monumental forms. It would be more consistent with truth and reason to say that the monumental forms adopted, having resulted from the use of materials possessing qualities other than those of iron, cannot be adapted to this latter material. The logical inference is that we should not continue to employ those forms, but should try to discover others that harmonize with the properties of iron. *(Discourses, XIX)*

The primary rule with regard to materials is to employ each of them in a manner appropriate to its distinctive physical properties.

Composition . . . should have its laws, or it would be only a fancy and a caprice. . . . Composition should have reference to two elements—the material made use of, and the processes that can be applied to it. The composition of a work requiring melted, wrought, or forged metal would not suit one that employs wood, marble, stone, or terra-cotta. Each industry or each process of manufacturing ought necessarily to possess a method of composition that shall be appropriate to the material made use of in it, and to the manner in which it is worked. The beautiful examples of past centuries, which we admire, follow these elementary principles.

To teach composition, you must first define these principles. The mistake in the instruction given in our schools has been in always presenting works that are indisputably beautiful to the pupils, without ever indicating to what they are applied, of what material they are made, what are the processes employed by the artists or artisans who produced them, and what is their place and purpose.

Thus it happens that, in the majority of our productions belonging to what is called industrial art, the most singular transpositions are brought to the attention.

In these matters, the want of a good education causes the reproduction in wood of works that belong more particularly to molten metal; and, in marble or stone, of forms belonging to stucco. In the composition of whatever relates to architecture and common articles, such as furniture, utensils, jewels, and gold and silver work, the first condition is to notice the particular properties in the material employed, and the mode of employing it, or the way it can be manufactured. For want of observation of these principles, one produces works that not only violate the most simple rules of good sense, but do not please, and offend reason as well as taste, and weary with their monotony. The charm of the best works of antiquity lies in their variety of form—the result of the nature of the material employed, and the way it is treated.

A tripod or a table of antique marble differs very much in appearance from one made of bronze or wood.

The first condition of composition is a knowledge of materials and their proper manufacture. . . .

There is not an art or trade in which the rules of common sense have been more disregarded than in the design of furniture. And yet wood is a material whose properties absolutely demand certain forms and a certain use. All wood is liable to swell and contract as the air is moist or dry, but in only one direction, transversely; for longitudinally the fibres of the wood neither lengthen nor shorten, though they expand or contract on account of dryness or dampness. It is therefore necessary to leave the wood to a certain extent free in a transversal direction, and to avoid the use of broad panels, for example, that are composed of several boards joined together, because the least dampness will cause them to start from their frames.

But, still worse, some have tried to reproduce in carpentry forms that are proper in a material that is not fibrous, and belong to a bulky material like stone or marble: columns, entablatures, and round pediments have been made in carpentry with parts or pieces glued or fastened together contrary to the properties of wood; some articles are turned by the lathe, although on account of its fibres, which are parallel to each other, wood permits the use of only flat or straight forms. If you look through works on carpentry, you will find that authors recommend wood to be used in ways contrary to its nature; that they think that their extravagances are the triumphs of art, or, to use a common expression, masterpieces.

When in any of our industries it is necessary to create, or make an article, it is well to proceed as Nature herself does, and take into account the purpose of the article and the qualities of the material out of which it is fashioned. An earthen or glass vase should not have the form belonging to one made of silver or bronze, and a piece of iron furniture should not resemble one made of wood. This is why it is well to perfectly understand the various industrial processes, so as not to deviate from them in designing objects supplied by them. *(Learning to Draw,* pp. 297–99)

Materials should be employed in a manner consonant with the formulation of a structure. Their proper use contributes to the clarity of structural expression; their misuse, on the other hand, diminishes the effectiveness of a design.

What then is implied in an acquaintance with the materials to be employed in a building? Is it to know whether the stone will resist frost or not? whether it will bear a certain pressure or not? Is it to be acquainted with the fact that wrought iron will endure considerable tension, while cast iron is rigid? Yes, certainly; but it implies more than this. It is to know the effect that can be produced by the use of these materials, according to certain conditions; a stone placed on end, or a monostyle, has a quite different meaning for the eye from that of an erection in courses; a casing of great slabs does not produce the effect of a facing of small flat bedded stones. An arch consisting of extradossed stones has an appearance quite different from that of an arch of notched voussoirs. A jointed lintel has not the strong look of a monolithic lintel. An archivolt of similar section built in several concentric rings, possesses other qualities and produces a different impression from those resulting from one built in a single ring. A perfectly close-jointed masonry, such as that of the Greeks and Romans, suits forms that cannot be made consistent with a masonry between whose joints there is a layer of mortar. Three stones with moldings, forming a door or window casing, environed by a plastered wall, answer to a necessity, and consequently exhibit an architectural form that is comprehensible and has a good effect; but a casing jointed in horizontal courses shocks reason and the eye. In the same way, stone jointing that does not coincide with the various architectural members, whose beds are not placed immediately above and below the stringcourses, socles, base moldings, etc., destroys the effect that a design should produce. To give the materials the function and strength suitable to their purpose, and the forms that most exactly express this function and strength, is one of the most important points in design. We can give a special style, a distinction, to the simplest structure, if we know how to employ the materials exactly in accordance with their purpose. A simple band of stone, placed in a wall, thus becomes an expression of art. A column, a pillar, shaped with due regard to the resisting power of the material in relation to what it has to sustain, cannot fail to satisfy the eye. Similarly a capital whose contour is designed with due regard to what surmounts it and the function it performs, always assumes a beautiful form. A corbeling that plainly shows its purpose will always produce a better effect than an undecided form that hides the strength needed by this architectural member. The adoption of a principle of unity and harmony in the expression of the various requirements indicated in a program—that is to say, a scale, a system of proportion, a style of ornamentation in harmony with the purpose of this structure, which has a meaning, and which also displays the variety proper to the diverse nature of the requirements to be satisfied—this is the point in architectural design in which the intelligence of the artist develops itself. (*Discourses*, X)

Historically, there have been a number of circumstances in which a structural formulation devised for one material has been continued after a culture has adopted another basic material with altogether different properties. This practice, discussed at some length in the passages on ancient Greece in Part I, was also noted with regard to Egypt and in a manner particularly appropriate to the issue at hand.

"It appears to me that things have undergone some change in this fertile region of Egypt since we first visited it some centuries ago. Its great men are beginning to erect dwellings much more sumptuous and durable than those of past times. . . .

"Our friends who inhabit the shores of the Nile are already employing large stones in these buildings of theirs; and though they still make walls of unbaked bricks and terraces of clay on timber joists, I believe that the wealthy persons of this country will someday be dissatisfied with such rude modes of building, and erect dwellings made entirely of durable materials. Who can tell if they will not deem even these limestones, which they have attained so much skill in working, too fragile, and try to get materials of a still harder kind?"

"That is a desire that I fully approve, for they would thus perpetuate for ages to come the forms first adopted."

"Be it so," returned Epergos; "but it seems to me that if they adopt materials different from those formerly employed, they would also do well to modify the forms of these buildings. Since in building they no longer confine themselves to tempered clay and reeds, it is unreasonable to adhere to the forms suitable to those primitive methods."

"Why should they change those forms?"

"Because they employ other modes of procedure."

"Always this mania for reasoning!" muttered Doxius.

Without noticing his companion's remark, Epergos continued: "These Egyptians used to make supports consisting of wood and bundles of reeds; now they are erecting stone columns; yet they try to reproduce in these hard materials, superimposed in layers, the appearance assumed by those materials composed of vegetable substances. I wager that if they take it into their heads to crown their edifices in like manner with layers of stone, they will give such crownings the form assumed by these projections of reeds and clay that appear so ingenious, and which, indeed, are so."

"Well! where would be the harm? It will thus be known that the early Egyptians constructed their dwellings with mud and reeds only; it will be known that they wished to preserve the remembrance of their first efforts; that they adopted a form of architecture that approved itself to them; that they were wise enough to adhere to it. Do you discover anything to find fault with in the palace we have just visited?"

"No, indeed; I think it perfect: everything about it is wisely and well conceived, and admirably arranged; but my reason none the less assures me that it is whimsical to simulate in stone a building of mud and cane. It would appear to me equally whimsical for our Aryans to reproduce in stone the houses formed with trunks of trees we once saw on the upper Indus." *(Habitations of Man,* pp. 35–37)

The proper handling of materials goes beyond the honest expression of their inherent qualities in the formulation of a design; it also includes the logistical preparation of materials before bringing them to the building site. Viollet-le-Duc was particularly eager to see the application of modern technology in both the preparation and delivery of materials. In this respect he anticipated quality control, total planning, and prefabrication.

In construction we are as it were attempting to ride two horses, one that is advancing and the other obstinately holding back; and while in private undertakings every endeavor is being made to discover appliances of an uncreasingly practical, economical, and truthful character, monumental art appears to take no heed of them, but to be desirous of maintaining methods that are no longer in harmony either with the requirements or the spirit of the age. *(Discourses,* XI)

Our builders find it convenient thus to possess themselves of a part of the highway for eight months or a year, to annoy the whole neighborhood, to encumber the streets with rubbish and building materials, and to sprinkle all who pass by with stone scrapings; this method will serve the purpose. But to construct a house in the workshop, the woodyard, and the factory, and to bring it ready-made like a piece of furniture, only requiring to be put up—that would necessitate fitting everything beforehand, foreseeing everything, arranging everything according to its destination as to place and time; that would require reflection, study, and prevision. It is much simpler to adopt the hand-to-mouth plan, to put up housefronts in the rough and cut the stones on the spot, to erect the shell, and then spend two or three months in piercing openings and holes in it in every direction—for the windows, the doors, the heating-apparatus pipes, those for gas and water, for the shopfronts, the sign-boards, the iron balconies, etc. etc. *(Discourses,* XVIII)

In many districts of France the architects are accustomed to have the stone sent from the quarry ready dressed. This plan offers certain advantages that are worth noting: only the required quantity and therefore only the required weight of stone has to be brought; it obviates the necessity of yards for the storage of stone previous to dressing; it prevents the sending of defective materials, since the dressing renders defects apparent—cracks, soft beds, etc. It necessitates on the part of the architect a very careful study of the jointing and the setting out of templates, since every piece ordered from the quarry must fit exactly into the place denoted for it in the drawing. We cannot ignore the fact that the material means of execution have their influence on the architecture. *(Discourses,* XIII)

It is evident that in a construction . . . everything should be prepared in advance. The various parts of the work can be executed in manufactories or special workshops and brought to the building ready fitted, so that they can be raised into place without further trouble.

A serious difficulty to be considered in building in the present day is that of yard space. Space has become so valuable in our populous towns that it would seem desirable to seek the requisite means for lessening as much as possible the area of these yards. For the masonry especially the custom of bringing to a building blocks of uncut stone, in which the stonedresser has to find all the pieces required for the building, entails the inconvenience of accumulating an enormous quantity of stone in pure waste, as the quantity will be lessened in the working. Since the stone is charged for according to the number of cubic feet supplied, and the carriage according to weight, it is clear that as from each block of stone a fourth or fifth of its quantity is cut away before the fixing, so many useless cubic feet of stone have to be paid for as well as the cost of its carriage, which profits no one, and for which the builder has to be indemnified. This needless outlay paid to the builder at the works has gone to pay part of the dues entailed and part of the expense of carriage. The cost of the stone used therefore includes in addition to its actual value that of the waste and the carriage of the waste.

If the size and shape of the stones, especially in the case of large buildings, were completely specified by the architect when giving the plans to the builder, the latter might order a great part of his stone from the quarries cut to shape, and thus would not be obliged to rent and occupy such large yard spaces. It would be a saving to him, and a proportionately less outlay would be incurred by the government and individuals.

If in slight masonry work, such as vaulting, certain methods were adopted that would obviate the necessity of having on the ground a stock of materials in the rough—if the parts of these slight structures came from a manufactory ready to be fixed—a still greater saving would be effected in the raising, the workmanship, and the time. Improvements in the art of building should be manifested in the saving of time, space, and labor. *(Discourses, XII)*

While steam, hydraulic, and gas lifting machines already mark a considerable progress as compared with the old windlass, the means for shifting heavy materials on the spot do not appear to be more economical, sure, or expeditious than those formerly used. Yet it would seem as if traveling cranes with moveable beams, to let down the stone where it is wanted, ought soon to replace the fixed hoist; in very large building works tramways are sometimes employed on the top of the scaffolding with trucks, so that by means of turntables stones may be moved to any point. But these are appliances that are only adopted for very considerable works, and have not been employed in ordinary buildings.

It would seem as if in our day, when machinery and manufactures supply every want, town buildings ought to be erected without occasioning any inconvenience, without hindrance to traffic or annoyance to the neighborhood, and with the precision that modern mechanical appliances insure. It is evident that very much still remains to be done if we would derive from these mechanical agencies all the advantages the public has the right to expect in the case of buildings that are not public works. *(Discourses, XIII)*

Part of the honest handling of material is to employ it in a building in the manner in which it has been worked. Materials previously unavailable in a certain format should not be altered to imitate the appearance of others employed in traditional methods of construction; rather, the mode of construction should be altered to accommodate the format of the new materials.

We bring into our building yards, on monstrous wagons, enormous stones sometimes cubing four or five yards. Do we proceed to take advantage of these splendid materials; will our architecture be in accordance with their strength? No: we set to work to cut in them meager pilasters, thin architraves, narrow stringcourses, so that in the building the stone will appear to consist of four or five pieces. We go so far as to work in it thin courses—yes, thin courses—with grooved joints, to imitate an architecture built with materials of less considerable cube. We saw these enormous blocks into pieces to form jointed lintels resting on iron bars. We erect masses of stonework, jointed without any regard to the form the building will assume; and when the whole is thus piled up, a host of stonecutters will come and dress down the rough rock to the shape that it shall have pleased the architect to adopt. Beds and joints will cross the sculpture or the moldings—no matter: for some years to come plaster-of-Paris tinted with ochre will mask these blunders. Thus it is that, though aided by extensive knowledge, and having at command the numerous and powerful appliances afforded by modern civilization and industry, it has come to pass that we are no longer able to give to our buildings the character, the expression, that we have always admired in the works of our predecessors, who were less favored in every respect than ourselves. *(Discourses,* XI)

Had the medieval builders possessed cast or rolled iron of considerable dimensions, they would not have employed such a material as they employed, stone. That would have necessitated joinings of too complicated a character, and useless work; they would on the contrary have sought contrivances more in harmony with the nature of metal. It is likewise evident, however, that they would not have failed to take advantage of the principles of elasticity that they were already applying to buildings of stone, and that they would have rendered the different members of their structure still more independent. *(Discourses,* XII)

The corollary of this principle is that architects, perceiving an advantageous structural formulation for which no manufactured material yet exists, should not hesitate to propose the production of a new format for the material. Without such initiative progress is not likely to occur.

It is not for manufacturers to anticipate the demand or to foresee the various kinds of ironwork that ingenious and scientific builders will require: it is for these to study the matter, and to indicate what is necessary for the realization of their projects. If each waits till the other begins; if builders, to excuse themselves from trying anything new, fall back on the insufficiency of manufactured appliances, and if, on the other hand, the manufacturers delay production till they receive orders, the present state of things may long continue. It must unhappily be confessed that hitherto it is not architects who have called forth the production of ironwork suitable for building, but civil engineers, and a few builders of special classes. Thus T irons, angle irons, rib irons, those of a U form, sheets of large dimensions and great thickness, have been produced; and though architects have taken advantage of these products, it must be confessed that they have done so with little discernment and still less economy. *(Discourses,* XVIII)

6 Planning Rationally

In nature, our author averred, the construction of organic creatures and their life functions are exactly coordinated (although it is difficult to tell whether the construction determines a priori *the function or the function has gradually refined the construction through the process of evolution). Viewed in the context of architecture, the lesson is clear: the design of any structure, be it a building or a piece of furniture, should be precisely determined by the function it serves in order to be appropriate and harmonious.*

"Now let us return to our bat of last evening. This animal, which generally causes aversion—which, you will presently learn, is a most foolish prejudice—is not only harmless but useful, because it eats very troublesome insects, like gnats for example.

"It is a mammal, which means that it does not lay eggs like birds: it gives birth to young, which it nurses; and you will see that it has other points of resemblance to the human race.

"Come near it. Do not put on that look of disgust: leave such airs to young ladies who are ready to faint if a bat enters their chamber.

"I will tell you, by and by, how the head resembles that of a man. Let us first examine the limbs (fig. 49). Suppose there is no membrane uniting them, and you see that the animal has arms and legs. These arms are fastened to the shoulders, like those of men, by triangular shoulder blades, and are each composed of a bone called the humerus, A, then of two bones, one of which is called the ulna, and the other the radius, B.

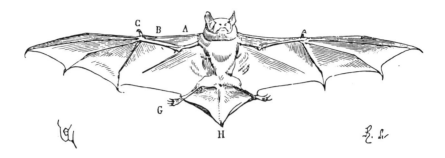

49. The bat.

Take hold of your forearm, and you will feel these two bones that enable you to turn your hand.

"But the hand of the bat is longer than its arm: with the exception of the thumb, C, which is small, the fingers are disproportionately long.

"These thumbs have at their ends very strong claws, which allow the animal to suspend itself from the sides of walls, or from the trunks of old trees.

"The legs are comparatively short, but, like yours, are each formed of a bone called the femur (the thigh), which is attached to the pelvis, and of two bones called the tibia and fibula, at the end of which is the foot. You see at G the small feet of the animal provided with very sharp claws. The vertebral column (the backbone) is prolonged like a tail at H, as in all the mammals. This is called the coccyx; and man also possesses it, only it is hidden under the flesh.

"Feel of the animal's chest, and see how full it is; here are the powerful pectoral muscles that enable the bat to work its arms and very long fingers, which are united by a membrane attached also to the neck, legs, and tail.

"If the bat falls to the ground it cannot fly, because its legs have not the strength to give it the first impetus to make it rise. So it clings to some wall or branch with its thumbs or feet, and remains there in the daytime; when evening comes, it opens its arms and drops, the membrane unfolding and forming a parachute; then, working its anterior limbs, it moves rapidly through the air without a sound from its velvety membranes. Of what a nice material these membranes are made! and how pleasant it is to have so fine a cloak, so ample and pliant, and

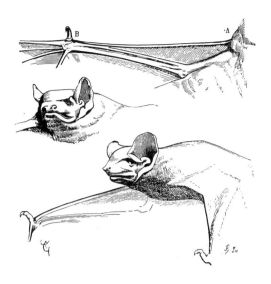

50. Details of the bat.

furred near the body, with which to wrap itself when it is still, and with which, when unfolded, to fly through space as swiftly as an arrow!

"Now let us examine (fig. 50) the arms and head of the bat.

"You see that from the neck, A, the membrane is attached to the base of the thumb of the hand, B, exactly as a cloak would be thrown over the shoulders, which you would extend with your hands in opening your arms. This cloak is attached to the back and legs, and to the tail of the animal, which serves it as a rudder. Few animals are better provided for, and it is very wrong for people to despise it.

"Its head is quite as interesting.

"Its broad ears, whose membranes are fastened under the jaw, are wonderfully arranged to perceive the slightest sound, and also to protect the eyes at the side, which enables it to aim at its prey without being turned aside by oblique rays of light. Thus the eye of the bat easily perceives, in a demi-light, the tiniest insects that flit about in the evening, and owing to its rapidity of flight seizes them on the wing; for you see that it has a large mouth, with sound incisor and molar teeth like yours and mine. . . .

"Human beings have at times tried to make a flying machine; but these fools (for one can hardly give them any other name) should first have observed the bat, which, of all winged animals, most resembles man.

"... It is well to closely examine every work of creation." *(Learning to Draw,* pp. 114–19)

When Jean saw around him all the objects collected at Pompeii and Herculaneum, he understood still better what M. Majorin told him the evening before about the application of art to the most common utensils, and how art was always made use of with a view to utility. He would have liked to draw all these objects, and M. Majorin was obliged to insist on his examining each of these admirable collections before choosing his subjects. They therefore visited the hall of sculpture, the pictures, and jewels; but naturally Jean returned to the antique articles and paintings that revealed an unknown world. M. Majorin now acknowledged the aptitude of his pupil, and afterward left him free to study and draw what most attracted him, either at Pompeii or Herculaneum, or at the museum at Naples.

As he was sketching a shovel and a pair of tongs (fig. 51), he asked his friend why the latter was provided with a kind of guard.

"Can you not guess?" asked M. Majorin. "Reflect a moment: there is a good reason."

"Oh, I know!" said Jean, after a moment's pause: "that the handle may not touch the ground, and that one may easily take hold of it."

"You see, when the tongs are left on the ground, as the profile A shows you, that the handle does not touch it. Thus a convenience becomes a motive for ornament. It is the same with the two little appendages that project from the shaft of the shovel, like the two ends of trimmed branches, and prevent the coals from falling toward the handle. But, in copying these objects, you must ask why such and such an ornament is adopted; for it is always because of some need; and that is why the ancients did not think the application of art to objects caused constraint, too often manifest in what we manufacture. *(Learning to Draw,* pp. 246–47)

For Viollet-le-Duc, some vernacular architectural traditions are admirable for their development of a rational structure based on local materials and in a manner harmonious with the local climate, topography, and culture. His analysis of a Southeast Asian house was one of the most notable examples of this interpretation.

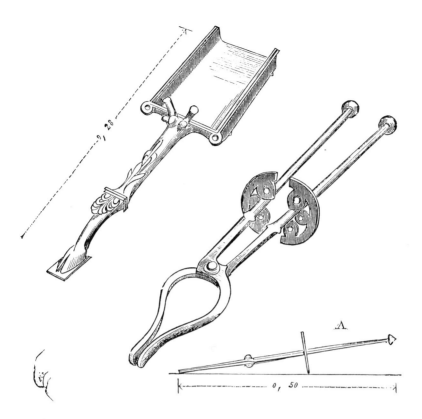

51. Ancient Roman shovel and
tongs, in the museum at Naples.

A plain covered with luxuriant vegetation stretched as far as the eye could reach; it was traversed by a wide river with a slow and muddy current. . . . On the banks of the river could be seen scattered habitations, which were built partly in the water, partly on *terra firma*. All these houses presented a gay appearance in the sun; for they were covered with brilliant colours. . . . One of the houses appeared more spacious and better ornamented than the others, and was surrounded by a garden. It consisted of a portico raised a few steps above the ground (fig. 52). This porch P, very low and deep, gave entrance into a central room A, lofty and lighted near the wooden roof that covered it by openings furnished with a trellis work of canes. On this room opened two side rooms B, very much less in height, and a narrow passage that led right and left to two covered balconies projecting on brackets C. One of these overlooked the river. Behind this gallery another wider one D led on to a terrace F, to two small chambers E, and to a long low building G, allotted to the servants and the offices, such as the kitchen and provision stores. On the terrace F were posts from which mats might be hung, enabling the occupants to enjoy the fresh air of the river under cover. A small landing stage descended from this terrace to the river to facilitate excursions on the water.

This building was constructed entirely of bamboos. Trelliswork of cane, tastefully composed, closed all the openings and allowed the air to circulate, while it subdued the glare of the sunlight. We give the view of this habitation on the entrance side (fig. 53) and the aspect of the porch (fig. 54).

Great roofs, made of thick bamboos, bent and covered with reeds very ingeniously disposed, sheltered the interior from the rain and heat; for these coverings were thick. Close mats made likewise of reeds enabled the openings to be hermetically closed during the night, and covered the floor. The building rested on a base consisting of large stones, perfectly fitting though irregular. The whole was painted outside and inside with lively colors, among which yellow and green predominated. In the principal room, whose aspect was cheerful, and whose agreeable temperature contrasted with the oppressive heat of the outer air, . . . the arrangement of the bamboos that formed the lofty ceiling was lighted by openings pierced above the entrance and on the side opposite (fig. 55). . . . The bamboo framing . . . made a large roof as light as it is strong. . . . The framework of the structure consisted entirely of bamboos of various thicknesses, intersecting and bracing at the same time in the simplest and strongest manner (fig. 56).

. . . All the parts of this house held together in combinations naturally suggested, and requiring little intellectual effort (fig. 57). To connect these canes at right angles, the builder had put crosswise, through one of them, a cylindrical piece of wood, which fitted, as a tenon would do, into the cylindrical cavities of the bamboos to be framed together: these pieces were secured by pegs. He saw that the light canes that composed the balustrades of the portico were joined according to the same method, and he perceived that the rudely carved heads that finished the ends of the horizontal pieces of the porch outside were merely a kind of cork fitted into the cylindrical cavities of those pieces (fig. 58).

. . . For the origination of the idea of so framing these canes of various length and thickness, the first condition was the possession of the materials. . . . In these vast and humid plains . . . these open-work habitation were the most suitable ones. (*Habitations of Man*, pp. 27–37)

STRUCTURAL HONESTY

In order to achieve an excellent structure one must maintain a scrupulous honesty in the formulation of the design. This truth begins with a very clear-headed and forthright idea of what is needed and continues with a careful control of the means. Such an outlook reflects the very fully articulated concern for morality in architecture enunciated some fourteen years earlier in John Ruskin's "The Lamp of Truth" (in The Seven Lamps of Architecture, *London, 1848).*

There are in architecture—if I may thus express myself—two indispensable modes in which truth must be adhered to. We must be true in respect of the program, and true in respect of the constructive processes. To be true in respect of the program is to fulfill exactly, scrupulously, the conditions imposed by the requirements of the case. To be true in respect of the constructive processes is to employ the materials according to their qualities and properties. What are regarded as questions purely belonging to art, symmetry, and external form are only secondary conditions as compared with those dominant principles. (*Discourses*, X)

While structural honesty may not necessarily produce a beautiful

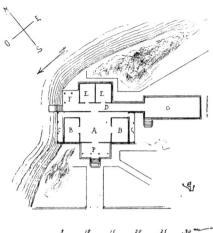

52. Plan of the primitive Chinese house.

53. View of the Chinese house.

54. Porch of the Chinese house.

55. Interior of the Chinese house.

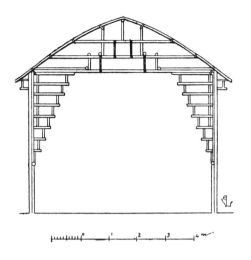

56. Diagram of the Chinese structure.

57. Bamboo framing.

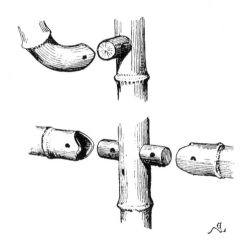

58. Ornamentation of the bamboo ends.

building it is certain that no beautiful building can be produced unless it conforms to this moral stricture.

In architecture truth is not sufficient to render a work excellent; it is necessary to give to truth a beautiful or at least appropriate form—to know how to render it clear, and to express it felicitously. Indeed, in the arts, although we make use of the most rigorous and logical reasoning, we often continue obscure and unpleasing; we may, in fact, produce what is ugly. But while conceptions based on the soundest reason sometimes produce only repulsive works, true beauty has never been attainable without the concurrence of those invariable laws that are based on reason. To every work that is absolutely beautiful there will be always found to correspond a principle rigorously logical. (*Discourses*, X)

Moreover, such a building must be animated by a guiding concept that simultaneously unites all the parts and controls the means for realizing the idea.

It is not enough to have succeeded in conveniently disposing the services of a public building or a private dwelling; to have succeeded in giving these arrangements the aspect befitting each of them. There must be a connection between the parts: there must be a dominant idea in this assemblage of services; the materials must be judiciously employed, according to their qualities; there must be no excess on the side of strength or slightness; the materials used must indicate their function by the form we give them; stone must appear as stone, iron as iron, wood as wood; and these substances, while assuming forms suitable to their nature, must be in mutual harmony. . . . Now, sincerity endows every work of art with a charm that engages the most cultured mind as well as that which is least so. . . . Whatever clearly explains itself, pleases and engages it. . . . The various materials we use posses different properties; and if we succeed in expressing these properties by the forms we give to our materials, not only do we thus open a vast field for variety and take advantage of infinite resources, but we likewise interest the public by this constant endeavor to give every object the form that befits its nature. . . . Not to deceive is the first rule that persons of taste lay down for themselves; how then can we credit with taste artists who in their works heap falsehood on falsehood? (*Discourses*, X)

Most of all the guiding concept itself must have honest simplicity.

"I think that art—in architecture at least—consists in being truthful and simple. You see in it only a form that charms or repels you: I look for something else; or rather I consider first whether this form is really the expression of a requirement—whether a reason can be given for its existence; and it charms me only so far as this condition is fulfilled, according to my judgment."

"You consider a barn, therefore, a work of art?"

"Certainly; if it is constructed so as to afford a suitable shelter for what it is intended to hold, it is, in my view, more admirable than an inconvenient palace, though decorated with colonnades and pediments." (*How to Build a House*, 144–45)

THE ILLS OF IRRATIONAL DESIGN

The ability to discern the path to honest design must begin with an awareness of the flaws of architecture that is irrationally conceived. For Viollet-le-Duc, such flaws existed in every sphere of architectural concern in the France of his day, beginning with the taste of patrons who commission works that conform to a fixed image and with the architects who accommodate them.

We have accustomed ourselves in France to decide everything, but especially questions of Art, by what is called sentiment. This is a convenient state of things for many persons, who presume to talk about Art without having ever had a pair of compasses, a pencil, a modeling tool, or a paintbrush in their hands; and professional men have gradually lost the habit of reasoning, finding it easier to take refuge in the conclusions of those amateurs who fill pages while really saying nothing to the purpose, and in so doing flatter the taste of the public while perverting it. Little by little, architects themselves, who of all artists should make good use of reasoning in their conceptions, have acquired the habit of concerning themselves only with appearances, and no longer trying to make these harmonize with the necessities of the structure. At last these necessities have come to be looked at by them as annoyances; they have concealed them so completely that the skeleton of an edifice—if I may so call it—is no longer in harmony with the dress it puts on. We see on the one hand a structure—often left to the mercy of contractors, who manage it as best they can, but naturally in subservience to their own interests—on the other hand a form that indifferently suits that structure. (*How to Build a House*, pp. 116–17)

Another cause of the flaw of designing for a fixed image is to be found in the education of architects. Trained to seek certain kinds of aesthetic effects in their compositions, they end by producing buildings that are anything but commodious to their purpose.

An attractive design is produced, a plan is drawn in obedience to academic rules that do not invariably accord with reason, and forthwith walls are built decorated with columns and banded with cornices; then, when this heap of stones has been covered in, worked down, and sculptured, presenting an assemblage of forms borrowed—no one knows why—from the remains of classical antiquity or the Renaissance, the question comes of allotting the huge building to a use of some sort. "Shall it be a God, a table, or a bowl," a palace, a government office, barrack, an assembly room, a stable, or a museum? Sometimes it will be all these in succession without difficulty. I say without difficulty, but I am wrong. It is now that the architect's embarrassment commences. Windows must be cut through floors and partitions, stairs must wind their way through dark stairways, considerable spaces must be lost because they cannot be lighted, while available apartments are too small; gas has to be used at midday in galleries, and closets are flooded with sunshine, carriage porches have to be placed before doors that were not constructed with a view to any such, and outside or inside blinds fitted to windows little adapted to receive them; small apartments have to be "entresoled" that they may not look like wells, and the ceilings of large rooms raised to make them habitable; suites of rooms receive none but borrowed light from arched porticoes through which nobody passes; that is, people must be condemned to live in apartments without air or light, for the satisfaction of giving the public the sight of magnificent galleries. (*Discourses*, VIII)

One of the most conspicuous examples of such an approach to design is Perrault's facade of the Louvre, which, though it provided a monumental backdrop, had nothing to do with the arrangement of spaces within. The flaws of procedure can be readily discerned by those with no pretension to architectural knowledge and give the art a bad name.

As early as Louis XIV's time rational method had been abandoned: the colonnade of the Louvre proves this, for there the architect's first thought was to erect an order imitating the Roman Corinthian, without concerning himself with the rationality of that order or its adaptation to the palace to which it is attached. This plan of reversing the reasonable order in architectural designs, that is to say, giving to form—a particular form—precedence before the simplest expression of a practical requirement, seems to us to be leading architectural art to its ruin; and experience daily proves that we are not deceived, for our public buildings are more and more losing the character befitting their purpose. Architectural design, instead of being a logical deduction from the various elements that ought to be taken account of in a building—e.g., the requirements, the habits, the tastes, the traditions, the materials, the method of employing them—has been reduced to an academic formula. This method, supported by a theory more and more vaguely enunciated, not by a true understanding and practical acquaintance with an art whose character is never defined, and which consequently cannot be discussed—which constitutes, I say it once more, a mysterious initiation, or rather a kind of protective patent, acquired by a blind submission—brings architects into a state of isolation if they submit to it, or leads them into the most extravagant vagaries if they free themselves from it. It entails moreover the serious disadvantage of giving a handle to the advocates of the "practical," who are disposed to see in works of art only a useless and ruinous luxury, having interest but for a very small section of society. How, in fact, can we defend the inconvenient magnificence of most of our public buildings against those who have so little difficulty in demonstrating their irrationality; and who, though unprofessional persons, can see that these architectural forms are out of harmony with the arrangements of which they are the casing? (*Discourses*, VIII)

Viollet-le-Duc's contempt for irrational design inspired some of his most fluent passages of invective. The following is perhaps the most memorable example of the kinds of inconvenience introduced in buildings for the sake of imposing a preconceived formal order.

The extent to which the absence of forethought on the part of architects is carried is incredible to those who have not observed it. For instance, in a public building erected not long ago, the gutters pass through the attics and form in each room, under the windows, a little trough covered with a board, where water may be drawn any rainy day;

and the downpipes, carried through the thickness of the walls, pour torrents of water into the rooms during a thaw; and all this for the sake of not interfering with the lines of a certain classical form of architecture. Generally, when we thoroughly examine these monumental facades, which seem to be built solely for show, we discover much poverty beneath this useless luxury of stone. Those who live behind their costly walls are soon made aware of it. Here you have gutters passing under your feet; there downpipes that periodically flood you and deafen you with their rush of water on rainy days. Elsewhere you have windows that cannot be reached without a ladder; rooms all but absolutely dark, or receiving their light near the floor; corridors that are never ventilated, and where you must light lamps in the middle of the day; enormous windows for small rooms; embrasures that hinder any direct light; accommodation narrow and insufficient side by side with considerable spaces wasted, disproportionate arrangements that seem in fact contrived to satisfy the needs of beings of a different race; perpetual sacrifices to external show—to monumental exigencies as costly as they are useless. Having these strange abuses of a misdirected art constantly in view, it is especially desirable to cling to true principles of construction, and to endeavor to practice them with more rigorous scrupulosity than ever. (*Discourses*, XI)

The most frequent justification for such follies in design is the insistence upon maintaining an unnecessary bilateral symmetry in architectural compositions.

I am aware that many well-meaning persons look upon the disregard of what are called the laws of symmetry as a kind of impiety, a contempt for ancient and sound traditions: as if the most ancient traditions, and consequently those that should be most respected by believers in traditions, were not in flagrant contradiction with these supposed laws, which are in fact very recent. There are some of these observances and ideas that each in his secret judgment or on the slightest reflection recognizes as absurd and false, but no one ventures to contravene. Each is waiting for his neighbor to display the requisite moral courage. All would gladly follow the movement, but are very careful not to provoke it. Symmetry is one of these unhappy ideas to which we sacrifice our well-being as far as our dwellings are concerned, and sometimes our common sense, and a considerable amount of money always. (*Discourses*, XVII)

THE VIRTUES OF RATIONAL PLANNING

What are the determinants of rational design?

In architectural art . . . there are two distinct elements that should always be considered, namely, necessity, to which we must submit, and the work of the artist's imagination. Necessity imposes the program: it says, I want a dwelling; I want air and light. But what is the work of the imagination? What is imagination? It is the power given to man to unite and combine in his mind things that have struck his senses. . . .

Swallows know that they must build their nest at such a time, and in such a situation; but all swallows' nests have resembled each other ever since swallows have existed. Man knows that he must make himself a shelter; but in the course of a few centuries he advances from the mud cabin to the palace of the Louvre. And why? Because man reasons, and his active imagination is nothing more than the application of reasoning to the passive imagination. (*Discourses*, VI)

ACHIEVING A RATIONAL DESIGN

The requisite procedure for producing a rational design begins not with artistic imagination but with a clear statement of the requirements and all the restricting factors. Most important is the formulation of a program that takes into consideration not only the most general issues relating to purpose but also those pertaining to local use. The design should take form only after all the various factors have been entered into the rational equation. Then, and only then, will an appropriate form come to mind. This form necessarily must originate with the plan, be developed in terms of structure, and only end with an aesthetic design, and that with all the details clearly subordinated to the whole. Each specific instance will have its appropriate design and one that is never wholly transferable to other circumstances. Appreciating the implications of Viollet-le-Duc's theoretical formulation, Louis Sullivan coined the memorable dictum "Form follows function," which pithily summed up the intentions behind the concept of rational planning and powerfully transmitted it to the twentieth century.

Since architecture belongs almost as much to science as to art properly so called, and as its conceptions are very largely dependent on reasoning and calculation, it must be allowed that design is not the result of a mere process of imagination, but is subject to rules methodically applied, and that it must take account of the means of execution, which are limited. If the painter or the sculptor is able to conceive and execute at the same time, and without having recourse to extraneous cooperation, it is not so with the architect. On the one hand, the requirements, the expenditure, the site restrict him within certain limits; on the other hand, the nature of the materials and the way in which they must be employed. If the architect is to design, he must before all things take account of the various elements that will affect his work. It would seem therefore that if architects are to be duly trained to design, they should, when a program of the requirements is submitted to them, be made acquainted with the various conditions that must be complied with in its execution. . . .

The main features of architectural programs change but little, for the needs of mankind in a civilized condition are the same with very trifling variations; but climate, traditions, manners, customs, tastes cause these programs to receive a particular interpretation, according to time and place. The requirements of a theater, for example, are the same both for the Athenians and the Parisians, as far as the purpose of the building is concerned. What were these requirements, and what are they still? Places for a large body of spectators, arranged so as to enable all to see and to hear; a stage and an orchestra for vocal or instrumental performers; rooms for assembling and apartments for the actors; promenoirs for spectators; commodious arrangements for entrance and exit. And yet a modern playhouse by no means resembles a theater of Bacchus. Why? Because side by side with the requirements that indicate simply the object of the building, there are others dictated by the manners and customs of the society that prescribes them. The mere fact that the scenic representations of the ancients took place in daylight, and that ours are given at night, obliges the two edifices—the ancient and the modern—to differ essentially in point of structure, internal arrangements, and decoration. If to the cardinal points of difference just noted we add the innumerable details that our habits in respect to theatrical arrangements impose—such as scenic effect, machinery, the division of the house into stalls and boxes, etc.—the result is the production of an architectural work that has little in common with that of the ancients but the name. Here then we have a program given at Athens and Paris respectively, to satisfy the same requirements; yet this program, from the mere reason that our habits are not those that the Athenians adopted, produces in the case of the two peoples two buildings greatly differing from each other. We may therefore regard it as a principle that in every architectural program there is a basis that varies little—which is destined to satisfy requirements almost identical in character in all phases of civilization—and a form prescribed by the habits of the time; that architecture is none other than the expression of this form: that the usages of society during any period must not be made to submit to certain architectural arrangements; but that these arrangements must be the outcome of customs and habits, which are necessarily variable. . . .

There is only one right method of design in architecture—that is, to comply with the conditions of the given program, and then to make use of what we know to find a form for all the requirements imposed by the habits of our times; a form moreover that must be beautiful and durable. But all who have long studied architecture, without being previously imbued with the prejudice of the schools, have been able to perceive that a form that was the simple expression of a necessity, were it even a commonplace one, acquired from this very circumstance a special charm.

Since every part of an edifice or construction should have its raison d'être, we are, in spite of ourselves, attacted by every form that indicates its object, as we are interested by the sight of a beautiful tree, all of whose parts, from its root clinging to the soil up to its remotest branches that seem to seek the air and the light, so clearly indicate the conditions of life and duration of these great vegetable growths. But if each part of a building should express the requirement that dictated it, there should exist intimate relations between these parts; and it is in the combination of the whole that the artist develops his natural abilities, knowledge, and experience. . . .

If an architect, in designing a plan, does not see the whole edifice before him; if it does not present itself complete in his brain; if he reckons on the abundant materials he possesses to apply to each part in succession a suitable form, the work will remain undecided; it will be wanting in unity, freedom, and character; and it will be decidedly bad, if, before studying the arrangements of the plan, he has resolved to adopt such or such a front, such or such a composition that has struck his fancy, or that is prescribed him by others who are strangers to art. Forgetfulness of these immutable principles, which are, as it were, the moral sentiment in art; want of method in study and the classing of the remains of ancient art; and deference to the fancies of the moment, have filled our cities with buildings justified neither by reason nor by taste, although their execution is sometimes of a high order. In the ancient world, with rare exceptions, and even during the Middle Ages (in France at least) we notice among architects a constant observation of the laws that constitute good taste, i.e., the absolute subjection of form, of appearance, to reason. When we forget these principles, we may have more or less skill and repute as decorators according as we interpret well or ill the fashion of the day; but we are not architects. . . .

To come closer to our subject, we may observe, for example, that in both the civil and ecclesiastical buildings of the Renaissance, the design of the ground plans is altered only as far as new habits require it. The plans of the palaces, chateaux, houses, or churches differ but very little from those of the fifteenth century, which again were but reproductions, with some slight modifications, of the arrangements of the fourteenth and thirteenth. The ground plan—that which determines all the others—is invariably the arrangement required by our civil or religious habits; the idea is always accommodated to the requirements of the time, it does not seek its starting point elsewhere; but when his idea has to be expressed, the architect takes possession of a foreign form, yet knows how to adapt it to the idea, because he proceeds methodically, and because he is above all a man representative of his times, and does not cherish the belief that a formula should be respected in preference to the faithful expression of practical requirements.

In the Middle Ages, as under the Roman Empire, the structure and purpose of a building are manifest from the very ground plan; the ground plan determines the whole: it is there that the power of the architect who designs is exhibited in its full energy; for in drawing his ground plan the architect has really had the solid edifice present to his mind's eye; and the arrangement of the details, when this first labor has been accomplished, is little more than an intellectual pastime. What pleases and must please in Roman buildings is their frankly determinate character, the clearness with which the details are subordinated to the whole. The same excellencies, under different forms, reappear in the good architecture of medieval times; that is to say, ground plans strictly dictated by the program and subordinated to the conditions of the construction: nothing redundant, conception clear from the foundations upward and methodically followed out, impulses of genius frequently exhibited, but always regulated by the reason and knowledge of the practical builder. (*Discourses,* VIII)

The very essence of art, as far as architecture is concerned, consists in knowing how to clothe every object with a form appropriate to that object, not in making a magnificent case and afterward considering how the requisite arrangements can be accommodated in that case. (*Discourses,* XVII)

RATIONALITY AND HISTORICAL TRADITION

For Viollet-le-Duc, each of the great historical traditions was so rooted in the cultural as well as the physical factors of its place of origin that it could never be wholly transferred to another locale. Hence, as much as the Romans and others might admire the Greek orders, their adoption of Greek forms would never result in the same kind of architecture. Greek ideas in a Roman context could never be anything more than a veneer.

On the other hand, this does not mean that borrowing cannot occur to positive effect. When the form or technique of one tradition fits the cultural and physical context of another, it can be appropriated to great advantage—as in the case of the Romans and vaulting. But in a fully rational procedure, if the borrowed element works better than a local custom then the custom itself could be dropped and the philosophy of the local tradition could continue unabated along another line of formal development.

"Taste is not in their blood, as is shown by the fact that they employ Greek artists whenever they wish to give to their dwellings the aroma of art. I can have no doubt, Mummius, that it was a Greek who was selected by you to build your porticoes and arrange the details of your villa."

"That is true; but it was I who prescribed the plan."

"I can well understand that: the Romans are expert in matters relating to general arrangements, and even construction; but when they have planned the building they call in a Greek to decorate it. Thus in all your public buildings as also in your houses, what belongs to the Romans can always be distinguished from what is due to the intervention of the

Greek artist. Whereas during the period of Athenian prosperity, the public buildings as well as the houses, both in their ensemble and their details, form a harmonious whole that was so complete that it was impossible to distinguish the structure from the decoration."

"So that," interrupted Caustis, "if the Romans do not take care, the Greeks will impose their arts on the masters of the world."

"Not at all!" replied Epergos; "the Greeks have never adopted vaulting, and the Romans will not abandon their architectural method, which is so well adapted for buildings on the large scale. Whatever orders or decorations in their particular taste the Greeks may lavish on the exterior or interior of the gigantic masses erected by the Romans, they will never be able to rob them of the Roman physiognomy and character. Is it possible that the rotunda that Agrippa is building for his Thermae can ever come to resemble a Greek edifice?—though Greek artists are working at the grand Corinthian portico in front of it. Would you in fact, Caustis, have me express my full conviction on the subject?—Greek art cannot be transplanted; everywhere else but in Attica it will show a stunted growth, or will become a monstrosity. The art that truly belongs to a people cannot develop itself elsewhere than on the soil from which it sprang, and under the conditions that produced it. Have you observed the two or three Greek temples that they have recently taken it into their heads to build in Egypt? They are not inferior in beauty or in any other respect to those that are built in Greece; yet, in presence of the Egyptian monuments, nothing could be more ridiculous. A similar result would ensue if anyone should take a fancy to build in Rome a temple in the style of those of Thebes. Let us leave things in the place in which they originated."

"It is a long time, Epergos," observed Doxius, "since you have said anything so sensible."

"Not quite so fast! I know what you would insinuate, and you would make me contradict myself. I say: 'Let us leave things in the place where circumstances have caused them to originate, but let us have the sense to take advantage of what these things teach us.' For example, the Romans found in Asia many architectural elements that have enabled them, in combination with what they already possessed from Etruria, to make those noble vaulted constructions that we admire; evidently they have acted wisely in taking advantage of these different elements, because, when we examine the matter thoroughly, we shall find that these elements are intimately related to each other; but where I cannot approve the judgment of the Romans so much, is in their attempting to unite the Greek architrave with the Asiatic vaults. These are contrary principles that can never be harmonized in an architectural work. If the Greeks should some day come to impose a style of art on the Romans, as they could no longer adopt the architrave, which allows of only small constructions, we should find that, considering the logical tendency of their minds, not being able to dispense with the vault, they would abandon the lintel once for all; and they would be right in so doing." (*Habitations of Man,* pp. 246–48)

7   Decorating Appropriately

HISTORICAL PRINCIPLES OF EMBELLISHMENT

For Viollet-le-Duc architectural ornament was no less important than for theorists and practitioners of premodern periods; indeed, he would have found an unornamented architecture unappealing and inappropriate. But he had clear notions about how and in what circumstances ornament should be employed. With respect to the past, he recognized three basic approaches to ornamentation—chiefly concerning figural sculpture, to be sure—in three different cultures of which he heartily approved: in the monuments of Egypt, Greece, and the (French) Middle Ages.

Does an architectural conception comprehend its ornamentation, or is the ornamentation an afterdesign of the architect? In other words, is the ornamentation an integral part of the edifice, or is it only a clothing more or less rich with which the edifice is covered when its shape has been determined? Among the various civilizations that have had a characteristic architecture, these questions have probably never been consciously proposed; but they proceeded as if these questions had been mooted, which, as far as our purpose is concerned, comes to the same thing. . . .

Various principles have been adopted in the ornamentation of buildings. The first, or oldest—that which most naturally occurs to the mind of the decorator—consists in deriving the ornamentation from the objects and materials employed in building.

The dweller in the forests erects his buildings with the trees he has felled; and the combination of the timbers and the leaves with which he covers them afford the earliest and most natural ornamentation. Accustomed to the forms thus suggested, when later on he migrates to countries that are not wooded, we may be sure that he will give the new materials he employs forms that are derived from timberwork. . . . The second principle of ornamentation is the result of a more perfect state of civilization: it consists in giving to the several members of the building forms not dictated by an unreflecting adherence to tradition, but, on the contrary, by thoughtful consideration; features deduced from the nature of the materials employed, the requirements to be satisfied, and the exigencies of the climate. The first method of decoration only was followed in ancient times by most of the Asiatic nations, with which we class Egypt. The Greeks were probably the first to adopt the second method. The first is not in conformity with logical deduction; the second is thoroughly rational. (*Discourses*, XV)

To put it another way, three distinct systems are recognizable in the styles of architecture known to us that have called in sculpture as a decorative accessory, and it seems hardly possible to imagine a fourth. The first and most ancient is that adopted by the Egyptians, but it is probable that they were not its inventors. This system consists, as is well known, in covering the bare spaces with a kind of continuous tapestry representing religious, heroic, or historic subjects, a tapestry that in no wise alters the principal lines of the architecture; and in placing colossal figures before pillars or pylons, or as ornaments, figures that are an essential part of the architecture, both in composition and method of treatment. Here sculpture and architecture seem, as it were, to have grown up together. The Greek monuments may be comprised among the offshoots of this system. Though much less lavish of monumental sculpture than the Egyptians, the Greeks also considered this kind of decoration as forming an essential part of the architecture. The metopes, tympanums, and friezes of the Parthenon are panels or tapestries in sculpture having no influence on the structural lines; and though we may not be acquainted with any Greek temple the walls of whose cella were covered with bas-reliefs from top to bottom, such may have existed, and the fact would not contravene the Greek idea of the application of statuary to architecture. (*Discourses*, XVI)

In the buildings erected by the Dorian Greeks, painting was always employed as a means of ornamentation, internal and external. In the best period of classic art, the Greeks did not use colored marbles in their large buildings. They built them of stone or white marble, coating the monochrome stone with a fine stucco and coloring it; when they used marble they selected white, and colored its entire surface. Color, therefore, was one of the most effective means of ornamentation; it served to distinguish the architectural members, and to give the several planes of the structure their due relief. . . . Among the Greeks all ornamentation, so far from falsifying, emphasizes the structure; moreover, it is always proportioned to the size of the building; it never breaks up the parts that should preserve an appearance of solidity; and it is effective in proportion to its sobriety and moderation. (*Discourses*, XV)

Next to this primitive system, of which we find specimens in Asia, we may class the Roman system. And by this we mean that which strictly belonged to the Romans, not their imitations of Greek art. The Roman system regards sculpture only as a decorative accessory, without any connection with architecture. Except in certain monuments whose characteristics in this respect we have particularized, viz., the column of Trajan and the triumphal arches, the Romans adopt sculpture as a kind of spoil with which they ornament their buildings: and in fact such was their actual procedure. (*Discourses*, XVI)

In the Roman buildings ornamentation is lavished without sufficient judgment, and aims rather at richness of effect than fitness and clearness. While the Greeks of the classical period made only a very moderate use of sculptured ornamentation, and confined their statuary to specially determined places, they covered the surfaces of their buildings with a coloring that when required, gave relief to the supports, while it subordinated the parts that did not support but served only as enclosures. The Romans of the empire, on the contrary, made it their chief object to employ all together, if possible, every decorative appliance—granite, jasper, porphyry, marble, painted stucco, bronze, and mosaic; they used all these with more profusion than discernment. With them, to charm meant to dazzle, to astonish; and they appreciated but slightly the refinements of Greek genius. Besides, it was a matter of no concern to them whether the ornamentation suited the material made use of or not; or whether that ornamentation belonged to the first or second of those two modes between which we have established a marked distinction, or borrowed at the same time from both. Every kind of decoration pleased them, provided it was rich. (*Discourses*, XV)

Lastly, we have the system adopted by the medieval artists—a system that restores to iconography the importance it had acquired in Egypt and in Greece, but that proceeds differently as regards the composition. This system does not allow of colossal sculpture, and groups the figures so as to present a striking scenic effect at a particular point. Bas-relief does not comport with it, as it does with Egyptian and Greek sculpture; the subjects have the effect of a tapestry covered with slightly projecting figures, but are all represented in full relief, except at some points near the eye of the spectator that are intended to appear as a kind of hanging. It does not seek, as do the Egyptian and Greek systems, to develop the sculpture on wide spaces or long friezes, but on the contrary to concentrate it on some points whose excessive richness and brilliant effects contrast with the less striking parts. It makes the sculpture form part of the structure more decidedly than the Egyptian and Greek systems; brings the former into close association with the latter, and even makes it accentuate the construction; in proof of which may be cited those portals that are so richly decorated, whose lintels, tympanums, jambs, or relieving voussoirs are clearly indicated by the sculptured arrangements, so that each object or figure is a piece of stone with a definite and useful function. The medieval artist in France, as much for reasons founded on the nature of the climate as from considerations of art, shelters his statuary and seldom allows its outlines to cut the sky. Moreover the statuary of the Middle Ages, like that of Egypt, India, and Greece, is always painted. This is equivalent to saying that those civilizations that really had schools of sculpture considered that this art could not dispense with painting. . . .

It seems to me that the name of monumental statuary can be applied only to that of which all the parts are connected with the architecture both in the idea generally and in the details of the execution. Egyptian sculpture, that of Greece, and that of the Middle Ages succeeded, by different means, in fulfilling these imperative conditions, and the last in date, the medieval, without abandoning the principle, furnished probably the greatest variety of expressions that can be obtained. (*Discourses,* XVI)

For modern usage the most important considerations for the application of ornament are 1) that embellishment shall be subordinate to the composition of a building as a whole, 2) that it should be applied to structurally significant locations, and 3) that its formulation should be appropriate to the material employed. One finds in Viollet-le-Duc's prescriptions the clearest and most explicit possible inspiration for the work of Louis Sullivan and, following him, Frank Lloyd Wright.

The main consideration is to put things in their proper place: ornamentation lavished in a facade till it becomes wearisome to the spectator would be pleasing were it confined to a few points in which it would find its appropriate position. In this respect the Orientals excelled us. In their buildings, however ornate the decoration, it never injures the effect of the masses; it invariably leaves points of repose, points moreover that are dictated by the structure; so far from wearying the eye, this decoration engages it, because it is put where it tells to advantage. . . .

However richly ornate a building may be, the ornamentation must be subordinated to the conception, in order not to weaken, disturb, or obscure its expression. I grant that in such a case the more lavish the ornamentation the more vigorously should the idea be expressed, and that it can be more easily manifested in a building that is simple than in one that is loaded with ornament. But it is plain that where an idea is wanting the temptation is strong to conceal feebleness of conception beneath a parasitical embellishment. . . .

In our opinion the best architecture is that whose ornamentation cannot be divorced from the structure. Whatever be the merit of a piece of carving—or of a decorative composition—if such piece of carving, or even such composition, can be removed without making it apparent that the edifice lacks something essential, that accessory is of small value, and perhaps even prejudicial. It needs no great practical knowledge to recognize the decorative features that an architect has added to a building, and that are not necessitated by the structure. For instance, ornamented panels are perfectly justifiable in woodwork, but they are utterly out of place in a stone pier. Medallions stuck against a plain wall, like pictures in a room, are evidently not an ornamentation suggested by a requirement of construction. Surmounting a door or a window with symbols more or less ingeniously designed, making the cornice of the opening remind us of a collector's chimneypiece covered with curiosities, cannot be considered veritable architectural ornamentation. Groups of figures placed on a pediment, and appearing to have escaped from it in order to be more at ease on the roof, make sensible persons long to push these escaping figures back into their frame. Little circular openings, filled with busts on their stands, may perhaps suit a gallery of portraits but have a most unmeaning appearance on an external facade. Curved or triangular pediments surmounting window jambs, keystones of arches whose exaggerated projection supports nothing, may be called, without too much severity, decorative makeweights. Apart from the expense they occasion, without any advantage to art, these commonplaces so greatly in vogue have a still graver fault—they weary and nauseate the spectator, and gradually lead to a distaste for all architectural forms. . . .

If there is one thing worthy of the architect's best considerations, it is the perfect agreement between all the parts of his building, that correspondence between the case and what it contains—the frank expression outside of the arrangements within, not only in point of structure, but of ornamentation, which ought to be in close alliance with it. (*Discourses*, XV)

One of the problems met in devising ornament for a modern architecture is that there is no established tradition of embellishment for modern materials. When iron, for instance, is to be frankly introduced into a structure, the pieces standard in manufacture should be embellished when they are produced; but they are not likely to be until that need is made evident by architects themselves.

Is it possible to give these iron trusses an architecturally decorative appearance? I think so; but this cannot be done by giving them forms appropriate to masonry. With our present appliances for iron structure, a decorative effect cannot be obtained except at considerable cost, for our manufactories do not supply us with the elements required for producing it. But the reason why our manufactories fail to supply them is that we have hitherto given iron only an accessory or concealed function in our great buildings, because we have not seriously considered how to make the best use of the material by giving it forms appropriate to its nature. (*Discourses*, XII)

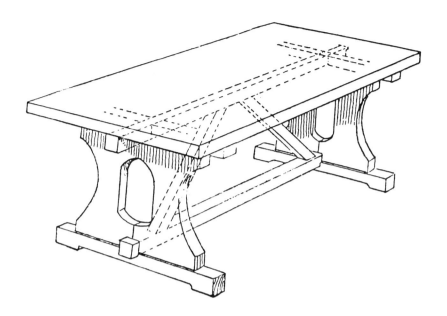

59. Rational composition of a table.

60. Decorative detail of the end of a table.

61. Rational composition of a
door panel.

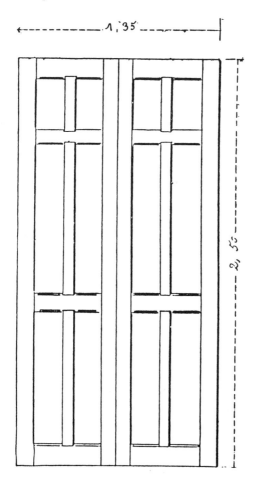

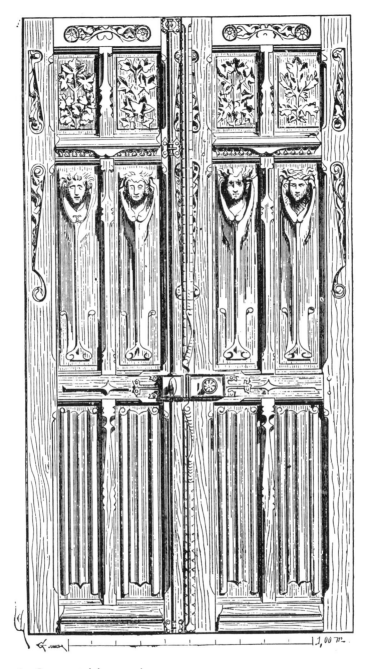

62. Ornamented door panels.

Viollet-le-Duc did not attempt to describe how the decoration of specific hypothetical modern buildings might be ornamented, except for a truss to be made of numerous small pieces of iron (see pp. 251–53), but he did offer some instances in which ornament might be employed in the decorative arts. At this point, his theoretical philosophy seems to coincide with that of the arts and crafts movement in England.

M. Majorin practiced his pupil in designing, but required him first to construct the object according to the material employed and the purpose for which it was intended. If it were a table, for example, Jean must design its correct form (fig. 59); then, taking one of the feet, the pupil tried to ornament it as its material and use required (fig. 60). If it were doors, the structure must be understood beforehand, in order to secure strength and durability while giving the panels only the width of a plank (fig. 61).

Then they added the ornaments, avoiding whatever might diminish the strength of the united parts (fig. 62).

Thus the teacher explained how it was well to leave the wood open at the right of the mortises, so that the panels might be free to enter the grooves between them; how sculpture that ornaments panels should contribute to strengthen them in their central, and especially their lower parts; how, in order to give more firmness to the crossbeams, they should be made thick, and thus a chance for ornament be secured; how it was necessary to provide places for the locks, that they might be properly fitted; how it was necessary to outline the moldings, according to the grain of the wood, and carefully observe the very exact laws of proportion belonging to every piece of carpentry. (*Learning to Draw,* p. 301)

8   Achieving Style

In the nineteenth century the most elusive goal of progressive architects was the creation of a distinctive modern style. Even through Viollet-le-Duc's lifetime there had been only a succession of style revivals, re-capitulating at some point nearly every period mode in the history of architecture. Viollet-le-Duc perspicuously recognized that the creation of a new style would occur only as the result of rethinking how a building ought to be put together, very likely employing new materials, in the light of clearly defined purposes. He observed that a design produced in this manner would necessarily have style; whether or not that style would become, or ultimately belong to, a period style was a different issue. In stating the problem in this manner he correctly placed the horse before the cart, and within a generation the grand procession into the modern era of architecture was under way.

What is style? I am not speaking now of style as applied to the classification of the arts by periods, but of style as inherent in the arts of all times; and to make myself better understood, I remark that independently of the style of the writer in each language, there is a style that belongs to all languages, because it belongs to humanity. This style is inspiration; but it is inspiration subjected to the laws of reason, inspiration invested with a distinction peculiar to every work produced by a genuine feeling rigorously analyzed by reason before being expressed; it is the close accord of the imaginative and reasoning faculties; it is the effort of the active imagination regulated by reason. . . .

In the present day we are no longer familiar with those simple and true ideas that lead artists to invest their conceptions with style; I think it necessary therefore to define the constituent elements of style, and in so doing, carefully to avoid equivocal terms and those meaningless phrases that are repeated with the profound respect that is professed by most people for what is incomprehensible. Ideas must be presented in a palpable form, a definite embodiment, if we would communicate them. Clearly to understand what style as regards form is, we must consider form in its simplest expressions. Let us therefore take one of the primitive arts, one of the earliest practiced among all nations, because it is among the first needed—the art of the coppersmith, for example. It matters little how long it took man to discover the method of refining copper and of reducing it to thin plates, so as to make a vessel with it fit to contain liquid. We take the art at the time when he had discovered that by beating a sheet of copper in a particular way he could so model it as to give it the form of a vessel. To effect this, all the workman needs is a piece of iron as a point of support, and a hammer. He can thus, by beating the sheet of copper, cause it to return on itself, and can make of a plane surface a hollow body. He leaves a flat circular bottom to his vessel, so that it may stand firm when full. To hinder the liquid from spilling when the vessel is shaken, he contracts its upper orifice, and then widens it out suddenly at the edge, to facilitate pouring out the liquid; the most natural form therefore—that determined by the mode of fabrication—is this (fig. 63). There must be a means of holding the vessel: the workman therefore attaches handles with rivets. But as the vessel must be inverted when empty, and to be drained dry, he makes the handles so that they shall not stand above the level of the top of the vessel. Thus fashioned by methods suggested in the fabrication, this vessel has style: first, because it exactly indicates its purpose; second it is fashioned in accordance with the material employed and the means of fabrication suited to this material; third, because the form obtained is suitable to the material of which this utensil is made, and the use or which it is intended. This vessel has style, because human reason indicates exactly the form suitable to it. The coppersmiths themselves, in their desire to do better or otherwise than their predecessors, deviate from the line of the true and the good. We find therefore a second coppersmith, who wishes to alter the form of the primitive vessel in order to attract purchasers by the distinction of novelty; he gives a few extra blows of the hammer, and rounds the body of the vessel that had hitherto been regarded as perfect (fig. 64). The form is in fact new, and all the town wishes to have vessels made by the second coppersmith. A third coppersmith, perceiving that his fellow townsmen are taken with the rounding of the base, goes still further and makes a third vessel (fig. 65), which is still more popular. This last workman, having lost sight of the principle, bids adieu to reason and follows caprice alone; he increases the length of his handles, and advertises them as of the newest taste. This vessel cannot be placed upside down to be drained without endangering the shape of these handles; but every one praises it, and the third coppersmith is credited with having wonderfully improved his art, while in reality he has only deprived a form of its proper style, and produced an unsightly and relatively inconvenient article.

This history is typical of that of style in all the arts. Arts that cease to express the want they are intended to satisfy, the nature of the material employed, and the method of fashioning it, cease to have style. The style of architecture during the declining years of the Roman Empire and that of the eighteenth century consist in the absence of style. We may follow custom in saying "The style of the arts of the Lower Empire," or of the reign of Louis XV; but we cannot say "The arts of the Lower Empire, or those of the reign of Louis XV, have style," for their defect (assuming it to be such) is that they dispense with style, since they show an evident contempt for the form really appropriate to the object and its use. If a Roman matron of the period of the Republic were to appear in a drawing room filled with ladies dressed in hooped skirts, with pow-dered hair and a superstructure of plumes or flowers, the Roman lady would present a singular figure; but it is none the less certain that her dress would have style, while those of the ladies in hooped skirts would be in the style of the period, but would not possess style. Here then we have, I think, an intelligible starting point for the appreciation of style. Are we then to suppose that style is inherent in one form alone, and that women, for instance, if they wish their dress to have style, must dress themselves like the mother of the Gracchi? Certainly not. The satin and the woolen dress may both have style; but on the condition that the shape of neither is at variance with the forms of the body; that it does not ridiculously exaggerate the former nor hamper the movements of the latter; and that the cut of the dresses in each shows a due regard to the special qualities of the material. Nature invariably exhibits style in

63. Primitive form of the copper vessel.

64. Developed form of the copper vessel.

65. Decadent form of the copper vessel.

her productions, because however diversified they may be they are always subject to laws, to immutable principles. The leaf of a shrub, a flower, an insect, all have style, because they grow, are developed, and maintain their existence according to laws essentially logical. We can subtract nothing from a flower, for each part of its organism expresses a function by taking the form that is appropriate to that function. Style resides solely in the true and marked expression of a principle and not in an immutable form; consequently, as nothing exists except in virtue of a principle, there may be style in everything. (*Discourses*, VI)

METAPHOR AS THE INSPIRATION FOR STYLE

To define the circumstances in which style is produced was one thing; to achieve it was another. The achievement required a leap of imagination of which Viollet-le-Duc himself was not capable, but he implicitly identified the vehicle that most effectively vaults the human imagination into new creative realms—namely metaphor. And he advanced two metaphors that were richly evocative of modernity in his own time, the machine and technology on the one hand and the natural organism and biology on the other. In his own mind the two metaphors were parallel in their applicability to architecture and very nearly interchangeable. The value of distinguishing them here chiefly lies in their having been separated after his lifetime, when each took on an independent life in the theory and works, respectively, of Le Corbusier and Frank Lloyd Wright.

The Machine
Unlike John Ruskin, who despised modern technology and industrially produced materials, Viollet-le-Duc welcomed both the new inventions produced by technology and the design opportunities presented by new materials. His memorable celebration of the steamship and the locomotive, quoted below, was to reverberate resoundingly half a century later in Le Corbusiers' Vers une architecture.

It was good to navigate with sails before the power of steam was known; nowadays that method—formerly excellent—is not good as compared to that furnished by modern appliances. We may say as much of the ideas, systems, and principles that regulate art. When ideas, systems, and principles are modified, the forms corresponding should be modified also. We admire a hundred-gun ship of war, rigged as a sailing vessel; we perceive that there is in this work of man—the principle being admitted—not only a wonderful product of intelligence, but also forms so perfectly adapted to their purpose that they appear beautiful, and in fact are so; but however beautiful these forms may be, as soon as steam power has supervened, they must be changed, for they are not applicable to the novel motive force; hence they are no longer good; and on the principle just now cited they will no longer be beautiful for us. In our days, when we are subjected to an imperative necessity, we subordinate our works to that necessity; thus far we are capacitated for acquiring style in art, which is nothing more than the rigorous application of a principle. We erect public buildings that are devoid of style because we insist on allying forms derived from traditions with requirements that are not in harmony with those traditions. Naval engineers in building a steamship, and machinists in making a locomotive, do not endeavor to reproduce the forms of a sailing vessel of the time of Louis XIV or of a stagecoach: they simply conform to the novel principles with which they have to deal, and thus produce works that have a character, a style of their own, as indicating to every eye a definite purpose. The locomotive, for example, has a special physiognomy that all can appreciate and that renders it a distinct creation. Nothing can better express force under control than these ponderous rolling machines; their motions are gentle or terrible; they advance with terrific impetuosity, or seem to pant impatiently under the restraining hand of the diminutive creature who starts or stops them at will. The locomotive is almost a living being, and its external form is the simple expression of its strength. A locomotive therefore has style. Some will call it an ugly machine. But why ugly? Does it not exhibit the true expression of the brute energy it embodies? Is it not appreciable by all as a thing complete, organized, possessing a special character, as does a piece of artillery or a gun? There is no style but that which is appropriate to the object. (*Discourses*, VI)

The great value of these metaphors, and particularly that of the machine, was that they could guide the formal imagination without imposing the influence of prior images. One of the greatest obstacles for those who would seek a modern architecture or modern decorative arts was the inability to forget the great examples of the past. By contrast, a metaphor was neither more nor less than a guide, while a monument from an older period offered only a pattern. And it was precisely the facile formulation fostered by employing patterns that made both buildings and furniture stale from the moment they were designed.

It should not seem strange . . . that the same people who know so well how to give grace to a machine by adopting exactly the form suitable to each organ erred so greatly in judgment and taste in the manufacture of furniture, utensils, and articles that are in daily use. For machinery, being of recent invention, does not follow any so-called tradition. It was necessary to create it in every part according to new ideas; and good sense caused forms to be immediately adopted that were perfectly appropriate. But as regards a table, armoire, or clock, it is quite different: the mind is haunted by a thousand previous examples; and instead of making them in the best way and under the most reasonable conditions, as one makes a machine, by taking into consideration the material and the duty required, one thinks of the furniture of Louis XVI or that of Marie Antoinette, Louis XIV, or the Renaissance, and an imitation is produced that will certainly go out of fashion, and be consigned to the garret as being too ridiculous an object to be shown. (*Learning to Draw*, pp. 306–7)

Nature: The Organism, the Crystal

Throughout western civilization architectural theorists have appealed to nature as a model for architecture, seeking to identify in it an absolute standard that cannot be questioned. Most frequently, the appeal is addressed to the proportions of the human body and, indeed, Viollet-le-Duc subscribed to that standard, as we shall see later in this chapter. Of greater importance, though, is his analogy between the construction of natural organisms and architectural structure, proposing that the one should serve as a model for the other.

For the most part, this analogy is employed in passing, as in the two following brief excerpts.

If we study with attention and without prejudices the principles applied in the masonry work of the thirteenth and fourteenth centuries, we shall soon perceive that the structure consists only of independent members, each fulfilling a determinate function. We no longer have, as in Roman architecture, concrete and homogeneous masses, but rather a kind of organism whose every part has not only its purpose, but also an immediate action, sometimes even an active one, as, for example, the flying buttresses and the vaulting arches. (*Discourses,* Lecture XII)

We . . . will produce a building, unassuming it may be, yet one in which not a detail shall be found that is not the result either of a necessity of the structure or of the requirements of it occupants. It will not cost us more on that account; and when the work is completed, we shall rest satisfied that there has been nothing disguised nor factitious, nor useless, in what we have produced, and that the architectural organism we have built will always allow us to see its organs, and how these organs perform their functions. (*How to Build a House,* p. 117)

The most explicit example of the organic analogy is in Learning to Draw, *in which both the issue of structural function and that of structural composition are raised. Here, the machinelike quality of organisms and the organic quality of machines are openly acknowledged, but curiously are not related to architecture* per se. *(There is, however, one notable instance in the* Discourses *in which the diagonal strut supporting a vault is composed of parts analogous to a hand, elbow, arm, and ball socket, quoted in this volume on pp. 241–44.)*

M. Majorin possessed excellent anatomical studies taken from nature, and began his second lesson by placing before Jean's eyes a drawing of life size, representing a human skeleton in profile (fig. 66) at A, and opposite a copy of a skeleton of a chimpanzee at B.

"Examine these two individuals attentively," he said. "Both have the same number of bones; and the difference between man and the chimpanzee, which is a monkey, consists only in the form and size of these bones. . . .

"Behold how well made are these bones of the leg (fig. 67) to carry the body. The femur is set in a cavity of the bone of the hips, which permits swaying from back to front, necessary in walking. The femur is bent to bring the weight of the body on the knee; then the tibia possesses a large head, provided with and strengthened by two cavities that receive the two rounded parts of the femur in order to insure the firmness of the leg in a lateral direction. The connecting rods of machines are always made in this way. The little bone called the patella is a lever to the muscles, and at the same time prevents the knee from bending from front to back. Then the tibia is straight, and placed edgewise in a manner to offer assistance in walking; and is aided by the fibula, which is a kind of support that prevents bending in a lateral

66. A, skeleton of a man;
B, skeleton of a chimpanzee.

67. Bones of a man's leg.

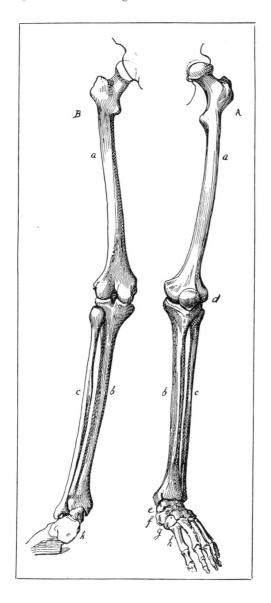

direction. The base of the tibia, which is also broad, bears on an intermediary bone, the astragalus, which permits the movement of the foot; and this intermediary bone bears on a strong bone, the heel or calcaneum, which serves as a lever and wedge. The bones of the metatarsus are curved like an arch, in order that the leg, bearing on the heel, may find, at a distance in front, a support and wedge. Therefore man, of all animals, is the only one who walks upright; while monkeys, which stand on their lower limbs, have more or less the position given by fig. 66, bent forward, and ready at need to make use of their long arms to prevent them from falling on their face.

". . . When you have studied and understood these principles of anatomy, you will examine with more interest and knowledge the machinery of the factory; for man, in the art of mechanics, seldom does more than apply these elements.

"Having neither these supple and strong ligaments that fasten the articulations of the bones, nor the tendons and muscles, man replaces these beautiful inventions with bolts, axles, or pivots, and eccentrics; but generally the organic parts of his best machines are made in conformity to the principles by which his body moves.

"Here is a clear illustration (fig. 68): at A, you see the lower end of the femur, and what are called the condyles, with the notch that separates them, in which is fitted the projection of the tibia, a, and at b the concavities of the joint. The ligaments, which unite the two ends of the bones of the thigh and leg and are attached to the sides, which are rough and pierced with little holes, permit the condyles, which are shaped like half spheres, to turn in the two cavities, b. What does the mechanic do to secure a like result? He joins the two parts, like the head of a compass, so that they will turn in one direction but not in the other.

"He fashions the two pieces B and C and unites them by a pivotal bolt: the head, a, which replaces the projection of the tibia, fits in the groove d; the cheeks, e, turn on the rest f, and the round shafts, like the bones, are strengthened at the joints.

"However, between the animal machine and those that we manufacture there is a great difference. We can, more or less perfectly, construct the parts of our machines in imitation of bones, tendons, and muscles; but to all of them it is necessary to communicate motion by an independent force—by water, air, or vapor, or by a horse, which are called motive powers. The animal machine has no need to be urged by a

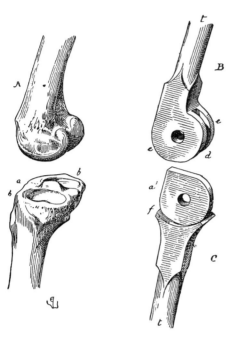

68. Application of the joints of the bones to mechanics.

69. Application of the play of muscles and tendons to mechanics.

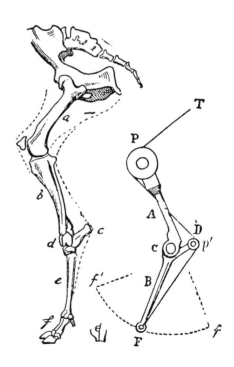

power independent of itself: it bears its motor in each of its organs. The discovery of a substance, or a combination of elements, that possessed the power that the muscles and tendons have of lengthening or shortening would be a very valuable one, for it would do away with many parts of very complicated machines; but we have none such, and we must, for the present, content ourselves with studying animal mechanism, and with borrowing from it all we can, that is to say, the principles applicable to the subject.

"I will show you, for example, how certain animal forms can be applied to mechanism. Here (at fig. 69) is the hindleg of a stag or a reindeer, or that of an elk or a large antediluvian stag, the arrangement of the bones of these swift animals being nearly the same. Their lower limbs have so much elasticity that they leap over large obstacles. The femur, a, is short and very strong; the tibia b, in addition, is very powerful at the upper end and has great freedom of action.

"But this is the calcaneum, c, the heel, which with us hardly extends beyond the union of the tibia and the fibula, and which here projects a good deal. Then come the bones, the astragalus, the cuboidal, etc., d; then the bones of the metatarsus, e, which are very long, while correspondingly short in the human foot; then, last, the phalanges f, only two of which aid in walking.

"Why is this calcaneum so prominent? To act as a lever to the tendons and muscles, whose duty it is to move the limb.

"Suppose we wish to construct, by an analogous process, a piece of machinery with a capacity for quick and powerful tension: we should have in A a shaft provided with a pulley, P, at its head; a second shaft, B, with a joint, C, and a projection, D, bearing also a pulley, p', at its end. By fastening a cord to a fixed point at F, and passing it along the grooves of the two pulleys, p' and P, and drawing it quickly at T, we give a sudden tension to the two shafts, which move to a straight line as at Pf; since, drawing the cord at its end T, we have shortened the irregular line, Pp'F. If the point f were placed at f', which the animal can do without difficulty, by drawing the cord, we should suddenly have described at this point f' the quarter of the circle f'f, and have thus caused a very quick forward movement from the point P, supposing this point f' to rest on the ground.

"With us it would be necessary to draw a cord at T to set the mechanism of our limb in motion. It is the tendons of the animal himself that having the power to contract or to extend at will, produce the effect caused by our cord, and permit him not only to make the movement we have just given to our piece of mechanism, but to return the limb to its first position, which we could do only by means of another process than that indicated in our figure. You see that while the calcaneum is useful to us in walking, and permits us to run, dance, and skip rope, being developed quite differently in the stag, it helps him to leap ditches and every obstacle met with in the forests.

"If ever you are a machinist, remember that to manufacture the parts of these machines, it will be useful to have some anatomical knowledge and to know how bones are made, why they are strengthened at a certain point, and why they have taken a certain curvature.

"One could write a treatise on mechanics having for its sole subject the curvature of the bones. But, if it is necessary to study at least the elements of comparative anatomy, one must draw a great deal in order to engrave on the mind the forms so suited to their purpose, the service required by the animal." (*Learning to Draw*, pp. 132–45)

A more minor appeal to nature for a structural metaphor is directed to the mineral crystal, especially for the composition of polyhedron vaults (see an example quoted in this volume, p. 246). The possibility of employing yet other analogies to nature is raised, prophetic of Buckminster Fuller and Paolo Soleri, to name only two such twentieth-century figures.

If we examine natural crystals, for instance, we shall find configurations the best adapted for vaulting of mingled iron and masonry. Most of the polyhedrons produced by crystallization present not only arrangements of planes that enable us to use girder irons of large size for covering considerable spaces, but likewise shapes whose appearance will be very pleasing. When the employment of novel materials is in question, we must not overlook anything that might be suggestive; we must seek everywhere for guidance, but especially amid those principles of the natural creation with which we cannot make ourselves too familiar if we are to originate in our turn. (*Discourses,* XII)

The Conditions of Beauty: Clarity
The conclusion to be drawn from his proposal of these various metaphors is that they provide the creative factor that permits the de-

signer to integrate the concerns for functional program, structural for-
mulation, and properties of materials. They make possible the unified
conception that gives the appearance of having been inevitable.

One of the conditions of beauty in an architectural work is that it
should impress all who see it as having been produced naturally without
effort—without occasioning trouble or anxious consideration to its
designer, that in fact it could not have been otherwise. In particular, it
should be free from those expedients that betray paucity of ideas, those
bits that bear the mark of studied effort, and the aim on the part of the
designer to astound and engage the attention of the passerby without
being able to satisfy his mind. To be clear, to be comprehensible without requiring an effort; this is, and always will be, the aim that the
architect should have in view. The highest praise to which the public
speaker can aspire is the remark on the part of the hearers: "That is just
what I thought; he exactly expressed my feeling." Similarly, in viewing
the work of the architect, every one should experience the impression
that the materials in combination do but reflect the anticipation of the
beholder—that the conception as realized is the only one that was
appropriate to the circumstances of the case. (*Discourses,* XV)

Scale
Finally, the attractive aspect of style in a design comes from the disci-
pline imposed upon its formulation. For Viollet-le-Duc this discipline is
derived from the application of a sense of scale. While scale can be
relative, a given module, it is more reliable if it is based on the absolute
proportions of the human body.

"This principle of unity and harmony in the expression of the various
requirements indicated in a program" is . . . neither symmetry nor
uniformity; still less is it an undigested medley of various styles and
forms of which it is impossible to give a rational explanation, even if
such a medley were skillfully composed: it is in the first place a rigorous
observation of the scale. But what is the scale? It is the relation of all the
parts to unity. The Greeks adopted as their scale not an absolute, but a
relative unity, what is called the *module;* this becomes evident in studying their temples; for it is certain that in their private dwellings the
Greeks kept in view the absolute scale, which is the human stature. But
regarding it as relative, the scale, by the very fact that it was the mod-

ule—that is, a component unity—established a harmonious relation between the parts and the whole in every building. . . .

With the medieval architects of France the only scale admitted is man; all the points of the building have reference to his stature . . . and from this principle necessarily springs the unity of the whole; it has also the advantage of presenting to the eye the real dimensions of the building, since the point of comparison is man himself.

If, while adopting the principle of the human scale, we employ a system of geometrical proportions, as the architects of antiquity and those of the Middle Ages evidently did, we unite two elements of design that compel us to remain true as regards the expression of dimension, and to establish harmonious relations between all the parts. We have here, therefore, an advance on the system of the Greeks, which had only employed the module and not the invariable scale. Why, then, should we deprive ourselves of this resource which we owe to the genius of the medieval artists? (*Discourses*, X)

9   Applying New Architectural Principles

Viollet-le-Duc looked forward to the creation of a truly modern ar-
chitecture that would have the originality and forcefulness of the great
period styles of the past. He regarded his own work—both designs and
theories—as nothing more than a preamble, but he was aware that he
had started on a new path.

We who are in midcareer may not hope to become the originators of
a new architecture, but we ought according to our ability to prepare the
ground, and with the knowledge of all the ancient methods and the aid
they can give us—not of some only, to the exclusion of others—seek
new adaptations in harmony with the materials and the means we have
at command. Progress always consists in passing from the known to the
unknown, through successive transformations of methods. It is not by
fits and starts that progress takes place, but by a series of transitions.
Let us therefore conscientiously endeavor to prepare for these transitions, and so far from losing sight of the past let us rise above it by
building upon it.

We shall now attempt to enter more fully upon the employment of
novel materials, and to deduce therefrom certain general forms of construction under novel conditions. (*Discourses,* XII)

It is not by the mingling of styles and combining, without reason or
principle, the architectural forms of various ages that we shall discover
the art appropriate to our own, but by making the introduction of
reason and plain good sense into every conception our first consider-

ation; making use of materials in accordance with their respective properties; with a frank and cordial adoption of industrial appliances, and instead of waiting for these to take the initiative, ourselves eliciting their production. (*Discourses,* XIII)

That buildings should be splendid is all very well; but at least let them be sensible and not designed chiefly for mere external show. . . .

The architecture suited to our times is not art that is a mere luxury, for the delectation of a few amateurs—a select portion of society; it must be an art that belongs to all, since in the case of public buildings it is paid for by all. It should therefore conform to the manners and habits not of a coterie, not of *a* public, but of *the* public. Let us then, while duly admiring—as we may do—the ostentatious splendors of Roman architecture or of that of the time of Louis XIV, cease to reproduce them; and endeavor not to improverish, despoil, and humiliate ourselves—which is unbecoming a great country—but to gain respect by a display of taste, thought, and good sense, rather than by an unjustifiable abuse of wealth. To bring the ornamentation of our buildings into accord with the sterling qualities of our national character, which is opposed to exaggeration and want of proportion, is a noble problem, to the working out of which the rising generation of architects should devote their best powers. It is the careful thinking out of the problem that can alone give birth to the architecture of the future; not the servile imitation and undigested mingling of features borrowed from previous times and previous styles of architecture. (*Discourses,* XVI)

Viollet-le-Duc's vision of a modern architecture was largely articulated in the context of his zealous advocacy of the use of iron in architecture. He saw in this product of modern industry the technological means to create structures that it had previously not been possible to build with traditional means. He saw in iron also the means to transport architecture away from formal tradition to a future limited only by technical ingenuity.

He was certainly not the first to recommend iron, much less the first to use it; indeed, he was also not the first to prescribe an iron frame (engineers had preceded him by decades). But it was his distinction in the context of polite architecture to propose that the design of a building should be devised in terms of the structural system appropriate to the needs of the program. Such a proposal flouted the widespread and time-honored custom of beginning with a formal image—usually based on the historical precedent of a period style—in which the functional requirements and the structural formulation were accommodated to the image.

While wrought iron is very useful in masonry when suitably employed, cast iron may serve numerous purposes. Cast iron notoriously possesses great rigidity; it is extremely durable, for it is less liable to decay than wrought iron; and when exposed to the air, as in supports, and when complicated joints and causes of fracture are avoided, it maybe regarded as unassailable by time. But it is evident that, in employing this material, forms of a suitable character should be given to it, and that it would absurd to simulate in cast iron, for example, columns of a diameter proper to stone supports. Hitherto we have not seen cast-iron supports for stone work except in very small buildings. Grand results might, nevertheless, be obtained by so employing it, on condition of adopting the equilibrated structure successfully carried out in our country by the medieval architects. In fact, while iron serves scarcely any purpose in monumental masonry such as we now conceive it, which is based on the principle of massive and concrete structure, it would find a rational and useful function in equilibrated masonry, by employing cast iron for rigid supports or wrought iron for ties. With these appliances we might erect vaulting in masonry on very slender supports, a thing hardly ever done. (*Discourses,* XI)

Hitherto cast or rolled iron has been employed in large buildings only as an accessory. Where edifices have been erected in which metal plays the principal part, in these buildings masonry ceases to take any but an exceptional part, serving no other purpose than that of partition walls. What has nowhere been attempted with intelligence is the simultaneous employment of metal and masonry. Nevertheless it is this that in many cases architects should endeavor to accomplish. We cannot always erect either railway stations, markets, or other immense buildings entirely of masonry, such buildings being very heavy in appearance, very costly, and not presenting sufficiently ample interior accommodation. A structure in masonry, regarded as an envelope protecting from cold or heat, offers advantages that nothing could replace. The problem to be solved for providing great edifices destined to accommodate large assemblages would therefore be this: to obtain a shell entirely of masonry, walls and vaulting, while diminishing the quantity of material and avoiding obstructive supports by the use of iron; to improve by means of iron on the system of equilibrium adopted by the medieval architects, but with due regard to the qualities of that material, and avoiding the too close connection of the masonry with the metal; as the latter becomes not only a cause of destruction to the stone, but perishes itself very quickly when not left free. Some few attempts have been made in this direction, but timidly—for instance by merely substituting columns of cast iron for stone pillars. Iron, however, is destined to play a more important part in our buildings; it should certainly furnish very strong and slender supports, but it should also enable us to adopt vaulting at once novel in plan, light, strong, and elastic, and bold constructions forbidden to the mason, such as overhanging projections, corbelings, oblique supports, etc. The use of rigid shafts or cast-iron columns as oblique supports is a means of which our builders have not yet thought; I hardly know why, for this system is fruitful in deductions. It somewhat contravenes the principles of Greek and even Roman architecture; but if we would invent that architecture of our own times that is so loudly called for, we must certainly seek it no longer by mingling all the styles of the past, but by relying on novel principles of structure. An architecture is created only by a rigorously inflexible compliance with modern requirements, while the knowledge already acquired is made use of, or at least not disregarded. . . .

Neither engineers nor architects have as yet succeeded in combining in a really satisfactory manner masonry with iron construction; and yet there are many cases in which the system of masonry building could not be superseded. It is scarcely possible to obtain a building satisfactory as regards the health of the inmates, warm in winter and cool in summer, unaffected by variations of temperature, constructed of iron alone. Masonry walls and vaulting will always present advantages superior to those obtained by any other method. We must therefore be content in most instances to continue to employ masonry. Can it then be combined with iron construction? Certainly it can; but under the condition that these two methods of building shall each preserve its characteristics, that they shall not be combined to their mutual injury. Cast or wrought iron, moreover, is liable to variations that must always be taken into account; it must therefore be allowed a certain liberty of movement, it must not be embedded in the masonry, and must retain its independent function. . . .

If we propose to use iron conjointly with masonry, we must give up the traditional methods of Roman structure. We have no longer to contemplate erecting buildings based on inert immovable masses, but to provide for elasticity and equilibrium. The distribution of active forces must replace an agglomeration of passive forces. For the attainment of these results, the study of the structure of the French medieval buildings can be of great service, for the architects of that period had already substituted the laws of equilibrium and elasticity for those of Roman structure; but it does not follow that we should imitate the forms they employed—forms that are admirable where masonry only is used but are unmeaning where iron and masonry are simultaneously employed. Had the medieval architects possessed the products of our metal manufactures, they would assuredly, in virtue of their logical and subtle intelligence, have adopted other forms. (*Discourses*, XII)

Viollet-le-Duc's proposals for the use of iron included one that L. S. Buffington in Milwaukee, claiming to have invented the skyscraper, attributed as the source of his inspiration (see Sigfried Giedion, Space, Time and Architecture, *5th ed. [Cambridge, Mass.., 1967], p. 206).*

A practical architect might not unnaturally conceive the idea of erecting a vast edifice whose frame should be entirely of iron, and clothing that frame—preserving it—by means of a casing of stone. . . . If, therefore, we undertake to encase an iron structure with a shell of masonry, that shell must be regarded only as an envelope, having no function other than supporting itself, without lending any support to the iron, or receiving any from it. (*Discourses*, XIII)

Along the same lines, the modern buildings he admired the most were structures so straightforward in design and so utilitarian in purpose as to be overlooked by critics and connoisseurs of fine architecture.

It would . . . be unjust to acknowledge that among recent buildings there are some of very considerable merit in point of art. I should mention as in the first rank the central market halls of Paris, which indicate so clearly the purpose to which these great structures are appropriated. I believe that if all our public buildings were erected with the same implicit deference to the requirements of the case and the habits of the population—if they indicated the means of construction as boldy—they would have a character proper to the age, and would also find for themselves beautiful and intelligible forms of art. In the example referred to, there has been a compliance with the requirements of the program and of the materials employed, and the result has been, in my judgment, a very fine building. Perhaps there may have been no deliberate intention to "produce a work of art." It were therefore to be desired that such an intention should be abandoned from this time forward; this would perhaps be the readiest way to secure works of art that should be the real expression of our civilization. (*Discourses*, VIII)

Viollet-le-Duc set out detailed descriptions of several hypothetical buildings, each illustrating a different type of solution to a structural problem. As he explicitly stated, none of them was ever intended as an example for emulation: it was the structural principle rather than the formulation that he regarded as useful to future architects. And, as has been often remarked, his hypothetical buildings (like his actual ones) did not manage to transcend the aesthetic limitations of the mid-nineteenth century or even foreshadow the style of the twentieth. Yet they did provide ample inspiration to younger architects, who saw in these schemes the beginning of a new way to conceive buildings.

THE MARKET HALL

The first scheme is a very famous demonstration of the value of diagonal iron struts as supports and also of the combining of different materials to serve various structural needs.

Let us suppose that we have to build—as is often done in the provinces—a large assembly hall over a covered marketplace (fig. 70). If we raise this hall in mason-work on rows of cast-iron columns in order to gain space and secure more air and light in the market, these supports must be tolerably numerous, and must be connected at their upper part by powerful stays, so as to hinder the superstructure from toppling over, and we shall have a rather inconvenient row of columns along the side of the street. If, on the contrary, we adopt a plan analogous to that shown in the section (fig. 71), it is evident that the hexagon whose half is drawn at *fabc* presents a stable figure, and that even the addition of the triangle *bdc* in nowise lessens this stability while the line *ce* remains unbroken.

With this elementary figure as our basis we may support the great hall over our marketplace as shown by the drawing A. On stone blocks *f*, solidly beded, placed at distances determined by the width of the bays, we set cast iron columns inclined at an angle of 60°. The capitals of these columns are held by the transverse wrought-iron girders that carry the joists of T-iron, from one another of which we turn barrel arches of brick. From the ends of the girders *g* may be suspended stirrups for the support of cast-iron shoes, to receive the springers of stone arches *f*, on which we shall build the walls of the hall, likewise of masonry. Bracket of cast iron, *i*, in two parts, secured by the tie-rods *j*, and whose thrust at foot will be counteracted by the triangles *opq, osq*, will sustain the longitudinal barrel vaults *k*, which will in turn support the main upper vaulting. One essential condition will be to bed the blocks *f* not on separate foundations, but on solid transverse walls; for it is important that the feet of the columns *f, g, a, b*, should not be able to lessen their distance apart under the pressure and thereby raise the columns of the inner triangle.

As staircases will certainly be required, and anterooms, and means for heating the upper hall, the general plan will be that represented in figure 72, and these two end buildings will hinder any movement of the lower bays in a longitudinal direction. The spaces *m* toward the street (fig. 71) sheltered by the incumbent arches will be very convenient for the buyers and for placing the stalls; moreover there is nothing to prevent the fixing of awnings at *n*.

It will be understood that it is not my purpose here to offer specimens of architectural style. That is not the question now; my purpose is simply to suggest to our younger professional brethren the proper method for proceeding in the search for novel elements of structure. . . .

Architecture cannot array itself in new forms unless it seeks them in the rigorous applications of novel methods of construction. Casing cast-iron columns with cylinders of brick or coatings of stucco, or building iron supports into masonry, for example, is not the result either of calculation or of an effort of imagination, but merely a disguising of the actual construction; no disguise of the means employed can lead to new forms. When the lay architects of the thirteenth century invented a system of structure different from any that had been previously used, they did not give to their architecture the forms adopted by the Roman or the Romanesque architects; they gave a frank expression to that structure and thus succeeded in originating new forms possessing a characteristic physiognomy. Let us endeavor to proceed thus logically;

70. Elevation of a market hall.

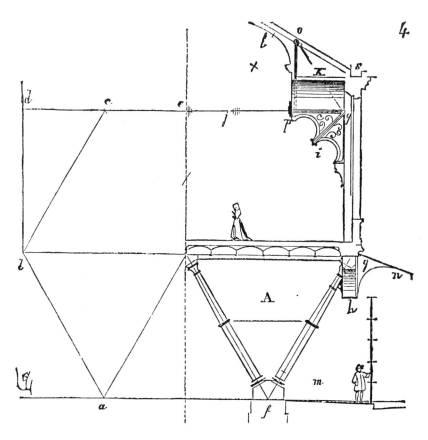

71. Market hall: method for support of the masonry structure on obliquely set iron columns.

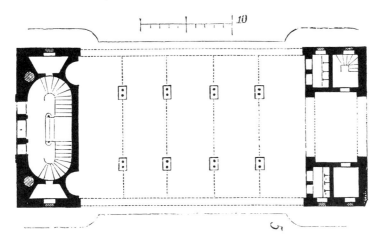

72. Plan of market hall.

let us frankly adopt the appliances afforded us by our own times, and apply them without the intervention of traditions that have lost their vitality; only thus shall we be able to originate an architecture. If iron is destined to plan an important part in our buildings, let us study its properties, and frankly utilize them, with that sound judgment that the true artists of every age have brought to bear upon their works. (*Discourses*, XII)

THE VAULT OF A GREAT HALL

This scheme for the vault of a great hall is actually a demonstration of how a medieval vault might have been made had its builders had structural iron at their disposal. To be sure, it is another important application of the diagonal strut, but the chief value is in the explication of the parts of the strut. Here, implicitly, he had devised structural membering according to organic principles, modeling it on the ball-and-socket joint of the hip and on the joining of upper and lower arm at the elbow.

When a building is substantially constructed and the vaulting is well made, the initial effort of thrust produced by the latter is very trifling, and a slight obstacle suffices to arrest its development (fig. 73). Supposing the arches and their springers to be of stone, and the vaulting of hollow bricks, each of the struts will at most have a weight of 15 tons to support. As a consequence of the obliquity of the strut a considerable part of the weight is divided vertically down the walls; the pull on the great lower iron brace will be reduced to an inconsiderable action, whose force, allowing for the weight of the wall itself above the shoes, and its direct resistance, will produce an effective action on the braces equal to 5 or 6 tons—a pull that need cause no apprehension. A structure of this kind would be very economical, for we see that only one part is required, either for the struts, the shoes, or the capitals (fig. 74).

On the scaffolding, which would serve for fixing the slanting columns, the centers (all alike) would be easily set up, and the vaulting, provided it is made in a particular way, may be turned without centering, or at least without lagging, as we shall explain presently.

This method of structure in iron and masonry fulfills the conditions that, in our opinion, should characterize such works. Thus the iron framework is visible, independent, and free to expand and contract, so that it cannot cause dislocation in the masonry, whether through oxidation or variation in temperature. The masonry, while concrete in parts, yet preserves a certain degree of elasticity, owing to the small arches that carry the whole. As the system of vaulting only takes up a very considerable height in proportion to the width of the interior, it allows of large windows comparatively elevated; it requires a minimum of materials and only thin walls, which (excepting the points of support) may be partly built of rubble stone. In the ironwork, the use of bolts, which are liable to be injured or broken, is avoided, bolts being employed only for fastening the tie-rods to the braces or collars. Figure 74 represents in detail at A one of the cast-iron capitals, with its dwarf shaft and spheroidal base at B; at T the collar of the upper tie-rods; at C the head of the struts; at D the foot of the same, and at E the shoe, with the branches of the tie-rods F and the keys G. It will thus be manifest that these fastenings are free to move, incapable of causing either ruptures or dislocations, and that they neither occasion trouble in fixing nor require fitting on the spot. (*Discourses*, XII)

THE ASSEMBLY HALL

The most famous of all of Viollet-le-Duc's hypothetical buildings, the assembly hall for three thousand people was a dramatic demonstration of how a vast space might be covered by a light structure, without any visual encumbrances. As an example to young architects it was a bold

73. The vault of a great hall.

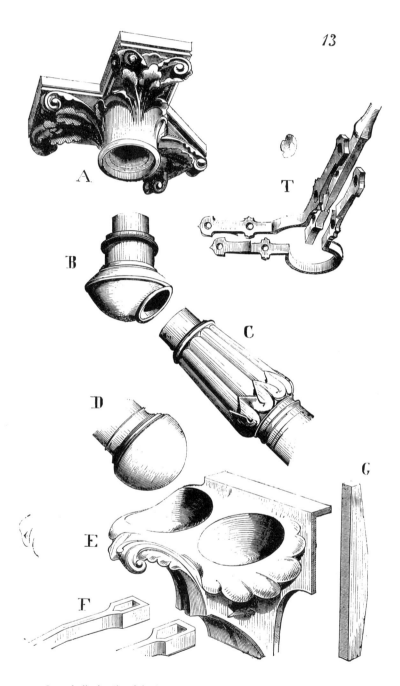

74. Great hall: details of the iron struts supporting the vaults.

argument for letting the building take shape from the structural accommodation of its program and also for letting the structure be frankly exposed to view. In addition, it was a forceful demonstration of the use of various materials in their different capacities without fusing them together in a detrimental bond.

To obtain the largest space possible with the least amount of solid is certainly the problem that has had to be solved by every style of architecture, when it has been necessary to build for the public. The crowd did not enter the Greek temples; and, as I previously mentioned, the citizens of the small republics of Greece assembled only in unroofed enclosures. While the Romans were the first to construct buildings in which great numbers were able to assemble under cover, the medieval builders, in working out a similar problem, endeavored to reduce as much as possible the quantity of masonry. The materials they possessed did not however permit them to exceed a certain limit, since these large buildings had to be vaulted. As they were not able to employ wrought or cast iron of considerable dimensions, it was only by contrivances of masonry—a system of equilibrium of thrust and counterthrust—that they succeeded in erecting spacious buildings such as our great cathedrals. But we possess those appliances that were wanting to them. Iron allows feats of construction hitherto unattempted, provided that material is employed with due regard to its nature. It is, I say once more, not the erection of market halls or railway stations that is in question, but covering in with masonry spaces that shall be amply lighted and present those arrangements for salubrity and durability that our climate demands.

Solid bodies such as polyhedrons, consisting of plane surfaces, appear to suggest the elementary forms applicable to the structure of mingled iron and masonry where vaulting is in question. The nature of the metal and the forms in which it can be manufactured do not favor the construction of iron arches, whether by means of plates riveted, or of trapeziums of cast or wrought iron bolted together.

Thus fashioned, iron framing becomes expensive, and only answers the purpose to which it is applied by being made excessively strong, so as to prevent its bending or breaking. But if we regard plate iron as a material specially adapted for resisting tension; if the masonry in conjunction with it be so combined as to prevent distortion of the ironwork; if we consider iron as easy to employ and connect in straight pieces, and if of these separate pieces we form a kind of independent network, and on this network of girders we rest the vaulting in separate parts, we shall thus have contrived a system of iron framework consistent with the nature of the material, and a method for covering wide spaces by means of a series of distinct vaults. Let figure 75 represent a polyhedron capable of being inscribed within a hemisphere, and consisting of regular sides forming octagons, hexagons, and squares. It is evident that if we set up a framework of iron in accordance with the lines of this figure, we shall obtain a perfectly strong network and shall be able to cover the various parts of this network with portions of vaulting. Starting from this simple principle, let us suppose that we have to vault a large concert hall, for example, capable of containing, inclusive of galleries, about 3,000 persons. Plan A (fig. 76) will meet these requirements. At a we shall have a vestibule for persons arriving on foot, at b vestibules for those coming in carriages, at c stairs leading up to the galleries. The hall, exclusive of the projections e, will have an interior width of 140 feet in both ways and a superficial area of more than 6,500 feet. At *ffffffff* is drawn the plan of the polyhedron shown in figure 75, and at B is represented the section across *gh*.

The framework of the iron polyhedron will rest on eight cast-iron columns, which direct the weight on the oblique struts *i*. These struts will also support the galleries *k*. The walls of the four projections will sustain the thrust of the whole system—thrusts that are, however, reduced to a very slight action. These projections will be vaulted (as shown in section C across *op*) on plate girders s, so as not to exert any thrust against the gables. It will be remarked that every rectilineal member of the framework is of equal length—a length of about 28 feet for the polyhedron as well as the other parts of the vaulting. We shall

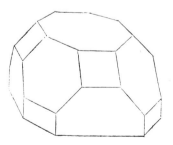

75. Geometry of a vault in the configuration of a polyhedron.

consider the form of these members and their ornamentation when we come to treat more specially of smiths' work.

The appearance of this structure is exhibited in figure 77. Owing to the strength afforded by the iron network, the portions of vaulting may be made of light material and be of slight thickness. We see that these portions of vaulting, in the spaces of the iron network, are divided with ribs that might be made either of terra-cotta or freestone, and that the intermediate spaces will be easily filled in either with pottery or with hollow bricks, flatways, or even with molded material in sections, as previously described. The centering of these vaults could be fixed on the framework itself, which remains independent and visible below the vaults, and which only supports them at the points where the dividing ribs abut. The largest space to be vaulted is that of the central octagon, 68 feet in diameter, whose weight, however, is lessened by the circular opening at the top. The hexagonal spaces are only 50 feet from angle to angle, and their oblique position causes the weight of their vaults to be directed on the cast-iron columns. Fully to illustrate the execution of this system of construction would require an amount of detail for which we have not space here; moreover, I have no idea of giving, in this example, anything more than one of the rational adaptations of the simultaneous employment of iron and masonry; of simply indicating the direction our efforts should take if we would get out of the routine to which architecture is confined, and seriously adopt iron in our large buildings otherwise than as a mere makeshift or a dissimulated means of construction. . . .

Suppose we had to erect an edifice of these dimensions, and that we covered in ths enormous space by means of the structural method adopted by the Roman architects or even by those of the Middle Ages, we could easily estimate the area it would be necessary to give to the solid parts relatively to the voids, in order to sustain a vaulting of masonry exceeding by 50 feet the dome of St. Sophia at Constantinople. It is no exaggeration to say that such an area would be at least three times as great as that given in our plan. Would it be even possible to build a spheroidal vault of these dimensions of masonry on pendentives? It has never been attempted. "But," it will be objected, "what proofs can you furnish of the stability of the system indicated here? It is merely hypothetical; granting its ingenuity, you give us no experimental

76. Section and plan of an assembly hall for 3,000.

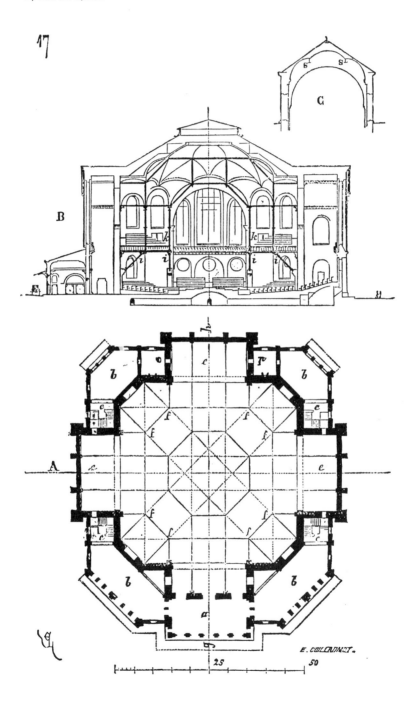

18

E. GUILLAUMOT.   MDCCCLXIV.

77. Interior of assembly hall.

proof of its practicability." As it is not in my power to build a hall of these dimensions to prove the excellence of this system, I can only maintain it by reasoning.

First remark that the main vault—that which replaces the masonry dome of a cupola on pendentives—stands at a distance of 18 to 20 feet clear within the masonry supports; that the iron framework of this central vault consists of members all equal to each other, having similar junctions, and all forming, at the meeting of these members, a pyramid of like angles; that consequently, were there no fastenings, these members so abut together as not to allow of their pyramidal summits giving way; that these rectilineal members, surmounted by arches of masonry carrying the soffits of the vaults, are maintained rigid and cannot become distorted; that their expansion is unrestrained, since each mesh of the network is surmounted by a vault that is independent of its neighbor; that moreover the total weight of the vaults resting on the central polyhedron does not exceed 375 tons; for the developed surface of these vaults (of the central polyhedron only) is at most 1,600 yards, and calculating the weight of these vaults, including the ribs, at 4½ cwt., per yard of surface, we are rather above than under the actual weight. If to this we add the weight of the iron, about 43 tons 2 cwt., we have for the entire weight of the central polyhedron, iron and stone, 418 tons 2 cwt. Each of the eight columns therefore supports a weight of 52 tons 5½ cwt., to which should be added a portion of the weight of the lateral vaulting, which will raise the weight on each column to at most 60 tons. It is easy enough to cast columns able to support the pressure. But these columns rest on struts leaning at an angle of 45°, which however are only 20 feet in length. The builder's chief consideration therefore should be directed to these oblique supports. Their thrust is to a great extent neutralized by the walls of the projections, and by the weight that bears on the interior summits of these walls. All that remains to be done, therefore, is to insure the strength of the braces that at their capitals hold the inclined columns in position. These braces will be of considerable strength, since they can be doubled or quadrupled in the height of the balustrade of the galleries. The central vaulting, firmly maintained by the horizontal stays placed between it and strongly abutting masonry, and by the lateral vaults, cannot give in any direction. The iron framework remains independent everywhere, and merely forms as it were the strings of bows in masonry. The joints may safely remain slack so as not to hinder the expansion, since the whole system of the framework consists in the combination of pieces, which, where there are no support, always form the apex of a pyramid. Allowing for some movement in so extensive a structure, it could not produce any mischief. The vaults, independent of one another, like the surfaces of the Gothic groined vaulting, are so constituted as to give with any movement without occasioning fractures or dislocations. (*Discourses*, XII)

THE IRON TRUSS

This truss was an eloquent demonstration of the argument that strong structural members can be constructed more efficiently with numerous small parts rather than a few large ones. Its chief value for the future, however, resided in the ingenious way in which ornament was made out of portions of the structural assemblage. Equally striking was the way in which the structural connections were so badly exposed. The flowing lines of the truss adumbrate the characteristic design of the Art Nouveau, the first generation of a truly modern architecture.

It must be acknowledged that girders of plate-and-angle iron have not a pleasing appearance in the interior of a building. An iron-box girder made in the shape of a wooden beam is all very well, but it is very heavy and expensive and does not present the appearance befiting the nature of iron. These box girders are not easily fastened on cast-iron columns; they require very widely spreading capitals. It would therefore appear that some other system should be adopted here. Accordingly we give a detail (fig. 78) of the system proposed. Cast-iron columns of moderate length are more easily procured than very long ones. The two columns that rise all the way from the ground to the underside of the gallery of the first floor are therefore made in two lengths—one of 26 ft. 6 in., the other of 23 ft. 6 in., fastened together at A with four bolts (see plan of capital a). The two other anterior columns also consist of a lower part, of 26 ft. 6 in., and a junction part of 4 ft. 6 in. in height, fastened together in the same way. At B we have the horizontal section of the part of the columns that receives the tranverse trusses c supporting the floor joists and the longitudinal bracing trusses g.

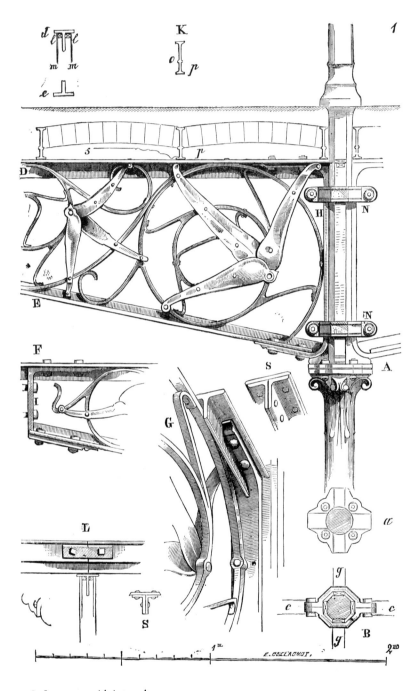

78. Iron truss with integral
ornament.

The transverse trusses supporting the joists consist of an upper bar D of single T-iron, whose section is represented at d, and an under bar E of single T-iron, whose section is shown at e. These bars are connected at their junction with the columns by vertical bands H, forming brackets, forked for the upper fastening as shown in detail G to allow a passage for the vertical flange of the T-iron. Similarly at the junction of the two half trusses (see detail F) bands, bent to an angle, receive the under T-irons, which abut against the face of these bands, and, forked, the upper T-iron, which alone is in one piece for the whole length of the bearing. The two bands, of which one is shown at L, are coupled by bolts. To render these trusses rigid, double scrolls (see section d at l) of 1¼ by ¾ inch iron are riveted on the flanges of the two upper and under T-irons; and the whole system is still further stiffened by leaf ornaments of sheet-iron m riveted on the outer faces of these scrolls. (*Discourses*, XIII)

THE IDEAL MANSION

The scheme for an ideal mansion amounts to Viollet-le-Duc's paradigm for devloping a plan from a complex program. Although he does not explicitly identify the principles underlying the design they could be readily inferred by his readers. Hence we can identify here the prototype of the zoned house or, to put it more abstractly, the organically conceived plan. Moreover, at every point function determines the form, resulting in emphatically asymmetrical elevations. Several different sizes and shapes of openings, irregularly placed, punctuate the varied masses of the structure. It is ironic that a scheme that was sociologically almost an anachronism by the time it was published should have been so important as a model for the modern house.

Everyone who wants a mansion built for him submits a program of his requirements. If he is incapable of doing so, it is for the architect to make up for his incompetence, or the indefiniteness of his ideas, by explaining his presumed wants to him and himself preparing the program. And to every architect worthy of the name, a program that is well drawn up and clear and not liable to any false interpretation is half the battle; on one condition, however; that he complies with it in every particular, that he completely satisfies it, that he will not content himself with mere aproximations, nor seek to control his failure to perform certain conditions of it under the seductive appearance of architectural prescription.

. . . Avoid external magnificence that adds nothing to the merit of the work, drawing largely on the client's purse without contributing anything to his comfort. . . . In the present day there is really no reason for the magnificent displays of frontage, and they interest no one. But I must recall this last statement: they do tend to keep up that brooding hatred that the less wealthy classes cherish against opulence and against those who make a foolish display of it to their own prejudice. I do not assert that we ought, as the Orientals do, to disguise the internal splendor of a palace behind bare whitewashed walls; but between that hypocritical semblance of poverty and the luxurious display that leaves no impression except in the mind of the envious, a rational *via media* may, I think, be found.

And the same may be said with regard to that symmetry whose abuse should be reprobated. It would be still more ridiculous to proscribe it absolutely and to design irregular plans for the mere love of irregularity. When the tenor of a program lends itself to symmetrical arrangements, it would be puerile not to take advantage of it; for we cannot be blind to the fact that circumstances often present themselves in which a symmetrical disposition is a satisfaction to the mind and to the eye. But the mind and eye must be able to take in this symmetry, whether in a public or private building: a result that is often produced in the interiors of houses but seldom on the outside, especially in dwellings that like large hotels, can only be seen in parts, and not altogether. However this may be, it would seem reasonable never to sacrifice absolute requirements, or rather arangements that ought to comply with those requirements, to symmetry. A bad arrangement is a nuisance felt constantly, while the pleasure a symmetrical arrangement produces is soon forgotten. . . .

One last remark suggests itself in reference to the building of mansions answering to our requirements. While we wish to present the intrusion of our domestics into our daily life, and desire that the former should as little as possible come in contact with the latter, on the other hand we have not so many servants as were kept in the mansions of former times. In fact, we may say that as compared with those days their number is now reduced to a minimum. We must therefore avoid the necessity of their having to traverse long distances. When we do not need their services, their presence is undesirable; but when we require a servant, we wish that there should be no delay in giving our orders. These habits require an easy and rapid concentration of the service, and communciations specially reserved for it.

Let us attempt, if not the complete fulfillment of this program—to which it would be ridiculous to pretend—to indicate at least the method to be followed in satisfying it. To do this we must present definite plans; this is the form of expression that excludes vagueness and ambiguity. Criticism is easy, but the realization of ideas that seem at first of the simplest and clearest order is a task of no small difficulty.

At the present day, still more imperatively than was the case in former times, we desire that the reception rooms of a mansion should be distinct from those reserved for privacy, simply because we receive a good many people with whom we have but the slightest acquaintance. The ground floor of a mansion should therefore be reserved for those receptions, and the first story for family privacy. But as crowds of visitors are sometimes entertained, the rooms destined to receive them must be so arranged that it may be easy to move about in them, and the means of entrance and exit may be easy; and so that isolation may be possible if, amid the crowd of persons we have to invite, there are, as generally happens, a select few who are more intimately connected. People should be able to find some better place of rendezvous than the embrasures of doors, if they wish to talk about their own interest or affairs. If we give a dinner, the hall in which we give it should be quite separated from the apartments reserved for evening receptions: for nothing is more disagreeable for those who come at nine or ten o'clock, than to be witnesses of the cleaning away of a large table, even with a side glance; yet the dining room must be very near the drawing rooms, so that one may pass directly from one into the others. Many other things are requisite: we want an awning to shelter the carriages; but those who come and go on foot—for in a democratic state of society there will be such, as well as people who keep their carriages—must also be able to come into the entrance hall without passing under the horses' noses; and there must be a closed vestibule where overcoats may be deposited. Between this vestibule and the reception rooms there must be a room where ladies may assure themselves of the state of their toilette, and where guests may prepare to be introduced. These antechambers must communicate readily with the servants' rooms of various functions. There must be a waiting room for attendants who receive overcoats and mantles, and who have to call the coachmen when the guests leave. A dressing room will be required for ladies whose attire may have been somewhat disarranged. But this antechamber must not be directly in view of the reception rooms, nor *vice versa*. The guests must not be imprisoned in one part of the public salons, but be able to make their escape at will. It should also be remarked that festive sounds and lights should not attract attention in the street.

As regards the private apartments, which we suppose to be in the first story, there must be a sufficient number of servants' staircases, besides the grand staircase, to insure the rapid and easy communication of the kitchens and servants' rooms with those apartments. And besides bedrooms with their wardrobes and dressing rooms there must be a waiting room, and antechamber, a dining room, and a drawng room for the family and intimate friends. Sun and air and light should be arranged for in every part, with aspects as favorable as possible, and ready exists and entrances, so that every inmate may come in without attracting attention.

As regards the servants' offices, underground kitchens should be avoided, as being unhealthy for those who live in them and undesirable as spreading the odor of cooking through the house. The kitchen, however, should not be too far from the rooms allotted to repasts. The pantry arrangements should be on a large scale, communicating directly with the kitchens and dining room. Of course there must be a backyard for the stables, coach houses, and kitchen; and so placed that the washing of carriages, or the grooming of horses, or the occupations of the scullery, may never be visible from the grand court.

Such at least have been the requirements of a well-planned mansion up to the present moment. . . .

. . . But let us consider our *hôtel,* the program of which we have just given in a summary form.

There is in every building, I may say, one principal organ—one dominant part—and certain secondary organs or members, and the necessary appliances for supplying all these parts by a system of circulation. Each of these organs has its own function; but it ought to be connected with the whole body in proportion to its requirements.

The plan (fig. 79) is sketched according to these principles, exhibiting the ground floor of a mansion of medium pretensions, taking the mansions in Paris as a standard.

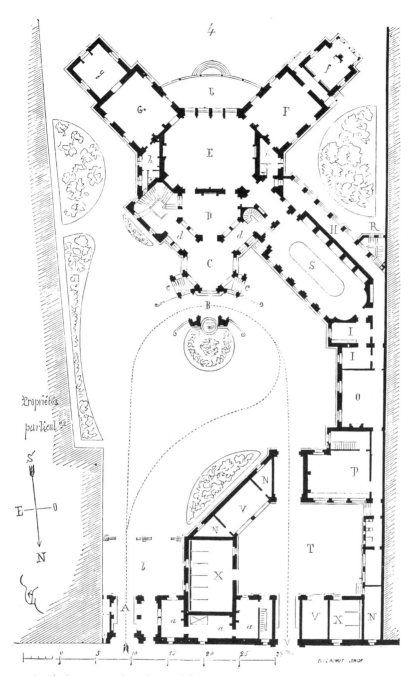

79. An ideal mansion, plan of ground floor. A, grand entrance; a, porter's lodge; b, forecourt; B, porte cochere; C, vestibule; D, first salon; d, galleries; E, drawing room; F, G, salons; f, smoking room; g, small parlor; H, servants' passage; I, pantries; h, i, ladies' and gentlemen's dressing rooms; N, harness rooms; O, servants' hall; P, kitchen; R, servants' stairs; S, dining hall; T, servants' court; V, coach houses; X, stables.

We suppose the ground it occupies to present the conditions most frequently met with in the midst of a great city—that is, with a frontage comparatively narrow and becoming broader toward the back. We need not insist on the advantages that buildings of this kind offer, built between a court and a garden, far from the noise of the street. But unless we have a very large space of ground at our disposal, mansions built between a court and a garden form a barrier separating them; the result of which is that on the side of the court the aspect is generally cold and gloomy, while on that of the garden there is complete isolation with a monotony of view and position. Besides, long rows of apartments or square returns make the arrangements of the house difficult, lengthen communications with the offices at certain points, and cause much space to be lost, if we would have a free circulation for the family and servants.

If, in order to avoid the inconveniences resulting from having a large building crossing the site—the building being two rooms deep—we adopt the block arrangement, we must provide air and light in the center; which cannot be obtained except by means of that objectionable English "hall" that our French customs will, I trust, not tolerate.

The abovementioned considerations have suggested the plan (figure 79), which consists of an octagon 65 feet in diameter, with two oblique wings on the garden site and a third wing, likewise oblique, overlooking the court.

Whatever the aspects of the site, the sun would thus dry and warm three-fourths of the walls at least; and supposing the position of the mansion to be as marked in the plan, there would not be a single aspect deprived of sun; each would have the benefit of its rays in turn.

At A is the grand entrance, with the porter's lodge at a; at b a forecourt closed by a railing, an arrangement frequently required if, for instance, the family are absent or are not accessible to visitors before a certain hour. At B is erected an awning for carriages, with a central entrance in the vestibule C. Two other side entrances with steps are provided at c. This vestibule C opens into a first salon D and two galleries dd one of which—that to the left—communicates with the grand staircase, and the other with a servants' staircase, the lobby of the dining room, and the passages leading to the pantries. Under the grand staircase, in the basement, is the room for attendants on guests. Glazed doors give entrance from the first salon, D, into the galleries, which are themselves glazed, so that when a levee is over the guests may easily disperse in the vestibule C, whence they can depart through one of three doors, two of which are for those on foot, who thus avoid encountering the carriages. While the first salon opens on the vestibule through a principal central door, it gives entrance to the great central drawing room E by two doors, both to avoid the direct view referred to above and to enable the guests to go out and in without passing through the same entrance.

It is customary for the master or the mistress of the house to present themselves at the entrance of their drawing rooms to receive invited guests or callers; it often happens, moreover, that only a few moments can be devoted to visits of this kind, and it is a very awkward thing to pass before the master or mistress of the house in departing when we have paid our respects to them on entering only a few minutes before. The two passages out enable us to avoid the inconvenience, either of failing somewhat in politeness or remaining prisoners.

The great central drawing room E opens on a conservatory or winter garden J, and obliquely on two salons F and G on the wing, which open likewise on the conservatory. The salon G, more particulary appropriated to ladies, is terminated by a small parlor g. The salon F opens on a gallery with two doors into the garden, and a smoking room f, the odors of which therefore cannot penetrate into the other apartments. At h is a dressing room with a closet for ladies; at i a similar arrangement for the other sex. These rooms may also serve as retreats in case of indisposition, or to conduct to the upper stories, either by the grand staircase or that of the servants. From the large drawing room E or the first salon D we pass into the great dining hall S, which has a passage H communicating with the kitchen, and pantries in its vicinity I. The servants' hall where they take their meals is at O, and the cooking kitchen and its appurtenances at P. The servants' passage H is entresoled; and the entresol and the gallery of the first story are reached by the servants' staircase. But we shall return to this arrangement directly. Around the servants' court T are coach houses V, stables X, and harness rooms N.

Let us ascend to the first story, allotted to family privacy (fig. 80). The grand staircase leads at A to a wide landing on the same level with a gallery B traversing the central part of the building, and leading to another gallery C, communicating with the offices. At D is a large study or parlor between the grand staircase and the servants' stairs, appropriated to the master of the house. This room opens on a terrace E covering the vestibule and lateral galleries. At F is an antechamber with a small waiting room G, and a private drawing room H and dining room I, with a pantry J in direct communication with the servants' staircase K descending to the kitchens. The gallery B therefore separates the apartments to which strangers can be admitted from the two rooms L with their dressing rooms M, and from the two apartments N, each furnished with an antechamber-salon O and dressing room P. Above, in the attics, are rooms for the children and for servants whose duties attach them more closely to the family. The roofing (fig. 81) is arranged in these buildings in the simplest manner and with no complicated combinations. The wings terminate in gables, an arrangement that allows of chimneys on gable walls and windows to light the attics, without adopting lateral dormer windows at these points.

Figure 82 gives a perspective view of this mansion, taken in a northeast direction.

It seems . . . that the grouping of the several parts of a dwelling around a center, besides greatly facilitating the domestic arrangements, tends to a better utilization of the ground occupied, and therefore to a real saving. Observation will show that reception rooms forming a series are very inconvenient, render the proper performance of servants' duties impossible, and cannot be made to accord with the custom, prevalent in our time, of receiving a large concourse of people. . . .

Further argument in its favor is needless; an examination of the plans drawn according to this method of grouping will show the advantages that can be derived from its application in the building of mansions, large or small. It would seem also possible to make a general application of oblique or polygonal plans in buildings of this kind, not conforming ourselves, when we have a free space at our disposal, to square plans that present parts in such positions as render them difficult to light and arrange, except by sacrificing space.

Without offering the preceding designs as a model to be followed—presenting them only as an application of a system that accords with modern requirements—it will be easily seen that this method allows us to gain numerous openings for light in every aspect, and leaves no places unoccupied. (*Discourses*, XVII)

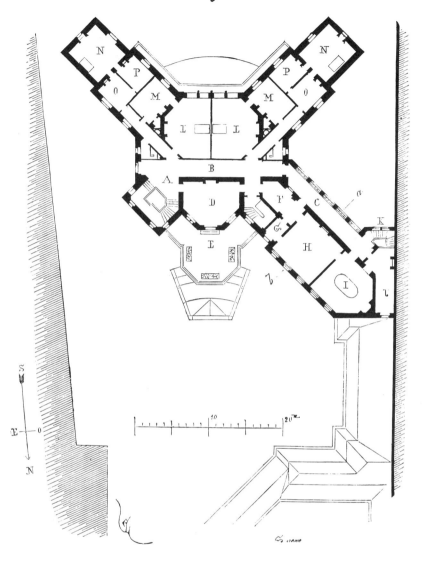

80. An ideal mansion, plan of first floor. A, grand staircase; B, central gallery;
C, gallery for offices; D, large study; E, terrace; F, antechamber; G, small waiting
room; H, private drawing room; I, private dining room; J, pantry; K, servants' stairs;
L, guest bedrooms; M, dressing rooms; N, master apartments; O, antechamber-salon;
P, dressing room. (Rooms for children and servants in the attic.)

81. An ideal mansion, plan of
roof.

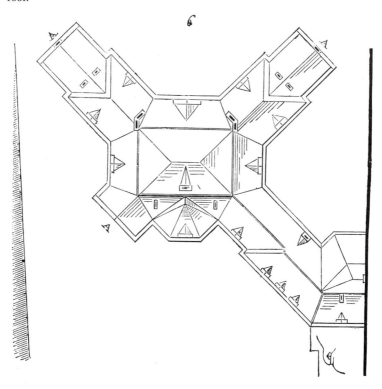

Viollet-le-Duc was a perceptive observer of the implications of socio-logical change for architecture. The following passage explains why the modern mansion of his time had many more rooms, arranged for much greater privacy, than the chateaux of earlier centuries. More important for our purposes, it points toward an understanding of the continued proliferation of private accommodations for each individual in luxurious households of the late twentieth century.

A social condition of aristocratic character introduces intimate, and, so to speak, familiar relations between superiors and inferiors, which disappear in democratic societies. Domestic architecture bears the impress of this change in manners. When the classes of society are separated by distances that cannot be crossed, those of the higher grades, assured that neither personal merit, nor intrigue, nor violence, will be able to rob them of their distinction, do not raise useless barriers between themselves and the subordinate classes; on the contrary, the very need of companionship soon gives rise to intimate relations connecting all ranks from the lowest to the highest.

Both in the chateaux and in the mansions the life of the noblesse was quite unsecluded; it was not deemed singular or reprehensible for the inmates of the dwelling, even those of an inferior class, to go in and out in every part of the building. Life was lived in common without inconvenience, because there was no reason to fear that subordinates would ever forget the social distance that separated them from their superiors.

It is not so in a democratic state of society; there the higher class require material barriers to protect them from the presumption and encroachments of inferiors. Such serious alterations in the habits of society are reflected in domestic architecture, in a number of precautionary details devised with a view to secure the independence of the master of the house, and to secure his domestic privacy from the curiosity of subordinates whom no moral tie attaches to the family, who are little devoted to its interests, if they are not unfriendly or envious.

We conclude from the above that domestic architecture in an aristocratic state of society may affect a breadth and simplicity in its arrangements that would be intolerable in a democratic condition, where each department in the dwelling must be distinct and definite, in proportion to the equality before the law that exists between masters and servants. (*Discourses,* XVII).

82. An ideal mansion, perspective
view of exterior.

IV RESTORING OLD ENVIRONMENTS

10 Defining the Nature of Restoration

The issue of restoration held no interest for the architects who pioneered and developed the modern movement. To them, the architectural theory of Viollet-le-Duc was useful precisely because it helped them to break free of the historical past and the theoretical tradition of earlier architecture. But in our own time, when preservation has assumed almost as great an urgency as the continued development of modernity, Viollet-le-Duc's ideas about the preservation of old buildings have acquired new import and offer valuable insights to patrons and builders alike.

The term restoration and the thing itelf are both modern. To restore a building is not to preserve it, to repair, or rebuild it; it is to reinstate it in a condition of completeness that could never have existed at any given time. It is only since the first quarter of the present century that the idea of restoring buildings of another age has been entertained; and we are not aware that a clear definition of architectural restoration has as yet been given. Perhaps it may be as well to endeavor at the outset to gain an exact notion of what we understand, or ought to understand, by a restoration; for it is evident that considerable ambiguity has insensibly gathered about the meaning we attach, or ought to attach, to this operation.

We have said that both the word and the thing itself are modern; and, in fact, no civilization, no people of bygone ages, has conceived the idea of making restorations in the sense in which we comprehend them.

In Asia, both in ancient and modern times, when a temple or a palace has become dilapidated, another has been, or is now, erected beside it. Its decay is not regarded as a reason for destroying the ancient edifice; it is left to the action of time, which lays hold of it as its rightful possessor, and gradually consumes it. The Romans replaced, but did not restore; a proof of which is that there is no Latin word corresponding with our term "restoration" in its modern sense. *Instaurare, reficere, renovare,* do not mean to restore, but to reinstate—to make anew. When the Emperor Hadrian undertook to rehabilitate several public buildings in ancient Greece and Asia Minor, he proceeded after a fashion against which all archaeological societies of Europe, had they then existed, would have protested: though he made some claim to antiquarian knowledge. . . .

We might say that it is as unadvisable to restore by reproducing a facsimile of all that we find in a building, as by presuming to substitute for later forms those that must have existed originally. In the first case, the good faith and sincerity of the artist may lead to the gravest errors, by consecrating what may be called an interpolation; in the second, the substitution of a primary form for an existing one of a later period also obliterates the traces of a reparation, whose cause, if known, would perhaps have rendered evident the existence of an exceptional arrangement. We shall explain this presently.

Our age has adopted an attitude toward the past in which it stands quite alone among historical ages. It has undertaken to analyze the past, to compare and classify its phenomena, and to construct its veritable history, by following step by step the march, the progress, the successive phases of humanity. . . . Our age is not satisfied with casting a scrutinizing glance behind it; this work of retrospection cannot fail to develop the problems presented by the future and to facilitate their solution. . . .

Many events have occurred since the presentation of the Inspector General's Report on the Historical Monuments in 1831; many discussions on art have been raised; still the seed first sown by M. Vitet has borne its fruit. M. Vitet was the first to interest himself seriously in the restoration of our ancient buildings; he was the first to enunciate practical views on this subject: the first to bring criticism to bear on work of this kind. The way was opened; other critics and other men of learning have entered upon it, and artists have followed in their track.

Fourteen years later, the same writer, faithful to the work he had so well begun, wrote the history of Noyon Cathedral; and in that remarkable work he thus bears witness to the stages passed through by the savants and artists devoted to the same studies:

In fact, to know the history of an art it is not enough to determine the different periods through which it has passed in any given place; it is necessary to trace its progress in all the localities in which it has appeared, to indicate the varieties of form it has successively assumed, and to present a comparative sketch of all its varieties, having regard not only to each nation but to each province of a country. . . . It is with this double view and in this spirit that almost all the researches undertaken among us in reference to medieval buildings during the last twenty years have been conducted. . . .

At that time M. Vitet had given up the Inspector Generalship of Historical Monuments; since 1835 its function had been entrusted to one of the most distinguished intellects of our time—M. Mérimée.

It was under these two sponsors that a first nucleus of artists was formed, of young men desirous of gaining an intimate knowledge of these forgotten arts; it was under their wise inspiration, guided always by severe criticism, that restorations were undertaken, at first with great reserve, but soon more boldly and on a more extensive scale. From 1835 to 1848, M. Vitet presided over the Commission des Monuments Historiques; and during this period a great number of buildings of the Roman and medieval periods in France were studied and also preserved from ruin. It must be observed that the idea of restoration was then quite novel. . . .

The unfortunate church of St. Denis was a sort of anatomical subject on which artists who first entered on the path of restoration made their first essays in restoration. During thirty years it suffered every possible mutilation; to such a degree in fact that its stability being endangered, after considerable outlay and when its ancient dispositions had been altered, and all the fine monuments it contained tumbled about, it became necessary to conclude this costly series of experiments, and to revert to the program laid down with respect to restoration by the Commission des Monuments Historiques.

We proceed, then, to explain the program now adopted in England and in Germany, which have preceded us in the path of the theoretical study of ancient art, a program accepted also in Italy and Spain, which seek in their turn to bring criticism to bear on the preservation of their ancient buildings. This program lays down at the outset the general principle that every building and every part of a building should be restored in its own style, not only as regards appearance but structure. There have been few buildings, particularly during the Middle Ages, built all at one time; or if so built, that have not undergone some considerable modifications, either by additions, transformations, or partial changes. It is therefore essential, previous to every work of repair, to ascertain exactly the age and character of each part—to form a kind of specification based on trustworthy records, either by written description or by graphical representation. Moreover in France each province has its own style, a school whose principles and practical methods should be ascertained. Data derived from a building of the Ile-de-France cannot therefore serve as a guide to restoration in an edifice of Champagne or Burgundy. These diversities of schools exist to a rather late period: they follow a law to which there are many exceptions. Thus, for example, while the fourteenth-century art of Sequanian Normandy bears a great similarity to that of the Ile-de-France at the same epoch, the Norman renaissance differs essentially from the renaissance of Paris and it environs. In some southern provinces the architecture called Gothic was at no time anything other than an importation: a Gothic building at Clermont, for instance, might be the product of one school, and at the same epoch a building at Carcassonne of another. The architect entrusted with a restoration should therefore be exactly acquainted, not only with the style appertaining to each period of art, but also with the styles belonging to each school. It is not in the Middle Ages alone that these diversities are met with; the same phenomenon presents itself in the buildings of Greek and Roman antiquity. The Roman buildings of the Antonine period, which cover the south of France, differ in many respects from the buildings in Rome of the same period. The Roman of the eastern shores of the Adriatic cannot be confounded with the Roman of central Italy, of Provence, or of Syria.

But to confine ourselves to the Middle Ages: difficulties multiply in problems of restoration. It has frequently happened that buildings of a certain period, or of a certain school, have been repaired again and again, and that by artists who do not belong to the province where the edifice is found. This has been an occasion of considerable embarrassment. If both the original and the altered parts are to be restored, should the latter be disregarded, and the unity of style, which has been disturbed, be reestablished; or, should the whole with the later modifications be exactly reproduced? In such a case the absolute adoption of one of the two alternatives may be objectionable; and it may be necessary, on the contrary, to admit neither of the two principles absolutely, but to proceed according to the special circumstances of the case. What are these special circumstances? It would be impossible to indicate all: it will suffice to call attention to some of the most important, so as to exemplify the critical side of the work. In preference to the possession of every other accomplishment—archaeological skill among the rest—the architect entrusted with a restoration should be a clever and experienced builder, not only in a general but a special sense; that is to say, he should be acquainted with the methods of construction employed at different periods of our art and in the various schools. These methods have a comparative value; they are not equally good. Some, indeed, had to be abandoned because of their defective character. Thus, for example, an edifice built in the twelfth century, which had no gutters unders the eaves of the roofs, had to be restored in the thirteenth century and furnished with gutters combined with escapes. The whole of the crown work is in a bad state; and an entire renewal is contemplated. Should the thirteenth-century gutters be done away with in order to replace the ancient twelfth-century cornice, of which traces are also found? Certainly not: the cornice-gutter of the thirteenth century should be replaced, retaining the form of this period, since there is no such thing as a cornice-gutter of the twelfth century: and to put a hypothetical one, pretending to give it the character of the architecture of that period, would be to commit an anachronism in stone. Again: the vaulting of a nave of the twelfth century had by some accident been partially destroyed, and rebuilt at a later period not in its primitive form but according to the mode then in vogue. This latter vaulting, threatening in its turn to give way, has to be reconstructed. Shall it be restored in its later form, or shall the primitive vaulting be replaced? Yes; because there is no advantage in doing otherwise, and there is a considerable advantage in restoring unity to the edifice. The question here is not, as in the previous example, that of preserving an improvement made on a defective system, but one in which we have to bear in mind that the later restoration was made according to the ancient method—which consisted in adopting the forms in vogue at the time, when an edifice had to be renewed or restored—whereas we proceed on a contrary principle, that of restoring every building in its own style. But this vaulting, which is of a character foreign to the first, and which has to be rebuilt, is remarkably beautiful. It has given occasion to the opening of windows adorned with fine painted glass. It has been contrived in harmony with a system of external construction of great value. Shall all this be destroyed for the mere sake of an absolute restoration of the primitive nave? Shall this painted glass be consigned to the lumber room? Shall exterior buttresses and flying buttresses, which no longer have anything to support, be left purposeless? No, certainly. We see, therefore, that in solving problems of this kind, absolute principles may lead to absurdities.

Suppose it were required to replace the detached pillars of a hall that are giving way under the weight they support, because the materials employed are too fragile and in courses that are not thick enough. At several different periods some of these pillars have been replaced, and sections given them that differ from the form originally traced. Shall we in renewing these pillars reproduce those various sections, and preserve the heights of the old courses that are weak? No! we shall reproduce the original section in all the pillars, and erect them with large blocks to prevent the recurrence of the accidents that have necessitated our operation. But some of these pillars have had their sections altered in consequence of changes that it was desired the building should undergo—changes that in respect of the progress of art are of great importance, such, for instance, as occurred at Notre-Dame in Paris in the fourteenth century. Shall we, in rebuilding them, destroy that so interesting trace of a project that was not entirely carried out, but that indicates the tendencies of a school? No: we shall reproduce them in their altered form, since these alterations may serve to throw light upon a point in the history of art. In an edifice of the thirteenth century, where the water ran off by means of drips—as in the cathedral of Chartres, for instance—it was thought necessary during the fifteenth century to add gargoyles to the gutters, for the better regulation of the escape. These gargoyles are in a bad state and have to be replaced. Shall we on the pretext of unity substitute gargoyles of the thirteenth century for them? No: for we should thus destroy the traces of an interesting primitive arrangement. On the contrary, we shall persist in following the later work, adhering to its style.

Between the buttresses of a nave, chapels have been afterward added. The walls beneath the windows of these chapels and the jambs of the windows do not in any way tie into the more ancient buttresses, but show clearly enough that these constructions are of later date. It is found necessary to rebuild both the exterior faces of these buttresses, which are decayed by time, and the enclosing walls of the chapels. Should we unite these two constructions of different periods, and which we at the same time restore? No: we shall carefully preserve the distinct jointing of the two parts—the unbondings; so that it may always be apparent that the chapels were afterward added between the buttresses. Similarly, in the unseen parts of buildings we should scrupulously respect any trace that may be seen to give evidence of additions and modifications.

In restorations there is an essential condition that must always be kept in mind. It is that every portion removed should be replaced with better materials, and in a stronger and more perfect way. As a result of the operation to which it has been subjected, the restored edifice should have a renewed ease of existence, longer than that which has already elapsed. It cannot be denied that a process of restoration is, in every case, a somewhat severe trial for a building. The scaffolding, the shores, the necessary wrenching away, and the partial removal of masonry shake the work, so as sometimes to occasion very serious accidents. It is reasonable, therefore, to expect that every building thus treated will lose something of its strength in consequence of this shaking; and this diminution of solidity ought to be counteracted by increasing the strength of the parts renewed, by improvements in the system of construction, by well-contrived tie-rods, and by providing better appliances for resistance. It need scarcely be observed that the choice of materials is a most important consideration in a work of restoration. Many buildings are threatened with ruin solely through the weakness or inferior quality of the materials employed.

While the architect entrusted with the restoration of an edifice ought to be acquainted with the forms and styles belonging to that edifice, and the school to which it owed its origin, he should, if possible, be still better acquainted with its structure, its anatomy, its temperament; for it is essential above all things that he should make it live. He ought to have mastered every detail of that structure, just as if he himself had directed the original building; and having acquired this knowledge, he should have at command means of more than one order for undertaking the work of renewal. If one of these fails, a second and a third should be in readiness. . . . While these problems that present themselves in the process of restoration incessantly puzzle and embarrass the builder who has not exactly appreciated those conditions of equilibrium, they become a stimulus to him who is thoroughly acquainted with the edifice to be repaired. It is a war that has to be carried on—a series of maneuvers that must be modified every day by a constant observation of the effects that may occur. . . .

Since all the edifices whose restoration is undertaken have a special destination—a particular use—the role of restorer of antique arrangements, now obsolete, cannot be assumed to the utter exclusion of the question of actual utility. The edifice ought not to be less convenient when it leaves the architect's hands than it was before the restoration. Speculative archaeologists very often disregard present requirements, and severely censure the architect for having made concessions to them; as if the building confided to his treatment were his own, and as if he were not pledged to carry out the program given him.

But it is in these circumstances, which frequently present themselves, that the intelligence of the architect is called into play. He always possesses the means of reconciling his role as restorer with that of artist commissioned to meet unforeseen requirements. Moreover the best means of preserving a building is to find a use for it, and to satisfy its requirements so completely that there shall be no occasion to make any changes. . . .

We must admit that we are on slippery ground as soon as we deviate from literal reproduction, and that the adoption of such deviation should be reserved for extreme cases; but it must be allowed that it is sometimes commanded by imperious necessities, which we cannot evade with a *non possumus*. That an architect should refuse to introduce gas pipes into a church, in order to avoid mutilations and accidents, is intelligible, for the edifice can be lighted by other means; but that he should refuse to lend himself to the formation of a heating apparatus, for instance, under the pretext that the Middle Ages did not employ this system of warming ecclesiastical buildings; and that he should thus expose the faithful to the risk of catching cold for the sake of archaeology is, to say the least, ridiculous. As this means of warming necessitates chimney stacks, we should proceed as a master of the Middle Ages would have done if he had been obliged to contrive them; and above all, not try to hide this novel feature; since the ancient masters, so far from dissembling a necessity, sought on the contrary to invest it with a becoming form, even making decorative features of such material requirements. An architect who, having to renew the roof of a building, should reject ironwork construction, because the medieval masters did not make iron framing, is in our opinion wrong; since by so doing he would obviate the terrible contingency of fire, which has so often proved destructive to our ancient buildings. But then, must he not consider the disposition of the points of support? Ought he to alter the conditions of equilibrium? If the timber framing weighted the walls equally, ought he not to seek a structural system in iron that would present the same advantages? Certainly: and he will make it a matter of special attention that the iron roof be no heavier than the wooden one. This is a consideration of the greatest moment. We have too often had to regret the overweighting of old work: the restoration of the upper parts of edifices with materials heavier than those originally employed. These oversights and negligences have caused more than one catastrophe. We cannot repeat it too often: the medieval buildings are planned with deliberate skill; their organism is delicate. We find in them nothing more than is required, nothing useless in their composition; if you change one of the conditions of the organism, you alter all the rest. Many point to this as a defect; in our judgment it is an excellence that we are too apt to disregard in our modern constructions, from which we might remove more than one member without endangering their existence. For what in fact is the use of science and calculation in construction if it does not enable us to accomplish the work with no more than the necessary appliances? . . .

Photography, which assumes every day a more important phase in scientific studies, seems to have appeared for the very purpose of aiding this grand work of restoration of ancient buildings, in which the whole of Europe has begun to take an interest.

In fact, while architects possessed only the ordinary means of sketching, even the most exact (the *camera lucida* for example), it was very difficult for them not to make some omissions—not to overlook certain scarcely apparent traces. Moreover, when the work of restoration was completed, it was always possible to dispute the correctness of the graphical reports—of what is called the existing state. But photography presents the advantage of supplying indisputable reports—documents that can be permanently consulted when the restorations mask the traces left by the ruin. Photography has naturally led architects to be still more scrupulous than before in their respect for the slightest vestiges of an ancient arrangement, and to take more accurate observations of the construction; while it provides them with the permanent means of justifying their operations. Photography cannot be too sedulously used in restorations; for very frequently a photograph discovers what had not been perceived in the building itself.

An all-important principle to be observed in restoration, and one that should not be departed from on any pretext whatever, is to pay regard to every vestige indicating an architectural arrangement. The architect should not be thoroughly satisfied, nor set his men to work, until he has discovered the combination that best and most simply accords with the vestiges of ancient work: to decide on an arrangement a priori, without having gained all the information that should regulate it, is to fall into hypothesis; and in works of restoration nothing is so dangerous as hypothesis. If at any point you have unfortunately adopted an arrangement that is at variance with the right one—with that originally followed—you are led by a course of logical deduction into a wrong path, from which it will be no longer possible to escape: and in such a case the better you reason, the farther you are from the truth. Hence, when, for example, the completion of a building partly in ruins is in question, before beginning it will be necessary to search for and examine all that remains; to collect the smallest fragments, taking care to note the point where they were found; and not to begin the work until their place and use have been assigned to all these remains, as with the pieces of a puzzle. If these precautions are neglected, the most annoying misconceptions may result, and a fragment discovered after the completion of a restoration may clearly prove that you were mistaken. It is necessary to examine the beds, joints, and dressing of the fragments collected in the clearing; for some kinds of tooling could only have been adopted with the view of producing a particular effect at a certain height. The slightest indications, even the way in which these fragments have behaved in falling, may not unfrequently show the place they occupied. In these difficult cases of rebuilding the demolished parts of an edifice, the architect ought, therefore, to be present during the clearing and entrust it to intelligent excavators. In erecting the new constructions he should as far as possible replace these old remains even if injured: this will furnish a guarantee for the sincerity and exactitude of his investigations.

We have said enough to show the difficulties that the architect commissioned with a restoration must encounter if he is in earnest in the performance of his duties—if he desires not merely to appear truthful, but to carry through his work with the consciousness of having left nothing to chance and of never having sought to practice a deception upon himself. (*On Restoration* [from *Dictionnaire raisonné*, vol. 8])

ON THE RESTORATION OF THE CATHEDRAL OF NOTRE-DAME DE PARIS

The following passage is a letter written in connection with Viollet-le-Duc's prospectus for the restoration of Notre-Dame. While it is much the earliest of all the texts in this volume, it demonstrates that most of his principles of restoration were already formulated early in his career. It is included here to provide an example in which some of the difficult decisions involved in restoring an actual building are being worked out. Perhaps most instructive is the fact that the principles he lays out at the beginning of the letter end up being violated by the time he gets down to specific items of the restoration.

Dear Minister,

Having been charged with drawing up the project of restoration for the cathedral of Paris, we are not deceiving ourselves about either the importance of the task you would confide in us or the gravity of the problems and difficulties we would have to resolve.

In such a project one cannot operate with too much prudence and discretion. To state it plainly, a restoration can be more disastrous for a monument than the ravages of the centuries and popular upheavals, for time and revolutions destroy but do not add anything. To the contrary, a restoration can, by adding new forms, obliterate a host of vestiges, the peculiarity, singularity, and antiquity of which add interest.

In this case, one truly does not know what is to be feared more, whether negligence that allows what is threatened with ruin to fall to the ground or ignorant zeal that adds, suppresses, and completes, and ends by transforming an old monument into a new one, devoid of historical interest.

Also, one understands perfectly that in view of such dangers archaeology is moved to restraint and that men deeply devoted to the conservation of our monuments have said, "In principle it is not necessary to renew; rather, brace, consolidate, and replace—as on the Arch of Orange—the utterly deteriorated stone with new blocks, but refrain from carving new moldings or sculptures."

We understand the point of these principles and we accept them completely, but they apply only when it is a matter of a curious ruin, a ruin without purpose and without actual utility.

For they should appear very exaggerated in the restoration of a building whose usefulness is still as real, as indisputable today as on the day of completion; of a church, in short, erected by a religion whose immutability is one of its fundamental tenets. In this case, it is necessary not only that the artist apply himself to propping up, strengthening, and conserving; he must also make every effort to restore to the building through prudent repairs the richness and brightness of which it has been robbed. It is thereby that he can conserve for posterity the unified appearance and the interesting details in the monument that has been entrusted to him.

However, we are by no means saying that it is necessary to suppress all the later additions to the original structure and to bring the monument back to its initial form. On the contrary, we think that each part, added in whatever epoch, ought in principle to be preserved, strengthened, and restored in the style appropriate to it, and this done with a reverent discretion, even with a total abnegation of all personal opinion.

The artist ought to remain entirely in the background, to forget his tastes and his instincts in order to retrieve and follow the thought that presided at the execution of the work he wishes to restore. It is not a matter, in this case, of making art but only of submitting to the art of an epoch that is no longer. Against the risk of being carried away in spite of himself by a more dangerous course, the artist ought scrupulously to reproduce what can appear defective to him not only from the point of view of art, but—we will go so far as to say—even from the point of view of construction. In effect, construction is essentially tied to form, and the smallest change in this vitally important aspect of Gothic architecture soon involves one in another, and yet another, and, bit by bit, one is led to modify completely the original system of construction in order to substitute for it a modern one; and that too often at the expense of form. Besides, in doing this one destroys one of the quaint pages of the history of building: the more real the improvement, the more flagrant the historical lie.

What we say for the conservation of the constructional system we say also for the strict conservation of the materials employed in the original forms—first for the sake of history and above all for the sake of art. In altering the materiality it is impossible to preserve the form; thus, cast iron can no more reproduce the appearance of stone than iron can lend itself to convey that of wood. For the rest, it suffices, in order to satisfy oneself, only to glance at the attempts of this sort that have been ventured—be it at Rouen for the spire of the cathedral, at Séez for the pyramidal buttresses, or at Reims for the archiepiscopal chapel. Wherever iron has replaced stone even the unpracticed eye cannot be fooled. At Rouen, as at Séez and Reims, cast iron has been able to reproduce only the naked forms, whereas the moldings and stone sculptures of the monuments were carved with the chisel and are impossible to mold in a single piece. But these are only minor disadvantages compared to the more serious ones that cast iron offers in terms of strength. In effect, without considering weight—which is very much more considerable than was foreseen before the great examples were made—a sharp change in temperature or an atmospheric commotion suffices to crack fragile cast iron as if it were stone. Moreover, this material not only never bonds with stone but for this reason is also a constant cause of ruin by oxidation, which one can never prevent. As for color, needless to say cast iron can never reproduce that of stone. And even when one covers it with a thick coat of paint the red oxide of iron destroys the paint so promptly that one must continually renew it. As for the argument of economy, it falls easily before the results of experience.

Another mode of restoration, employed for some years, presents a still more deplorable result. Here we speak of mastics, cements, and finally all materials foreign to stone—which have never been successfully bound to stone—means that are always destructive in matters of masonry. The application of these cements (and even worse, the use of iron—a new cause of ruin) necessitates the defacement of all the parts one wishes to restore, only producing a result that offers no chance of durability and leaves afterward no vestige of what had originally existed. Admitting even that the medium might be durable, the appearance of mastic will never be that of stone. Difficult to employ, with a sere quality that can never reproduce either the frankness or the grain of stone, this material retains its appearance of modeled paste. What we have just said experience has proved: whenever they are used these cements detach from the stone, crack, and decompose in the air. What will remain when they fall off?

But people have not limited themselves to restoring sculpture in this way but have gone so far as to replace old stone with new and then glued on the ornaments! In such cases we think the reason of economy was involved above everything else. Oh, well! Sculpture in soft stone is not more expensive than sculpture in cement and the skilled worker always prefers to work in stone. There is, then, only the difference of the price of the material, but this difference is not in the favor of cement if one counts the cost of the cramp irons—which it is necessary to use—and the difficulty of making it stick. In addition there is the waste of a large part of this cement, which can be used only when fresh.

These incentives, Minister, more than suffice for us to believe that we ought to reject entirely the use of cast iron, mastic, and all the materials foreign to the original construction, in the restoration project that we now have the honor to submit.

As for the restoration of both the interior and exterior bas-reliefs of the cathedral of Paris, we believe that it cannot be executed in the style of the period. We are convinced that the state of mutilation (not so serious in other respects) in which they are found is very preferable to an appearance of restoration that would only be very remote from their original character; for where is the sculptor who could retrieve with the point of his chisel this naivete of past centuries? We think, then, that the replacement of all the statues that embellish the portals, the gallery of kings, and the buttresses can be executed only with the aid of copies of existing statues in other analogous monuments, and of the same period. Models are not lacking at Chartres, Reims, Amiens, and on so many other churches throughout France. These same cathedrals will offer also the models for the stained-glass windows that it will be necessary to replace in Notre-Dame, models that it would be impossible to invent and that it is much wiser to copy.

The principles that we have just set forth, applicable according to our lights to all restoration, should not be forgotten when it is a question of a monument as important as the cathedral of Paris—this remarkable edifice, located in the center of the capital and under the eyes of authority, visited every day by so many intelligent and enlightened persons.

There, it is necessary not to hestitate and make excuses but to proceed with confidence, take no risks, and be sure to succeed. In order to arrive at this result it is necessary to decipher the texts and consult all the existing documents on the construction of this building, descriptive as well as graphic. We must study above all the archaeological character of the monument and finally gather all its treasured traditions.

It is thus that we have taken into account the slow accretion of Notre-Dame and have hypothetically restored each part according to its own period. Through these careful studies we have been able to ascertain the different phases of its construction from the twelfth through the fourteenth centuries.

In the execution of the important project that we have the honor to submit, a project composed of twenty-two sheets of drawings and an estimate of all the costs, we shall remain constantly faithful to the principles that we have set forth above on the restoration in general. We shall resolutely resist all modifications, all changes, all alterations, as much in regard to the form and materials as to the system of construction. It is with a reverent respect that we have researched even the slightest evidence of forms, however altered by time, weather, or the hand of man. And when we have lacked this information it is with the aid of actual documents, engravings, and, above all, in applying these authorities to the monument that we shall proceed with the restoration.

Far be it from us to foster the idea of "completing" so remarkably beautiful a work of art; that is an arrogance that we would not have countenanced. Does one believe, for example, that this monument would gain by the construction of spires (in an otherwise very hypothetical form) above the two towers? We think not. And even assuming a total success, one would perhaps obtain a remarkable monument but this monument would not be Notre-Dame de Paris.

To give back to our beautiful cathedral all its splendor, to restore to it all the richness of which it has been despoiled, such is the task imposed upon us. The building is surely beautiful enough that it would be pointless to want to add anything to it.

As for the structural strengthening, we shall not speak of it here; all the details of this work are scrupulously set down and worked out in the prospectus.

We shall not be concerned, then, only with the restoration, strictly defined. We have already pointed out numerous degradations that betray the activity of the architect Parvy in the repairs made on Notre-Dame. It is with the aid of a precious drawing belonging to a M. Depaulis, and above all in carefully consulting the remains that have escaped the hammer of the masons, that we shall be able to restore the rich framing of the rose and the beautiful sheaves of foliage that unfold at each angle of the buttresses.

Before this architect, Soufflot had already dared to set his hand on the justly admired sculpture of our cathedral. Finally, the vandals of 1794 finished the work of destruction in pulling down all the statues, the kings and the saints—nothing was spared. In our restoration we propose the replacement of all the lost statues, because everything is related in this ensemble of statues and reliefs and one cannot leave incomplete so admirable a text without risking making it unintelligible. It is in taking some examples from our ancient cathedrals that we shall be able to reestablish the twenty-eight kings in their niches, Christ blessing in the midst of the twelve apostles in the embrasure of the central portal, the eight figures of the portal of the Virgin, and the eight Romanesque statues of the Saint Anne portal.

In the four niches of the pilaster buttresses we replace also Saint Denis, [Synagoga, Ecclesia], and Saint Stephen. On the empty pedestals of the gallery of the Virgin we shall replace also the beautiful statue that has come to be esteemed by this name, as well as the angels that accompanied it—and the statues of Adam and Eve between the buttresses of the towers.

We shall replace the hideous acoustic hoods, currently gnawing at the clusters of columns of the great windows of the towers, with an analogous system that, while preserving the belfry, will leave visible the ample proportions of the windows and no longer spoil the original exterior construction.

If from the western facade we pass to the transept facades, some important degradations still disfigure almost completely the appearance of the monument. We shall have to rebuild the walls of the nave chapels—with their old decoration of gables, niches, statues, and gargoyles—as well as the buttresses crowned by pinnacles and the statues that surmount them, as shown by the documents and above all by the remains of the decoration still *in situ*. In effect, the buttresses have retained the brackets of their gargoyles and the cornice that supports the pinnacles, as was documented by Corrozet's text, which we quote. ("The full height is supported by flying buttresses, at the top of which as a diversion are square and triangular pyramids, with effigies of kings and other personages who are within and above.") At the extremities of the transept some important restoration efforts are necessitated by the poor state of the fabric. The two great rose windows, especially that of the north, are fallen into ruin and that of the south, which was restored by the cardinal de Noailles, will soon require a complete reconstruction.

The restoration of these rose windows, embellished with beautiful stained glass, requires a scrupulous examination of their construction, faulty from the beginning, for which it will be necessary to devise some modifications. Perhaps without changing their interior and exterior profiles, we can give them a much greater strength by thickening their tracery. The upper rose and the two spires flanking the northern gable are in the saddest state: the character of these important features of the edifice is so altered and their stability is so precarious that we shall have to renew them almost entirely, but with proportionately less regret since the ornament of the two portals has been marred and totally altered. The restorations we propose will bring back to these beautiful facades all the elegance they have lost. In the nave and choir, the renewal of the tracery cusps of all the tall windows will necessitate the reconstruction of the upper part of their mullions. Above the chapels of the choir, from the south flank to the apse, the pilaster buttresses that receive the pressure of the flying buttresses have been flanked by heavy masonry constructions with the aim of strengthening them. These accretions, poorly contrived, only pretending to support and with the most unfortunate effect, ought to be removed and the pilaster buttresses repaired in order to reduce them to their original thickness.

One of the gravest problems of the restoration is certainly that underlined by the repair of the tribune windows. These windows, as we have said in the historical section of our report, do not belong to any style. This makeshift construction, made in the time when the builders had probably abandoned the idea of doubling the tribunes of the first story, is in a state of dilapidation that it is mandatory to repair. Already in the fourteenth century the architects, struck by the ugliness of these openings, replaced those of the apse with large transomed windows that present the same drawbacks as those of the nave and the choir, making unavoidable the replacement of the simple pitched roof with terraces and gutters. Three questions arise here: ought one to preserve the actual windows of the tribunes and replace them in their bastard form? Ought one to restore them in the style of the fourteenth century? Or better, ought one to reconstruct them in the twelfth-century style of the tribunes?

We do not feel that we should adjudicate such a delicate question. Although in our drawings we have indicated the restoration of the windows in the style of the tribunes, we have not considered the problem resolved. Here are the considerations that we have directed toward this feature:

To continue the windows in the style of the fourteenth century, namely that which had been begun on the apse, would be a defective option with respect to construction, as we have said. To renew them according to their temporary form would be to confirm a curious fact, seeing that it provides proof of a scheme for a double tribune. But wouldn't it be childish to sacrifice the appearance of the flanks of Notre-Dame to this fact? Wouldn't an inscription or a tracery on the stone fulfill the demands of archaeology?

In any case, we have thought that in our drawings it would be appropriate to replace the ugly openings with windows in harmony with the general style of the facades, if only to facilitate the solution of this difficult problem.

On the apse, a major restoration ought to complete the rich appearance of the chapels, namely, on the last two buttresses, whose jutting crowns—removed or destroyed—were replaced in the fifteenth century by two blunt little pyramids. These features are entirely discordant with the beautiful bell turrets of the choir. These pyramids, now in a very bad state, displaced large pinnacles ornamented with columns and statues, such as were made for many monuments of the fourteenth century. It is difficult on this point not to renew these pinnacles with a sense of certainty because the pedestals and even the bases of the columns are still in place.

It remains only to speak of the central flèche, constructed in timber and covered with lead. The flèche, which completes so beautifully the cathedral of Paris, stands 104 feet from the highest roof ridge up to the rooster on the top. The engravings of Israel Sylvester and, above all, a precious drawing by Garneray permit us to restore it completely.

A minute swabbing appears to us to be the first operation to undertake on the interior of Notre-Dame in order to know the state of the vaults, which can be less sound than one supposes, and to recover the traces of painting. Some partial investigations give hope in this respect. However, the means of execution of this work appears to be of the greatest importance. It is evident in this case that only the brush and the sponge can be used and that scraping ought to be totally ruled out. We must say, however, that should the cleaning not give us some positive proof of a general system of painting formerly adopted on the interior of Notre-Dame, we do not think that this feature ought to be adopted. Up to now we have admitted painting only as decoration of the chapels or of certain parts of the church.

As for stained glass—although in our prospectus we have reserved for it a chapter of its own—we believe nevertheless that the execution of painted windows would be one of the most splendid means of interior decoration. Nothing equals the richness of these transparent pictures, which are an indispensable complement to the monuments of this epoch. Also, among our drawings we have presented a specimen executed in the manner of the windows of the cathedral of Bourges. You have wished, Minister, to communicate to us a request from Monseigneur the archbishop concerning the lowering of the organ loft. We are quite ready to recognize all the disadvantages of its present form, as pointed out by Monseigneur the archbishop. Unfortunately, this loft was constructed in the thirteenth century with the purpose of resisting the pressure of the gallery arches that carry the two enormous towers. The destruction or even the lowering of this loft could present great dangers, then, which it would be imprudent to provoke. As for the archaeological question, it has too little importance relative to the issue we have just raised to warrant speaking of it.

In a restoration like that of Notre-Dame, it is impossible not to try to harmonize all the accessory objects with the design of the edifice, above all when they are really important. Thus, we shall replace the convoluted grills and the bad taste of the galleries with grills more in sympathy with the architecture they accompany. Examples of iron strapwork are not lacking at Rouen, at Saint-Denis, at Saint-Germer, and even at Notre-Dame—on the beautiful doors of the west facade.

We have given in our drawings a restoration of the choir of Notre-Dame, as it was before 1699; but this work is only an archaeological study not meant for execution, because we think that it would be unfortunate to destroy without good reasons a historical souvenir as important as that. Actually, it would be foolhardy to destroy decoration executed so luxuriously, if not with taste, in order to replace it with some forms of which there remain only some descriptions or some rather vague information. In any event, if one ought to change anything in the actual decoration of the choir of Notre-Dame it could only be after completion of the exterior restoration and the whole of the interior work. Perhaps then one could extricate just the piers and the ribs of the hemicycle that are enveloped in massive encasements of red marble, then remove the paintings and reveal the ribs above the bas-reliefs of the fourteenth century? As for the choir stalls, even though they are not at all in harmony with the edifice, enough reasons plead in favor of their conservation that it is unthinkable to destroy or remove them. If we have not rendered in our drawings the choir of Louis XIV it is only that it retains no interest under the rubric of art and that there is no usefulness in reproducing it. . . .

(Report addressed to the Minister of Justice and Religious Rites)

Select Bibliography

Abraham, Pol. Viollet-le-Duc et le rationalisme médiéval. Paris, 1934.

Aillagon, Jean-Jacques. *Le Voyage d'Italie; Viollet-le-Duc, 1836–1837.* Florence, 1980. (Exhibition catalogue.)

Architectural Academy Design Editions. *Eugene Emmanuel Viollet-le-Duc, 1814–1879.* London, 1980. (Twenty short essays, bibliography, and biographical chronology.)

Auberson, Paul, ed. *Viollet-le-Duc: centenaire de la mort à Lausanne.* Lausanne, 1979. (Exhibition catalogue with nine essays.)

Auzas, Pierre-Marie. *Eugène Viollet-le-Duc, 1814–1879.* Paris, 1979.

Bercé, Françoise, Bruno Foucart, et al. *Viollet-le-Duc: Architect, Artist, Master of Historic Preservation.* Washington, 1987. (Exhibition catalogue of Viollet-le-Duc drawings.)

Boudon, Paul, and Paul Deshayes. *Le Dictionnaire d'architecture: relevés et observations.* Brussels, 1979.

Centre National des Lettres. *Actes du Colloque International Viollet-le-Duc, Paris 1980.* Paris, 1982. (Thirty-one essays.)

Foucart, Bruno, et al. *Viollet-le-Duc.* Paris, 1980. (Exhibition catalogue, comprehensive Viollet-le-Duc exhibition at the Grand Palais, Paris; sixty-two short essays, six appendices.)

Frankl, Paul. "The Rational School in France." In *The Gothic: Literary Sources and Interpretations through Eight Centuries.* Princeton, 1960. Pp. 563–78.

Gout, Paul. *Viollet-le-Duc: sa vie, son oeuvre, sa doctrine.* Paris, 1914.

(Principal printed source for biographical material, written by the architect-in-chief of the Monuments Historiques.)

Hoffman, Donald. "Frank Lloyd Wright and Viollet-le-Duc." *Journal of the Society of Architectural Historians* 28 (1969), 173–83.

Mark, Robert. *Experiments in Gothic Structure.* Cambridge, Mass., 1982.

Middleton, Robin D. "Viollet-le-Duc, Eugène Emmanuel." *Macmillan Encyclopedia of Architects.* New York, 1982.

Middleton, Robin D. "Viollet-le-Duc's Academic Ventures and the Entretiens sur l'Architecture." In *Gottfried Semper und die Mitte des 19 Jahrhunderts.* Zurich, 1976. Pp. 240–54.

Pevsner, Nikolaus. *Ruskin and Viollet-le-Duc: Englishness and Frenchness in the Appreciation of Gothic Architecture.* London, 1969.

Rieff, Daniel D. "Viollet-le-Duc and Historic Restoration: The West Portals of Notre-Dame." *Journal of the Society of Architectural Historians* 30 (1971), 17–30.

Saint-Paul, Anthyme. *Viollet-le-Duc: ses travaux d'art et son système archéologique.* Paris, 1881.

Summerson, John. "Viollet-le-Duc and the Rational Point of View." In *Heavenly Mansions and Other Essays on Architecture.* London, 1948. Pp. 135–58.